Birds at Risk

Lammergeier, or **Bearded Vulture,** a rare bird of mountains in southern Europe, though it has re-established itself in some areas. *Photo. Eric Hosking*

Birds at Risk

RALPH WHITLOCK   **A COMPREHENSIVE WORLD-SURVEY OF THREATENED SPECIES**

MOONRAKER PRESS

© 1981 Ralph Whitlock
First published in 1981 by
MOONRAKER PRESS
26 St Margaret's Street, Bradford-on-Avon, Wiltshire
SBN 239.00207.5
Set in 10/12½ pt Times New Roman by Butler & Tanner Ltd,
Printed and bound by Colorcraft Ltd, Hong Kong

Contents

Birds illustrated

Colour

PHOTOGRAPHS
White-winged Dove
Nene Goose
Red Bird of Paradise
Brown-capped Weaver
Avocets
Galapagos Penguin
Ipswich Sparrow
Cape Sable Sparrow
Seychelles Fody
Ashy-headed Goose
Cereopsis
Red-cockaded Woodpecker
California Condor

PAINTINGS BY MATTHEW HILLIER
Peregrine Falcon
Crested Honeycreeper
Great Bustard
Racket-tailed Hummingbird
Laysan Duck
Red-breasted Goose
Collared Dove
Greater Prairie Chicken
Golden Eagle
Bald Eagle
Noisy Scrub-bird
Black-tailed Godwit
Imperial Pheasant
Everglade Kite
Kaui Oo
St Kilda Wren
Bittern
Ivory-billed Woodpecker
Japanese Cranes

DUST JACKET
Rothschild's Grackle
Photo. Eric Hosking

Black-and-white Photographs

Maps drawn by T. Stalker Miller

Introduction

The eastern sage who, when required to produce a statement which would be true under any circumstances devised the formula 'This too will pass', stated a profound but regrettable truth. The *status quo* is never permanent, and nowhere is this more relevant than in the field of ecology. If evolution is a history of the survival of the fittest, then the extinction of those not so fit is a necessary corollary. It holds true for both individuals and species. Death is the inevitable fate of every weak, sick or aged individual, and extinction that of every species slow to adapt.

The extinction of species is, then, a natural phenomenon—it has been occurring throughout geological time. To any observer who could have looked down on the earth 200 million years ago the extinction of the huge and ubiquitous dinosaurs would have seemed wildly improbable, yet they have all gone. Man cannot be blamed for everything.

Yet undoubtedly Man has to accept responsibility for the extermination of many species in more recent times, probably many more than was realised until the last two or three decades. Recent research has suggested that the impact of Stone Age man on the larger fauna was cataclysmic: even eighteenth- and nineteenth-century men with firearms were hardly more destructive.

The remarkable collection of fossils from the asphalt deposits or tarpits of Rancho La Brea, a site now in the centre of Los Angeles, California, provides an outstanding example of the depredations caused by early Man. Here open pools of tar, exuding from bituminous sands, lie on the surface and still trap small mammals in their treacherous scum. Superficially they look like pools of water, reflecting the blue sky and drifting white clouds, but any animal venturing to step into them to quench its thirst is speedily trapped by the viscous material. Between 15,000 and 10,000 years ago the tarpits, in a climate perhaps even drier in summer than it is now, attracted an intriguing cross-sample of the fauna of the region. Among the larger mammals were the Ancient Bison (*Bison antiquus*), an animal considerably larger than the present-day American Bison; the American Mastodon (*Mammut americanus*); the Columbian Mammoth (*Mammuthus columbi*); the Emperor Mammoth (*Mammuthus imperator*); the Mylodon or Ground Sloth (*Parasnylodon harlani*); the Nothrotherium (*Nothrotherium shastense*) and the Megalonyx (*Megalonyx jeffersoni*), which were also ground sloths; the American Camel (*Camelops hesternus*); and the Western Horse (*Equus occidentatis*); as well as numerous smaller species, including antelopes, rabbits, and various rodents. Assembled to feast on such of these herbivorous animals as became trapped in the tar were an horrendous company of ferocious carnivores. There were the Dire Wolf

(*Canus dirus*), one of the biggest wolves ever to exist; the Short-faced Bear (*Tremarctothenium simum*) which was as large as the giant Kodiak Bear of Alaska; the Similodon, or Sabre-tooth Cat (*Similodon californicus*), which resembled the African Lion in size; the Great Lion-like Cat (*Panthera atrox*), which has been likened to a giant Jaguar; and two extinct species of Puma, as well as an assortment of Coyotes, Foxes, Badgers, Skunks and Weasels.

Birds were represented by no fewer than 126 species or types, to which more may be added, for the excavation of the deposits is by no means complete. They included the Teratornis (*Teratornis merriami*), a condor-like Vulture far larger than any modern bird capable of flight, with a wing-span of 12 feet. Other large birds now extinct were three other species of Vulture, several Eagles, a Stork, a Turkey and a large Owl. In all, 24 species of the mammals and 22 of the birds which clustered around the tarpits of La Brea are now extinct. Radio-carbon dating and other modern devices have now established that the catastrophe overtook them between about 11,000 and 8,000 years ago. It is probable that men first found their way to the American continent about 30,000 years ago via the land that then occupied the present position of the Bering Strait, and spread gradually and at first in very small numbers, southwards. By 10,000 B.C. the population of America must have been growing quite rapidly, and a link between human activities and the extermination of many of the larger fauna of La Brea would seem logical, especially as human bones and weapons, including the atlatl, have also been found in the tarpits.

Although to us Stone Age man seems a primitive savage, to other species he could be reckoned as an efficient and relentless destroyer. Three thousand years is a relatively short period to accomplish the extermination of such a large and varied fauna as that of La Brea. Even today the armoury of tribes at the same low cultural level is surprisingly extensive. Physically weak compared to its prey, Man has perfected the techniques of killing at a distance and of the trap and the ambush. The atlatl was a spear-thrower, corresponding roughly to the bow-and-arrow of the Old World. Nets, snares and concealed pits were important features of the stock-in-trade of hunting Man. Primitive tribes were doubtless adept at stampeding herds of frightened animals over the edge of a cliff, as American Indians in more recent times have demonstrated. Many mammoths, it seems, were killed in this way. The use of the blow-pipe and poisoned dart, still practised by tribes in South America and New Guinea, was probably widespread. Decoys and the art of camouflaging oneself in the skin of an animal so as to approach a grazing herd are devices with a long history.

The catastrophe which befell the fauna of La Brea was exceptionally sudden and dramatic for the reason that in America Man was a newcomer. Current theories maintain that Man originated in Africa, a million or two years ago. Through the long eons of slow development the species shared its environment with the other African fauna, with which it inevitably established a kind of working compromise. As each new advance was made, so the many associated species learned to live with it. American fauna had no such conditioning period—men appeared in their midst, fully armed with intelligence and weapons, and they stood little chance of survival. It is likely that the same conditions accounted for the extinction of the mammoth, the Irish elk, the northern rhinoceros and other large northern animals as skin-clad men followed the retreating ice northwards in Europe and Asia at the end of the last Ice Age. The impact of destructive Man on an unprepared fauna was thus very similar in the Stone Age to that of men armed with firearms on the larger animals and birds of America, Africa and dozens of remote islands in later periods.

A law of Nature is that no parasite or predator entirely eliminates the species on which it feeds. To do so would be tantamount to committing suicide. When the balance between Man the hunter and his quarry showed signs of becoming tilted against the victims an instinctive reaction seems to have occurred. The taboos imposed by primitive tribes against eating the flesh of certain animals or of eating it only at certain seasons are probably examples of this. Sometimes such taboos had to be imposed by a privileged caste, aristocratic or priestly, as, for instance, the protection of deer in royal forests or chases by draconian laws in northern Europe in the early Middle Ages. Deer were normally the only source of fresh meat for the royal household in winter and so vigorous steps were naturally taken to preserve an adequate stock. In the Faeroes, Iceland and other northern isles the annual harvest of sea-birds' eggs from the cliffs was strictly controlled when they were essential to the islanders' existence.

The chief criterion governing early attempts at conservation, which these are, was the *permanent* residence of the predator, Man, in a fixed area. Because he was at least partially dependent on a seasonal cull or harvest he took care that a basic stock was preserved for the future. The arrangement has failed when men have found themselves suddenly in a new environment. With little thought of the future, they have indulged in an orgy of destruction and have not realised or cared that they were indulging in an 'overkill' until it was too late. It happened in north America in the nineteenth century, when the extraordinarily plentiful Passenger Pigeon was harried to extinction and the bison only narrowly escaped the same fate. It had happened in the Mascarene Islands in the seventeenth century, when the Dodo, the Solitaire and allied species were ruthlessly clubbed to oblivion. Something like it must have happened in western America 10,000 years ago.

Because of their powers of flight birds, of all creatures, ought to be relatively safe from the predatory instincts of Man. Although traps, decoys, blow-pipes and other ingenious devices can be used to encompass their destruction, they have the means of escape from the straightforward hunt with its climax in hand-wielded weapons, so effective against large mammals. It is not surprising, therefore, that many of the species that have become extinct over the past three or four centuries have been flightless birds. The Dodo, the Solitaire, the Moa and the Great Auk are among the best-known examples. Other factors must have been involved in the extermination of the giant birds of prey of California, notably the monstrous Teratornis. Such a large species was undoubtedly a tempting target for missiles, but the killing must have been for sport, for it is difficult to imagine the primitive Amerindians eating the flesh of these carnivorous birds. Possibly the Teratornis perished through food scarcity, as its normal prey was steadily obliterated by these new-comers. Direct interference is not the only impact Man has on other species.

In recent times Man's effect on the environment has been at least as significant as his predatory habits. As the human race has multiplied excessively so it has altered, modified and often polluted its habitat. Grassy plains have become deserts, forests felled to make room for farmland; swamps have been drained, valleys drowned to create reservoirs, and monstrous towns have proliferated like amoeba. Some birds and mammals have proved as adaptable as Man himself to these cataclysmic changes, but many others have not been able to move fast enough and so have paid the penalty to the law of Nature, 'Adapt or perish'.

However, it is as well to reiterate that no species lasts for ever. It has been calculated that the natural life-span of a bird species is around two million years (for mammals, about 100,000 years). By the end of that period the species has either become extinct or, by the slow processes of evolution, has been transformed into something new. Man's role, therefore, has in many instances been merely to hasten a natural process. One can envisage that the Dodo, for example, was inevitably a doomed species: adapted over the ages to life in a paradise free from predators, it had become such a slow, defenceless creature that sooner or later it was bound to meet its nemesis.

This book surveys the present scene. It examines the events which have brought species currently at risk into peril and assesses their chances of survival. It investigates the fate of those species which have foundered and the factors which give threatened species in the 1980s a better hope of escaping extinction.

Foremost among those factors is an awareness of the need for conservation which has developed and is growing just in time to save many of the species at risk. Restricted habitats have been declared sanctuaries, educational campaigns have been launched, protective laws passed, wardening has become more effective, and zoo-banks have been established. Obeying the law 'Adapt or perish', too, many species have shown themselves remarkably adaptable to a changing environment. In particular, many have come to terms with life alongside human neighbours, in some instances, though not in all, with human assistance. The mutual respect and tolerance displayed by humans and birds in city parks is most encouraging.

Failures

Before surveying the contemporary scene it will be salutary to take note of the increasing group of species that have plunged into the ultimate abyss of extinction. A study of their fate may serve to draw attention to existing species on the same dangerous downward path and may suggest ways by which they may avoid encountering the same doom.

It is generally conceded that between 130 and 140 bird species have become extinct since the world opened up to Europeans, say within the past 250 years. An analysis of a list of 137 species compiled by the author provides the following data: 57 of the extinct species inhabited small islands; 60 species lived on islands of intermediate size; ten species belonged to large islands (though an additional 20 or so should be added if the species of Moa of New Zealand are reckoned in); eight species were found in continental countries, chiefly North America.

Of the extinct birds whose habitats were islands of intermediate size, 25 were indigenous to the Mascarenes and 26 to Hawaii, thus accounting for the greatest proportion of them. The other islands were Fiji (two species), Guadeloupe, in the West Indies, (two), Martinique (two), the Solomon Islands, Kangaroo Island (off the South Australian coast) and King Island (in the Bass Straits).

The small islands which have lost species are the Bonin Islands (five species), the Carolines (two), the Chatham Islands and the Auckland Islands (12), the Society Islands, including Tahiti, (six), Norfolk Island (two), Lord Howe Island (seven), the Line Islands (two), Bering Island (two), Guadalupe, the Mexican island off the coast of Baja California, (five), the Riu Kiu Islands, the Kuriles, Wake Island, Samoa, Macquarie Island, Tanna (in the New Hebrides), Tristan d'Acunha, Culebra (West Indies), the Seychelles, Comoro Islands, Marie Galante Island (West Indies), Antigua and neighbouring islands, Stephen Island (an islet off the New Zealand coast)—each of which lost one—and sundry islets in the North Atlantic where once the Great Auk nested.

The large islands include New Zealand (four species, but about 24 if the Moas are included), Jamaica (three), Cuba, Puerto Rico and Tasmania (one each).

Of the continental losses, six refer to North America, one to India (assuming the Pink-headed Duck is really extinct) and one to Korea.

The Mascarene Islands

The Mascarene Islands, situated in the wastes of the Indian Ocean east of Madagascar, fall into the intermediate category as regards size. They are neither tiny nor large. Réunion has an area of about 1,000 square miles, Mauritius 720 square

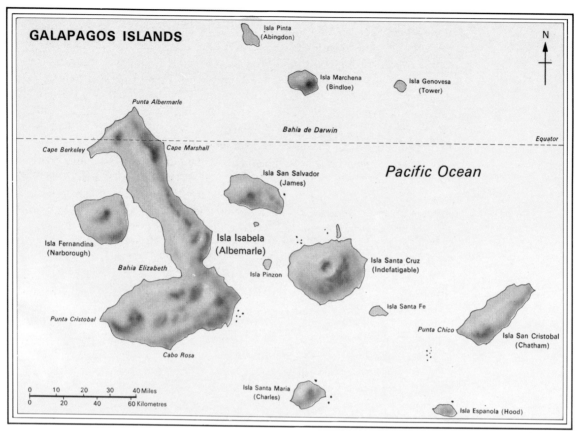

GALAPAGOS ISLANDS

N

Isla Pinta
(Abingdon)

Isla Marchena
(Bindloe)

Isla Genovesa
(Tower)

Punta Albermarle

Bahia de Darwin

Equator

Cape Berkeley   *Cape Marshall*

Pacific Ocean

Isla San Salvador
(James)

Isla Isabela
(Albemarle)

Isla Fernandina
(Narborough)

Bahia Elizabeth

Isla Pinzon

Isla Santa Cruz
(Indefatigable)

Punta Cristobal

Isla Santa Fe

Punta Chico

Isla San Cristobal
(Chatham)

Cabo Rosa

Isla Santa Maria
(Charles)

Isla Espanola (Hood)

| 0 | 10 | 20 | 30 | 40 Miles |
| 0 | 20 | 40 | 60 Kilometres |

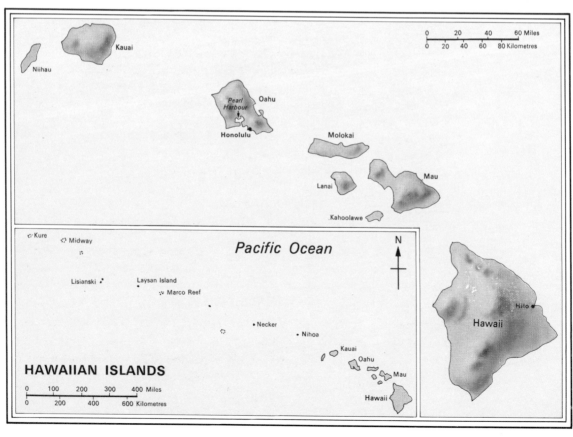

Kauai

Niihau

Pearl Harbour   Oahu

Honolulu

Molokai

Lanai   Mau

Kahoolawe

Kure   *Midway*

Pacific Ocean   N

Lisianski   Laysan Island

Marco Reef

Necker   Nihoa

Kauai

Oahu   Mau

Hawaii

Hawaii

Hilo

HAWAIIAN ISLANDS

| 0 | 100 | 200 | 300 | 400 Miles |
| 0 | 200 | 400 | 600 Kilometres |

| 0 | 20 | 40 | 60 Miles |
| 0 | 20 | 40 | 60 | 80 Kilometres |

miles, and Rodriguez 43 square miles. The fate of their avifauna glaringly illustrates the perils associated with species that are confined to islands. Although the tally of extinct birds of the Mascarenes has been put at 27, the exact figure is open to doubt. Some of the lost species are known only from skeletal remains or from dubious descriptions. Whether all of them could be classified as species or were only sub-species (and therefore in an intermediate stage of evolution) is another matter on which there is some difference of opinion. Incontrovertibly, however, they were peculiar to the Mascarenes and have now disappeared.

THE DODO (*Raphus cucullatus*) The fact that the Dodo has passed into proverbial English in the phrase 'as dead as a dodo' suggests the bird as a suitable candidate for prime position in this chapter of species irrevocably lost. Unless some future miracle of science makes possible the re-creation of extinct species (as has already happened though under decidedly more favourable conditions with the extermi- nated and resurrected Aurochs), no human eyes will ever again gaze on this ungainly, ill-fated but endearing bird.

Not many years ago an enthusiastic idealist demanded that Mauritius and the other Mascarene Islands which relieve the immensity of the Indian Ocean should be returned to their aboriginal inhabitants, not realising that when those islands were discovered by Portuguese sailors about the year 1507 they had no human inhabitants at all. Because they had remained in blissful isolation from the rest of the world for so many millennia, the Dodo and its associated species on the other islands of the group had specialised to an extraordinary extent. They had lost the power of flight, were grossly fat, moved only slowly and, naturally but disas- trously, nested on the ground. Long centuries of immunity from predators had made them trusting and unsuspicious. In appearance the Dodo was a caricature of a bird. Its exaggeratedly plump body was covered with grey down rather than properly-formed feathers; its wings were vestigial; a ridiculous tuft of tail-covert feathers served instead of a tail; it had an inordinately heavy, hooked bill and big, clumsy feet. It weighed up to 23 kg.

No Portuguese records of the Dodo have been discovered, and it is assumed that the decline of the species began with the annexation of Mauritius by the Dutch in 1598. For some years after that date the island was not permanently inhabited but served as a provisioning station, where vessels could replenish supplies of food and water. To augment the food supplies the Dutch evidently turned loose num- bers of pigs and goats. Later, in 1644, they established a permanent penal-settle- ment and began to fell the forests and develop the land for agriculture. Cats, dogs, rats and monkeys (macaques) were also introduced, some unintentionally, some deliberately. Ships calling in for provisions naturally exploited the easily captured Dodos, and accounts of Dodo-hunting expeditions and the subsequent salting down of carcases have survived. Apparently the flesh of the bird was no great culinary acquisition, for one account admits that 'even long boiling would scarcely make them tender', though the breast received more favourable comment than the rest of the meat.

The last recorded Dodo was seen on Mauritius in 1680. When the inquisitive François Leguat visited the island in 1693 he found no trace of it, so by that time it was presumably extinct. The species thus survived the human impact by only about 175 years. Its previous history may be conjectured as follows. As Mauritius is a volcanic island unattached to any continent by a former land-bridge, the ancestors of the Dodo presumably flew to the island. They are thought to have been related to the Pigeons or perhaps the Rails, but doubt still exists. The island paradise where they found themselves was so free from predators that they had no need to develop defensive characteristics; they lost the power of flight and the need for a covering of feathers. Their food, which is thought to have been fallen fruit and roots, was evidently so abundant that they became fat and heavy. Survival being easy, they needed to lay only one egg per year to maintain their population. They laid it in the easiest place—on the ground.

On Man's arrival they were assailed on every front. They had to contend not only with direct predation by Man but by indiscriminate assaults by the animals he had introduced, especially pigs. The destruction of their habitat was the final blow. Man could hardly have conducted a more efficient extermination campaign if he had planned it. The Dodo had no chance at all.

THE SOLITAIRES (*Raphus solitarius* and *Pezophaps solitaria*) It seems that the other islands of the Mascarene Group also had large flightless species of birds, now extinct. The Solitaire of Réunion (*R.solitarius*) is known only from pictures and descriptions; no remains of it have been discovered on the island, which causes some writers to doubt whether the species ever existed. The descriptions and pictures show a large bird very similar to the Dodo but white or yellowish white. One account, however, speaks of one bird having a bluish colour. Some modern writers, having studied the available evidence, think there may have been two distinct species on the island—one a white Dodo, possibly an albino; the other a bird more closely resembling the Rodriguez Solitaire. The evidence is so thin, however, that we cannot be sure. Both species, if there were two of them, were extinct by the middle of the eighteenth century.

The Mascarene Islands are not a closely-knit group. Although Réunion, the largest, lies only about 120 miles west of Mauritius and between it and Madagascar, Rodriguez is situated in the remote ocean 365 miles east of Mauritius. Visited by mariners from time to time at earlier dates, Rodriguez was settled in 1691 by a party of Huguenot refugees, whose leader was the already-mentioned François Leguat. Although they stayed for only two or three years, Leguat has left a detailed description of the Rodriguez Solitaire. Apart from numerous bones which have been found in caves and ravines, a secondhand account by the Abbé Pingue, an astronomer who visited the island in 1761 but never saw a bird, and incidental references by other visitors comprise our total information about the species.

François Leguat, however, was an excellent observer, and his records contain not only descriptions of the bird itself but also accounts of its habits and behaviour. The Rodriguez Solitaire was evidently a bird of about the same size as the Dodo but much more active and athletic. It had a long neck, which it held erect. Like the Dodo it was covered with a kind of down rather than fully-formed feathers, but it seems to have taken pleasure in preening itself. Unlike the Dodo, it could 'run very fast, principally among the rocks, where a man, agile as he may be, will have trouble in catching them'.

The quotation is from an anonymous writer of about 1730 who also states, 'they have a little lump in the wings which has a sort of musket-ball at the end, and this serves them in defense. ... They never fly, having no feathers in their wings, but fight with them and make a great noise with their wings when they are angry, and

16

Crested Honeycreeper

Great Bustard

Racket-tailed Hummingbird

Laysan Duck

the noise is quite like thunder....' Leguat also refers to this sound, which he says could be heard 200 yds away. It seems that the noise was associated with a territorial display in the course of which the birds, both male and female, made vigorous and spectacular attempts to drive off intruders. If the display were ineffective they had no inhibitions about resorting to actual force, and in the numerous skeletal remains wing-bones with healed fractures have been found, apparently indicating severe buffeting. Although the Solitaire would seem to have been better equipped for survival than the Dodo, its nesting habits tended to make it decidedly vulnerable. Like the Dodo, it laid only a single egg, and the young bird remained helpless and dependent on its parents for several months. The nest was a mound of vegetation, some 18 in. high, built on the ground. The dangers to a ground-nesting bird with such a long period of immaturity are obvious. The animals introduced by Man, notably pigs, must have wrought more havoc than Man himself.

Men, however, found the Solitaire good eating—better than the Dodo. From at least early in the eighteenth century the island was used as a provisioning station, and expeditions were even sent from Réunion to stock up with birds (presumably Solitaires) and tortoises (in which the island abounded). Before the end of the century the Solitaire was extinct.

THE APHANAPTERYX (*Aphanapteryx bonasia* and *Aphanapteryx leguati*) When the Mascarene Islands were discovered by Europeans early in the sixteenth century, they found on Mauritius a bird the pictures of which are reminiscent of a kiwi. It was, in fact, a flightless rail, to which the name Aphanapteryx has been given. Wings and tail had become atrophied, and the plumage too seems to have degenerated, much as in the Dodo and Solitaire. The legs were sturdy and rather long, the beak long and down-curved. The bird was variable in size but comparison with a domestic hen is not unreasonable. Several of the birds were brought to Europe in the seventeenth century and were kept for a time in zoos, where they attracted the attention of artists. From surviving paintings and descriptions one gathers that their general colour was reddish brown, with lighter underparts. Sufficient numbers of bones have been discovered on Mauritius to confirm that a large rail to match the illustrations did live on the island.

For the Rodriguez Aphanapteryx (*Aphanapteryx leguati*) there are no records, but the evidence of bones is conclusive. These show that the Rodriguez species was distinctly smaller than the Mauritius bird. François Leguat who, as already stated, was on the island from 1691 to 1693, describes a bird which may have been an Aphanapteryx, though modern scientists tend to think it was more likely a species of *Porphyrio* imported from Madagascar. Leguat's birds were fat, heavy and flightless, good to eat, and either grey or blue in colour.

Both species of Aphanapteryx had passed into oblivion by the middle of the seventeenth century, experiencing the same fate as the Dodo and Solitaire and for much the same reasons.

OTHER EXTINCT BIRDS OF THE MASCARENE ISLANDS At least 24 other species of land birds and freshwater birds, present on the Mascarene Islands when they were first visited by Europeans, have subsequently become extinct. The exact number is uncertain as some of the reports are of doubtful provenance. Many of the species are known solely from their bones. Each of the three islands had a flightless Heron or Night-Heron. Of the Mauritius Heron (*Ardea* or *Nycticorax mauritiana*) only the bones have been found, but descriptions of the Réunion Heron (*Ardea duboisi*) and the Rodriguez Heron (*Ardea* or *Nycticorax megacephala*) have survived. The seventeenth-century missionary, Abbé Dubois, describes the Réunion Heron as a bird with grey plumage, 'each feather spotted with white, the neck and beak like a heron, and the feet green.' It was evidently appreciated as a table dish, for the Abbé comments that it was 'very fat and good'. Doubt has been cast, however, as to whether this was a distinct species, there being a suspicion that it might have been a heron or egret brought over from Madagascar.

Two writers, one of them the Huguenot Leguat, the other an anonymous writer shortly before 1730, describe the Rodriguez Heron. The latter states, 'There are not a few Bitterns which are birds which fly only a very little, and run uncommonly well when they are chased. They are the size of an Egret and something like them.' Leguat describes them as being 'as big and fat as capons', and mentions that lizards were one of their favourite preys.

With at least one of the four extinct species of parrot we are on firmer ground for this bird, the Russet Parrot (*Mascarinus mascarinus*), was exhibited live in zoological gardens in Europe, one as recently as 1834 in the garden of the King of Bavaria. It was a greyish-brown bird, about 14 in. long, with a big red beak and some black feathers on the forehead. It inhabited Réunion but may have occurred on Mauritius as well.

The anonymous writer to whom we are indebted for the description of the Rodriguez Heron (he wrote a report entitled *Relation de l'Isle de Rodriguez* for the Ministère de la Marine in Paris about the middle of the eighteenth century), also describes a Rodriguez Parrot (*Necropsittacus rodericanus*). It was, he says, as large as a cockatoo, with an enormous beak and a large head to match; it also had a long tail. He mentions that there were three distinct kinds and that they were abundant.

Bones prove that a large parrot, to which the name *Lophopsittacus mauritiana* has been given, existed on Mauritius. Like the Rodriguez Parrot, it had a huge bill and may have been nearly related to that species. Paintings and sketches indicate that the bird was probably blue or grey and had a crest, though it is not certain that the pictures in question relate to this species.

Early in the eighteenth century the Abbé Dubois reported a black-necked parrot on Réunion and a picture of it by Daubenton, dated 1783, survives. It has been given the name *Psittacula krameri eques* and may have been a sub-species of *Psittacula echo*, still found on Mauritius.

The existence of the Mauritius Blue Pigeon (*Alectroenas nitidissima*) is well authenticated, for three skins survive in museums (in Paris, Edinburgh and Mauritius). Nearly related species still live in Madagascar and on the Seychelles. The bird, apparently a fruit-eating species, seems to have been abundant and its extinction is rather a mystery. Evidently a campaign in 1775 against all vermin, which included most species of birds, had much to do with it. The last live specimen was reported in 1826, but the bones of what seems to have been an allied species have been discovered on Rodriguez.

Until the 1830s Réunion had a large crested starling, of which a score or so mounted specimens have survived. Locally it was known as the Calandre or Huppe (*Fregilupus varius*), but little is known about it. A similar but somewhat smaller species, now also extinct, lived on Rodriguez. The Réunion species was predominantly brown and brownish grey, with head, neck and underparts light grey and a whitish crest. An early eighteenth-century account describes the Rodriguez starlings as 'a little larger than a blackbird, and have white plumage, part of the wings and tail black, the beak yellow, as well as the feet, and make a wonderful warbling. I say a warbling, since they have many and altogether different notes. We brought up some with cooked meat, cut up very small, which they eat in preference to seeds.' This is from the anonymous report, *Relation de l'Ile Rodrigue*, submitted to the French Ministère de la Marine in 1760.

That same report mentions a brown Owl (now described as *Athene murivora*) on Rodriguez: 'It eats little birds and small lizards. They almost always live in trees, and when they think the weather will be fine they utter always the same cry at night. On the other hand, when they think the weather will be bad, they are not heard.' Bones of this bird have been found on Rodriguez. Another Owl, which seems to have been a kind of Barn Owl, lived on Mauritius but is known only by excavated bones.

The bones of extinct species of Coot, Goose and Darter have also been found on Mauritius.

The Lost Birds of Hawaii The havoc caused by the arrival of Europeans among the birds of the Mascarene Islands is matched by that accomplished in an even shorter period among the birds of Hawaii. The first known European to visit the Hawaiian islands was Captain Cook (in 1778), more than 250 years after the exploitation of the Mascarenes began, but in the two centuries that have since elapsed between 20 and 30 species of birds have been exterminated.

The Hawaiian Islands stretch in a great arc, some 1,600 miles long, in the North Pacific Ocean about midway between California and Japan. They are large islands—larger than the Mascarenes: Hawaii proper, the biggest of the group, having an area of over 4,000 square miles, Maui being 728 square miles, Oahu (on which the capital city, Honolulu, is situated) 698 square miles and Kauai 543 square miles, with numerous smaller ones. Some of the lesser islands are sprinkled around the larger in the main group, but others are strung out, like the lesser outer planets of the solar system, in the immensity of the ocean. Outermost of all is remote Ocean Island, with Midway Island, Laysan and sundry other atolls and reefs forming a tenuous link with Hawaii proper. Laysan, Midway and the other ocean islets are mostly of coral formation, flat and low-lying. The main islands of the group are, on the other hand, spectacularly mountainous, having been created by now extinct volcanoes. The great island of Hawaii has three mighty mountains, of which the largest, Mauna Kea (the White Mountain), rises 13,784 ft above sea level. The islands of Oahu, Kauai, Molokai and Maui also possess majestic mountains, the last-named having a volcanic peak of more than 10,000 ft.

Most of the islands lie just within the tropics and are exposed to the north-east trade winds which, striking the towering mountains, produce a torrential rainfall. On the windward side of the mountains rainfall often exceeds 100 in. a year. The chain of islands is not well served by ocean currents. The North Equatorial Current, which flows steadily westwards from Central America after following the Californian coast southwards, passes well to the south; the North Pacific Current, which sweeps eastwards from Japan, has its course about the same distance to the

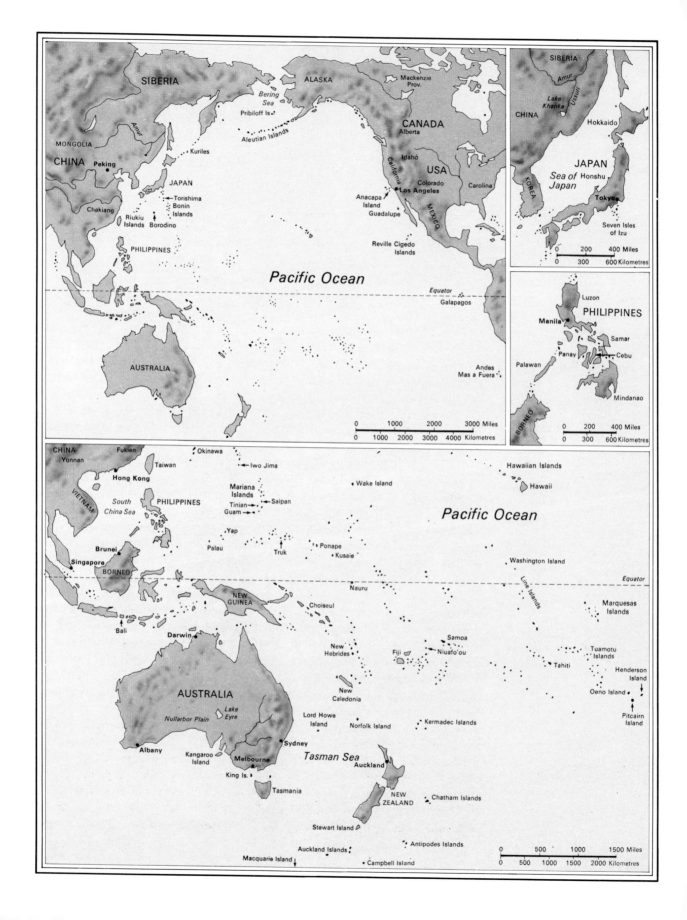

north. Nevertheless sufficient forms of life have found their way across the ocean to develop in the islands a luxuriant flora and a prolific fauna.

The formation of most of the islands occurred probably in the Pliocene period, about five million years ago, though some of them are much younger. In time the main islands acquired a clothing of dense tropical forests, some of them of tree ferns and most tangled with vines and burdened with epiphytes. At present most of the forests survive in the altitude-zone of 2,500 to 6,000 ft. At some period in the past the forests descended almost to sea level, as they still do on the island of Hawaii, but whether the lower-altitude forests disappeared entirely through human activity or whether they were affected by changes of climate is not known.

The first human colonists are thought to have been Polynesians from Tahiti. Radiocarbon dating indicates that they were certainly there by the middle of the tenth century A.D., and may have arrived four centuries earlier. How much destruction of the native forests and other changes in the environment can be attributed to the Polynesians before the arrival of the Europeans in 1778 is a matter of some controversy. The general opinion seems to be that their inroads into the forests were not very considerable but, on the other hand, they were apparently responsible for the introduction of pigs, which subsequently roamed wild and must have caused some destruction of other wild life. Since the European irruption at least 26 species and sub-species of native birds have become extinct, most of them within the past century.

The most specialised of Hawaii's indigenous birds are a group known as the Drepanids (*Drepanididae*), or honeycreepers. They are small, finch-like birds, the largest, the Akialoa, being less than eight in. long. Some have long, down-curved bills, and in one, the Akiapolaau, the upper mandible is more than twice as long as the lower. One group, however, the *Psittirostrinae*, have large, heavy, finch-like beaks. Their antecedents are doubtful. One school of thought maintains that they are most nearly related to the Buntings and are probably descended from birds blown over from North America eons ago. Other authorities consider that their origin is Central American and that their nearest relations are the tropical honeycreepers found there. Of the 22 species once resident on the islands, eight have become extinct and eight are in grave danger.

THE GREATER AMAKIHI OR GREEN SOLITAIRE (*Loxops sagittirostris*) This species was first identified in the foothills of the mountain Mauna Kea, Hawaii, in 1892 and became extinct within ten years. The destruction of its forest habitat to make room for sugar-cane plantations undoubtedly hastened its end, but its status must have been precarious before that.

THE LANAI ALAUWAHIO (*Loxops maculata montana*) The island race confined to the small island of Lanai (area—only 141 square miles) became extinct in the early decades of the present century, due primarily to more intensive settlement and the destruction of the forests. Allied sub-species are still found on some of the other islands, though in reduced numbers.

THE OAHU AKEPA (*Loxops coccinea rufa*) This tiny bird, less than five in. in length, survives in the sub-species indigenous to Kauai, Hawaii and possibly Maui, but the

Oahu race became extinct about the beginning of the twentieth century. It was a bird of mountain forests.

THE HAWAIIAN AKIALOA (*Hemignathus obscurus obscurus*) The Hawaiian race of the Akialoa, a tiny, insect-eating bird with down-curved bill, is certainly extinct. Sub-species confined to the islands of Cahu and Lanai are probably so, though there is just a possibility that a vestigial population survives. Kauai has a similar though distinct species (*Hemignathus procerus*) which is very rare.

THE NUKUPUU (*Hemignathus lucidus lucidus*) The typical race of this species inhabited Cahu, where it was last seen in about 1860. It probably lived in a lowland forest area which was cleared about that time.

THE MAUI NUKUPUU (*Hemignathus lucidus affinis*) The race of Nukupuu, an insectivorous species, found on Maui, was first described and last seen in the 1890s. It apparently occupied a high-altitude habitat on Mount Haleakala.

THE GREAT KOA FINCH (*Psittirostra palmeri*) A seed-eating species apparently confined to a restricted area on the western side of Hawaii island. Last seen in 1896.

THE LESSER KOA FINCH (*Psittirostris flaviceps*) Some specimens of this species, collected from a party of Great Koa Finches in 1891, are the only examples ever recorded.

THE KONA FINCH (*Psittirostris kona*) A heavy-billed, seed-eating bird, not unlike the European Greenfinch, formerly found in a very restricted locality on the slopes of Mount Mauna Loa in the western side of Hawaii island. Last recorded in 1894.

THE ULA-AI-HAWANE (*Ciridops anna*) One of the smallest of the honeycreepers, only just over four in. long, this species seems once to have been fairly widespread on Hawaii island but to have become extinct by the 1890s, though there have been a few subsequent unconfirmed reports.

THE MAMO (*Drepanis pacifica*) A species once widespread in the forests of Hawaii Island, this handsome black-and-yellow bird used to supply the skins and feathers from which the feather cloaks of Hawaiian kings were fashioned. It remained not uncommon until the late 1870s and early 1880s, when its extinction was brought about by feather-collectors with guns.

THE BLACK MAMO (*Drepanis funerea*) The species of Mamo confined to the island of Molokai. When first discovered and described in 1893 it was already rare, owing to the destruction of the forests in which it made its home. Last seen in 1907.

THE HONEY-EATERS (*Meliphagidae*) Although similar in appearance to the Drepanid Honeycreepers, the birds of the family *Meliphagidae* are not nearly related. Most members are found in Australia and the eastern Indonesian islands but some on the islands of the Pacific, including five on the Hawaiian islands. Four of the

Hawaiian species have, however, become extinct. They are: THE KIOEA (*Chaetoptila augustipluma*), found on Hawaii island and last seen in 1859; THE HAWAIIAN OO (*Moho nobilis*); MOLOKAI OO (*Moho bishopi*); OAHU OO (*Moho apicallis*).

The name Oo is, incidentally, pronounced 'Oh-oh' in the typically mellifluous Hawaiian manner. Hawaii's Oo may have survived till the 1930s, and there is still a species of Oo probably living, though very rare, on Kauai.

THE HAWAIIAN THRUSHES (*Phaeornis*) Five thrushes of the genus *Phaeornis* originally inhabited the Hawaiian islands, but three are now extinct. Those which have earned obituaries are: THE LANAI THRUSH (*Phaeornis obscurus lanaiensis*), which became extinct in the 1920s or 1930s; and THE OAHU THRUSH (*Phaeornis obscurus oahensis*), which was apparently last recorded about 1825. Related races still exist on Hawaii and Kauai. They are brown forest birds and excellent songsters.

THE HAWAIIAN RAIL (*Pennula sandwichensis*) This small brown rail, less than six in. long, formerly inhabited a restricted area on the eastern coast of Hawaii island. It seems to have become extinct towards the end of the nineteenth century.

THE LAYSAN HONEYEATER (*Himatione sanguinea freethii*) This species, also known as the APAPANE, is a Drepanid once found on the remote coral island of Laysan. It is thought that strong winds must have once blown a small number of Apapanes from the main islands of the archipelago to the islet of Laysan, far to the northwest. In the course of evolution the Laysan birds became distinctly paler and warranted sub-specific status. However, as the whole island measures only two miles by one, its hold on life must always have been somewhat precarious, and its eventual disappearance seems to have been in some way associated with the introduction of rabbits to the island. Perhaps they destroyed its habitat.

THE LAYSAN MILLERBIRD (*Acrocephalus familiaris familiaris*) Surprisingly this species, on its remote Pacific islet, belongs to an Old World genus, *Acrocephalus*, and is nearly related to the European Reed Warbler. Its extinction, which occurred about 1923, seems to be associated, as with that of the Laysan Honeyeater, with the introduction of rabbits to Laysan, A related species, the Nihoa Millerbird, still maintains a very precarious existence on the island of Nihoa, westernmost of the main group of Hawaiian islands (q.v.).

NOTE Pages 50–56 give details of an even greater number of Hawaiian birds which are teetering on the edge of extinction. Even now some of them may be lost beyond recall. The chapter discusses the several interlocking factors which produced such a holocaust of native birds on these attractive islands.

The remarkable Avifauna of New Zealand

The archipelago of New Zealand has had no land connections with any other part of the world for at least 130 million years. Somewhere about that point in geological time it became severed from the land mass of Gondwanaland, the conjectured great southern continent of the Jurassic period, and drifted away northwards to an independent career. The separation occurred before mammals appeared in the world, and in consequence New Zealand, before its discovery by Man, had no native mammals except for a few bats whose ancestors had evidently flown there. It had, however, a few species of primitive reptiles and amphibians, including the remarkable Tuatara lizard, which existed in Permian times and has changed very little since. It also had a unique collection of large flightless birds.

THE MOAS In the islands that later split off from the main land-mass of Gondwanaland flightless birds had the opportunity to evolve through long millennia of relative tranquillity. In New Zealand in particular they were harassed by no mammalian predators and had little competition: here and in Madagascar they achieved impressive stature. The largest Moa stood more than ten ft high; the extinct Elephant-bird (*Aepyornis*) of Madagascar was equally large and weighed more than half a ton.

The ecological niche occupied by the Moas of New Zealand was that of grazing animals, similar to that of antelopes and zebras in Africa and deer in Europe and North America. They lived entirely on vegetation, especially grasses. They had small heads, with stout beaks and long necks, and legs as massive as tree-trunks. More than 20 species of Moa have been described from skeletons and other remains, though the exact number is a matter for some controversy. All are now extinct, though some have been so for only a few hundred years, and there are suggestions that a few may have survived into the nineteenth century.

The Moas are divided into two families, the *Dinornithidae* which comprises the Moas proper, and the *Anomalopterygidae*. Of the Moas proper there were six species, the largest of which was the ten-foot-tall *Dinornis maximus*. The smallest species was about the size of a Turkey, as was the *Anomalopteryx*, the smallest of the *Anomalopterygidae*. One of this latter family, the *Megalapteryx*, was still in existence when Europeans began to visit New Zealand.

New Zealand lies some 1,200 to 1,300 miles south-east of Australia but was first colonised not from that continent but from the islands twice as far away to the north and north-east. A massive Polynesian invasion by the ancestors of the Maoris occurred about A.D. 1350, but apparently there was an earlier settlement by smaller groups around A.D. 1000 or 950.

The chronology of the extermination of the Moas is uncertain. It seems that the fourteenth-century settlers found Moas so plentiful that they tended at first to neglect their traditional cultivation of crops in favour of hunting, only reverting to agriculture when game began to be scarce. Certainly they hunted Moas, frequent remains of bones and eggs having been found in Maori kitchen-middens. Naturalists investigating the status of the extremely rare Takahé (*Notornis*) in the Takahé Valley in 1948 found on excavating the site of a hunter's shelter the bones of not only the *Notornis* but the *Megalapteryx*, the date being fixed at not earlier than 1785. On the other hand, some authorities consider that the Giant Moa (*Dinormis maximus*) was extinct or nearly so before the fourteenth-century Maoris arrived. They suggest that a deterioration in the climate of New Zealand in the centuries before the arrival of the Maoris weakened and reduced the numbers of many of the species of Moa. A much heavier rainfall, too, caused the forest to invade the grassy plains, particularly in North Island, which were the most favoured Moa haunts. The impact of predatory human beings tipped the scales towards extinction.

The Polynesians also introduced two predatory animals, the dog and the Polynesian rat, to a land which had no indigenous carnivores. And as the human population multiplied they claimed for agriculture more and more of the dwindling area of grassland. Whatever happened, however, in the prehistory of New Zealand, most of the Moas had vanished before the advent of Europeans, and very few Europeans ever saw one.

OTHER LOST BIRDS OF NEW ZEALAND European traders began to call at New Zealand soon after Cook's rediscovery of the islands in 1769. Until 1840 there was much internecine war between Maori tribes, aided and often instigated by Europeans. Following the establishment of a British protectorate in 1840 European settlement proceeded on an increasing scale, often to the detriment of the Maoris, whose land was illegally seized. A series of Maori wars in the 1860s was the result, but from 1870 onwards the country settled down to a stable existence, with increasing prosperity. Over the 150 years of European settlement large areas of land have been claimed for agriculture. At the beginning of the period nearly 70 per cent of the country was still covered in forest, but the proportion has now been drastically reduced, and felling continues. To the dogs and Polynesian rats introduced by the early Maori settlers have been added cats, stoats, weasels, the Australian opossum, brown rats and black rats, all of which take a toll of birds and their eggs, as well as the domestic pigs, cattle, sheep and rabbits, which tend to destroy habitats. Nostalgic settlers from Europe have also brought in familiar birds from their homeland, with the result that no fewer than 43 species of European birds, including Goldfinches, Song-Thrushes, Blackbirds and the ubiquitous House-Sparrows are now well established there. A few species of Australian birds, too, including the Australian Silvereye and the Welcome Swallow, have within the same period found their way to New Zealand and have now become common.

All these changes have naturally had an effect on the indigenous birds of New Zealand, and it is perhaps surprising that not more than four, with the exception of the Moas, have become extinct, though many others are extremely scarce. One of the extinct species was that most interesting bird, the HUIA (*Heteralocha acutirostris*), which suddenly disappeared into oblivion in the early years of the present century. Distantly related to the Crows and Starlings, the Huia had evolved in the isolation of New Zealand into an elegant black-and-yellow creature with a remarkable divergence beween male and female. The male had a rather short, strong bill, similar to that of a Starling, whereas the female's was long, slender and downcurved. When feeding, the male broke through the bark and dead wood of decaying trees to get at the fat grubs feeding there, while the female followed, probing more daintily into the soft heartwood.

The Huia, a bird of subtropical forests, was never really abundant in New Zealand, its population being concentrated in a forest area in the southern part of North Island. There it was regularly hunted by the Maoris, who valued its white-tipped tail-feathers very highly for ceremonial purposes, though they were careful to maintain a viable population by imposing religious taboos on the killing of the birds. Unfortunately Europeans took note of the decorative value of the feathers, and a vogue developed in curios in which they featured. Huia skins began to fetch high prices, and the species was doomed. The last bird was recorded in 1907. Certain other factors may have played a secondary role in the extinction of the Huia. It lost much of its habitat through the felling of forests, though considerable areas of suitable woodland remain. Predatory animals probably destroyed many eggs and nests. There is also a suggestion that introduced species, notably the Indian Mynah, may have brought with them new diseases and parasites. But, beyond much doubt, commercially-minded Man was largely responsible for the Huia's demise. Unhappily the bird had two characteristics which made it especially vulnerable. Locating it was easy because of its lovely, bell-like call-note, for which it was sometimes known as the Bell-bird; while, having lived for so long in a land where it had hardly any enemies, it was inordinately tame.

Another extinct New Zealand species is the Stephens Island Wren (*Xenicus lyalli*). Stephens Island is a tiny offshore island near the north coast of South Island. The Wren was evidently an excessively local species, confined to the island and never seen alive by any ornithologist. It is known only from about 20 specimens brought in by the lighthouse-keeper's cat in the year 1894. This single animal apparently wiped out the entire population, which must have been very small.

The North Island race of the NEW ZEALAND LAUGHING OWL (*Sceloglaux albifacies*), known as the WHEKAU by the Maoris, has been extinct since the 1890s. Its South Island counterpart survives but is very rare. A ground-living, ground-nesting species, it probably fell victim to introduced predators which destroyed its nest and young.

The NEW ZEALAND QUAIL (*Coturnix novazeelandiae*) was the only game-bird native to New Zealand. In the 1840s it seems to have been reasonably common, for in about 1848 29½ brace were shot on an estate in the Nelsom province of South Island in a single season; 30 years later it was extinct. One is inclined to put the responsibility on introduced predators, to which a ground-nesting bird would naturally fall victim, but a disturbing fact is that other ground-nesting game-birds, including the Pheasant and several Australian species of Quail, introduced during those same 30 years, have flourished. The probability is, therefore, that these imported game-birds brought with them some disease to which the native Quail had no immunity, a state of affairs paralleled in the encounters of Europeans with sundry primitive peoples.

In addition to these four species, which must now be considered irretrievably lost, New Zealand still possesses a number of allied species and sub-species which have become extremely rare. Mention of them will be found on p. 72. Several have at times been written off as extinct, only to be restored to the list of surviving species by the unexpected discovery of a small population lingering in some remote region.

The Chatham Islands

Some 370 miles east of New Zealand but still on the same continental shelf, the Chatham Islands comprise one fairly large island of 372 square miles, another (Pitt Island) of 24 square miles, tiny Mangare Island and a few islets and rocks. After being visited frequently by whalers and traders, the islands were permanently settled in the nineteenth century and now have a population of about 500, as well as numerous cats, pigs, dogs and rats, which have played havoc with the indigenous bird population. Three local bird species and one sub-species have been extirpated within the past 150 years.

Two of these were flightless RAILS (*Rallus dieffenbachii* and *Rallus modestus*). The first became extinct before the middle of the nineteenth century, the second lasted until nearly 1900. Another casualty was a FERN-BIRD (*Bowdleria rufescens*), a member of the *Sylviidae* family and therefore related to the European warblers. All three of these species nested on the ground and were therefore extremely vulnerable to introduced predators. The fourth species was the CHATHAM ISLAND BELLBIRD (*Anthornis melanura melanocephala*), a subspecific form of the New Zealand Bellbird which is still not uncommon. It is also nearly related to the Oo of Hawaii (*see* page 52). Extermination on the main Chatham Islands was undoubtedly due to human interference, chiefly by the destruction of habitat and the introduction of alien predators, but the bird's disappearance from the uninhabited islets, notably Little Mangare, remains unexplained.

In addition, the Chatham Islands also once possessed a raven-like bird, the Kaka Parrot (still found in New Zealand), a large Rail, a large Coot and a very large Swan. All these are known only from excavated bones.

Lost birds of the Auckland Islands

The Auckland Islands are less hospitable than the Chatham Islands, lying 200 miles south of the southern tip of New Zealand and therefore 200 nearer the Antarctic; they are swept almost incessantly by westerly gales. There are eight islands in the group, of which the largest are Auckland and Adams Islands, the total area being 234 square miles. There is no permanent human population, but in the early decades of the nineteenth century the group was much visited by sealers and whalers who introduced dogs, pigs and, accidentally, rats.

Most of the indigenous Auckland Island birds survive, but two species have become extinct. The AUCKLAND ISLAND MERGANSER (*Mergus australis*) was once widely distributed on South Island, New Zealand, and after its extermination there found its last sanctuary on the Auckland Islands. Here it survived until the early years of the present century, when visiting sportsmen virtually eradicated it. The other indigenous species that has vanished, the AUCKLAND ISLAND RAIL (*Rallus muelleri*), disappeared somewhat earlier. A ground-nesting species, it was presumably eliminated by introduced predators.

Fortunately, another flightless species, the AUCKLAND ISLAND FLIGHTLESS TEAL (*Anas aucklandica*), has survived all hazards and is fairly common.

Lord Howe Island

Lord Howe Island, a mountainous island of about five square miles in the wastes of the Tasman Sea, some 300 miles east of New South Wales, has the distinction of having lost about two-thirds of its indigenous bird species since its discovery by Europeans. When first visited in 1788 it seems to have had 12 species or sub-species of resident land-birds, only four of which now survive.

The casualties comprise:

WHITE GALLINULE or SWAMP-HEN (*Porphyrio albus*) This was apparently a white sub-species of the PURPLE GALLINULE (*Porphyrio porphyrio*) which is still quite common in Australia and New Zealand. They were described by Arthur Bowes, who visited the island in 1789, as 'white birds resembling Guinea Fowl' and were apparently abundant.

LORD HOWE ISLAND PARROT (*Cyanoramphus novazelandiae subflavescens*), a sub-species of the NEW ZEALAND PARROT or KARARIKI (*Cyanoramphus novazelandiae*), which is still to be found on South Island, New Zealand, and on some of the smaller islands.

LORD HOWE ISLAND FANTAIL (*Rhipidura fuliginosa cervina*), a sub-species nearly related to the Fantails of Australia and New Zealand and to the European Penduline Tit.

LORD HOWE ISLAND FLYCATCHER (*Gerygone igata insularis*) was a sub-species of the GRAY WARBLER or RIRORIRO (*Gerygone igata*) of New Zealand.

LORD HOWE ISLAND PIGEON (*Columba vitiensis godmanae*) is known only from two paintings, one made in about 1790, and by a mention in an account of a voyage in 1788, the writer remarking significantly that he saw 'large fat pigeons . . . sitting on low bushes and so insensible to fear as to be knocked down with little trouble'. The bird was evidently related to Pigeons of Fiji and other Pacific islands.

LORD HOWE ISLAND STARLING (*Aplonis fuscus hullianus*) was said to have been plentiful in the first decades of the present century and, starling-like, to have been a bit of a nuisance to the settlers, eating the fruit in their gardens.

LORD HOWE ISLAND THRUSH (*Turdus poliocephalus vinitinctus*) was a bird nearly related to the English Blackbird (*Turdus merula*) and was a sub-species of a species still common in Indonesia, the Philippines and some of the Pacific islands.

LORD HOWE ISLAND WHITE-EYE (*Zosterops strenua*) was the island representative of the White-eye family, species of which are widely distributed in Africa, Asia and Australasia. Until about 1918 it was extremely common on the island and did much damage to garden crops.

The Lord Howe Island casualties occurred in two stages. The first followed the settlement of the island by Europeans in 1834. Within about 40 years the Gallinule, the Pigeon and the Parrot had become extinct, the first two through being killed for food, the last because of the damage it did in the settlers' gardens. (There is a possibility, though, that the Gallinules and the Pigeons had their populations considerably reduced by visiting whalers and sealers before permanent settlement occurred.) The second disaster to strike the island's wild life followed the wreck of a ship in 1918. Rats escaping from the wreck made themselves thoroughly at home on the island and were very largely responsible for the extermination of the Fantail, Flycatcher, White-eye, Starling and Thrush. Owls introduced to control the rats, however, did nothing to help the dwindling population of indigenous birds.

It is curious that certain other small species have managed to survive. A species nearly related to the extinct WHITE-EYE (*Zosterops lateralis tephropleura*) is still plentiful.

Norfolk Island

Some 300 miles east-north-east of Lord Howe Island and 400 miles north-west of the northern tip of New Zealand, Norfolk Island is a pleasantly temperate island of about 13 square miles, discovered by Captain Cook in 1777. Its indigenous bird population seems to have been 15 species of which, in remarkable contrast to the

28

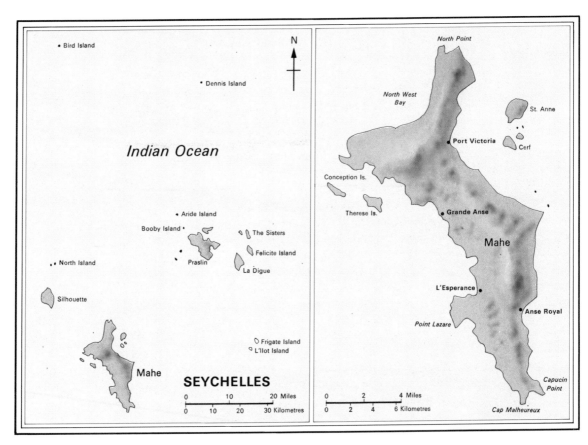

N

Indian Ocean

Bird Island

Dennis Island

Aride Island

Booby Island

The Sisters

Felicite Island

North Island

Praslin

La Digue

Silhouette

Frigate Island

L'Ilot Island

Mahe

SEYCHELLES

| 0 | 10 | 20 Miles |
| 0 | 10 | 20 | 30 Kilometres |

North Point

North West Bay

St. Anne

Cerf

Port Victoria

Conception Is.

Therese Is.

Grande Anse

Mahe

L'Esperance

Anse Royal

Point Lazare

Capucin Point

Cap Malheureux

| 0 | 2 | 4 Miles |
| 0 | 2 | 4 | 6 Kilometres |

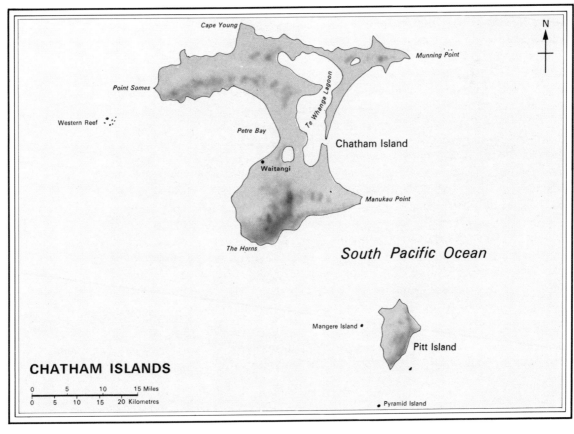

N

Cape Young

Munning Point

Point Somes

Te Whanga Lagoon

Western Reef

Petre Bay

Chatham Island

Waitangi

Manukau Point

The Horns

South Pacific Ocean

Mangere Island

Pitt Island

CHATHAM ISLANDS

| 0 | 5 | 10 | 15 Miles |
| 0 | 5 | 10 | 15 | 20 Kilometres |

Pyramid Island

casualty-rate on Lord Howe Island, only two have become extinct. These were: the NORFOLK ISLAND PARROT (*Nestor meridionalis productus*), a sub-species of the New Zealand KAKA (*Nestor meridionalis*) and evidently a forest bird, nesting in the fine woods of Norfolk Island pine (*Araucaria*) which clothed much of the island; and the NORFOLK ISLAND PIGEON (*Hemiphaga novaseelandiae spadicea*), similarly the local sub-species of the NEW ZEALAND PIGEON (*Hemiphaga novaseelandiae*) still to be found in the forests of New Zealand, while the Chatham Island race also survives and is apparently in no danger of extinction.

In addition THE BIRD OF PROVIDENCE (*Pterodroma solandri*), a Petrel, was exterminated on Norfolk Island at an early date, though it still survives on Lord Howe Island. The casualties on Norfolk Island were caused almost entirely by the establishment there of a penal settlement in 1788, the convicts and their guards being at times required to live off the land. The name, Bird of Providence, reveals how the hapless members of the little colony regarded the Petrels, which apparently they managed to exterminate within the first two years. The impact of human beings on the age-old ecology of the island was here so sudden and overwhelming that other species which were never recorded and of which we have no knowledge may have been eliminated at the same time.

Macquarie Island

Macquarie Island, which has an area of about 100 square miles, lies some 1,000 miles south-east of Tasmania (of which it is a dependency) and so is well on the way to Antarctica. Its harsh climate and almost incessant westerly gales make the growth of any other vegetation than tussocky grass and moss impossible. The only human inhabitants are the members of an Australian research station. But remoteness and an inhospitable environment were no safeguards against the depredations of Man. Of the five species of land birds known to have bred on the island, two are now extinct.

One was the MACQUARIE ISLAND RAIL (*Rallus philippensis assimilis*), a sub-species of a Rail still found in New Zealand, with relations on certain other Pacific islands. The other, the MACQUARIE ISLAND PARROT (*Cyanoramphus novazelandiae erythrotis*), a near relation of the Lord Howe Island sub-species which is extinct, and the Norfolk Island sub-species which survives and apparently flourishes, as well as the species type, which is still found in New Zealand.

Although Macquarie Island was without permanent human inhabitants until the establishment of the research station, it was visited from time to time by sealers from the early nineteenth century onward. As well as themselves killing the native birds, the sailors left behind them dogs, cats and, involuntarily, rats, which adapted to life in this inhospitable land and lived by preying on the birds and on each other. The birds were at a disadvantage in that, in the absence of trees, they had to nest on the ground under tussocks of grass, where of course they were extremely vulnerable. A contributory factor was the introduction, by Man, of the Weka (*Gallirallus australis*) from New Zealand, a tough and aggressive bird which doubtless bullied the native Rail and competed with it for food and territory.

The Pacific Islands

A remarkable feature of the list of extinct birds of the islands of the broad Pacific is the number of Rails it contains. Already in this survey we have encountered six, and there are at least six others, as well as a number of species and sub-species which are now dangerously rare. We have also noted an extinct rail, the Aphanapteryx, in the Mascarene Islands. Rails are not conspicuous birds, largely because of their reluctance to take wing. They prefer to conceal themselves by skulking in marshes or undergrowth, and in countries with a large human population their presence is often undetected even in semi-urban areas. Yet evidently they are at times great travellers, for they are among the few species which have established themselves on the remotest oceanic islands. In addition to the extinct Rails mentioned above there are many other island races which survive by the most tenuous of margins. The extinct Rails of the Pacific islands comprise the following:

RED-BILLED RAIL (*Rallus pacificus*) once lived on Tahiti, but little is known about it, and it has been extinct for many years.

SAMOAN WOOD RAIL (*Pareudiastes pacificus*) was a native of Savaii Island, of the Samoan group. It was last recorded in about 1873 but as it is highly secretive, probably nocturnal and confined to remote mountain fastenesses, it may just possibly survive. If it is extinct, cats and rats are doubtless to blame. Both the Samoan and the Fijian rails were almost flightless.

WAKE ISLAND RAIL (*Rallus wakensis*) was the sole land bird inhabiting the lonely coral atoll of Wake Island, in the north central Pacific. It was formerly fairly plentiful in the dense scrub which covered the island but was probably extirpated during the war by a Japanese garrison who are known to have run short of food.

KUSAIE ISLAND RAIL or CRAKE (*Aphanolimnas monasa*) formerly lived on Kusaie Island, which is a volcanic isle of some 42 square miles in the Caroline group, 1,000 miles or so east of the Philippines. The island seems to have been a favourite rendezvous of whaling ships, which were careened there in the early years of the nineteenth century, and the Rails, which were too small and insignificant to be of much interest to the sailors, were probably exterminated by rats escaping from the ships. The bird has not been seen since the 1870s.

IWO JIMA RAIL (*Poliolimnas cinereus brevipes*) was resident on Iwo Jima island, one of the Kazan, Volcano or Sulphur group which lie some 750 miles due south of the main island of Japan. It probably became extinct in or about the 1920s through the activities of domestic and feral cats. Apparently in times of drought the birds wandered from their forest and swamp habitats and, approaching human settlements, were snapped up by prowling cats.

There is a suspicion that in addition to these species there may have been many others on small Pacific islands, exterminated before they were ever recorded. A number of the Pacific islands also possessed Parrots which have become extinct. Most of them belonged to the New Zealand and Pacific genus *Cyanoramphus*, of which several sub-species have already been mentioned. Tahiti had two species of *Cyanoramphus* Parrot, both of which disappeared in the nineteenth century: the TAHITIAN PARROT or PARAKEET (*Cyanoramphus zealandicus*) and the RAIATEAN PARROT (*Cyanoramphus ulietanus*). The latter was found on the neighbouring island of Raitatea or Ulieta. Both have been so long extinct that little is known of them or of how they met their fate.

Species of *Cyanoramphus* Parrots still have small populations on the Kermadec Islands and Antipodes Islands, where at the moment they are safe from disturbance. Only one of the Kermadecs has a small human population, while the Antipodes are uninhabited, and few introduced animals have become acclimatised.

One of the surprising survivals of the Pacific is the TOOTH-BILLED PIGEON (*Didunculus strigirostris*) of the Samoan archipelago. This bird, which seems to be related to the extinct Dodo and Solitaires of the Mascarene Islands, might have been expected to succumb to interference by humans and feral animals, as so many other island species have done, but it is not even on the threatened list. However, several other Pacific pigeons and doves have slipped into oblivion. One was the highly specialised CRESTED PIGEON (*Microgoura meeki*), which inhabited the island of Choiseul, in the Solomon Islands. It is known from specimens collected in 1904.

Even more obscure is the history of the TANNA DOVE (*Gallicolumba ferruginea*), which is known only from a drawing and description of a bird obtained in 1774. Tanna is one of the southernmost islands of the New Hebrides, now Vanuatu. The Bonin Islands, 600–700 miles south of Tokio, used to possess their own species of Wood Pigeon, the BONIN WOOD PIGEON (*Columba versicolor*), found on only two of the small islands. They were probably eliminated by human interference, being of a suitable size for eating when other food was scarce. Other lost birds of the Bonins were the BONIN GROSBEAK (*Chaunoproctus ferreirostris*), which was probably extinct before the middle of the nineteenth century; the BONIN NIGHT HERON (*Nycticorax caledonicus crassirostris*), a sub-species of a species which is still widely distributed in the islands off eastern Asia; and the BONIN THRUSH (*Zoothera terrestris*), a species known only from specimens collected in 1828. Cats and rats were probably responsible for the disappearance of the Grosbeak and the Thrush, but the Night Heron may have been subject to direct human interference, for it was a large bird (standing two feet high) of striking appearance, with two long white plumes dangling from a black crown.

The Riukiu Islands, which form an extensive chain extending from southernmost Japan to Formosa (Taiwan) and include the large island of Okinawa, have lost a Kingfisher and probably a Thrush. The RIUKIU KINGFISHER (*Halcyon miyakoensis*) is supposed to have lived only on Miyako Island, one of the southernmost of the archipelago, and is known only from a single specimen collected there in 1887. The YAKUSHIMA THRUSH (*Turdus celaenops yakushimensis*) belonged to the island of Yakushima, not far from the Japanese mainland islands. It has not been recorded since 1904.

Mention has already been made of the Kusaie Rail, an extinct species which once inhabited the remote easternmost island of the Carolines. Kusaie also had a species of Starling, the KUSAIE ISLAND STARLING (*Aplonis corvina*), which apparently became extinct in the 1830s or soon afterwards. Starlings are usually able to adapt themselves, and this species was a large and robust bird, so its disappearance seems strange. Probably its Achilles heel was its nesting habits, of which nothing is known, for they may have exposed it to the depredations of rats which, escaped from whaling ships, swarmed on the island. A smaller allied species of Starling (*Aplonis opacus*) has survived evidently because of its habit of nesting in holes in trees.

Wading birds, which are celebrated long-distance travellers, may seem unlikely candidates for extinction, but the Pacific has two on its list. The TAHITIAN SAND-

32

PIPER (*Prosobonia leucoptera*) is one. It did not long survive the discovery of Tahiti by Captain Cook in 1773, and rats are generally blamed for its extermination. It was, of course, a ground-nesting species.

Christmas Island and Washington Island are two members of a group known as the Line Islands, for the reason that they straddle the equator, about midway between America and Asia. The second extinct wader of the Pacific, the BARRED PHALAROPE (*Aechmorhynchus cancellatus*), is extinct only as far as Christmas Island is concerned. It is still found on a number of the small islands of the Tuamotu archipelago, to the south-east. Washington Island had a duck, a sub-species of the American Gadwall and known as the WASHINGTON ISLAND GADWALL (*Anas strepera couesi*), which has disappeared, probably through excessive shooting. The unlikely emergence of a sub-species on such a small remote island is largely due to the presence there of a sizeable freshwater lake—an almost unique occurrence. Presumably at some time storm-blown Gadwall alighted there and found it a con-genial habitat.

In the north Pacific the Aleutian Islands had lost a sea-bird, the SPECTACLED CORMORANT (*Phalacrocorax perspicillatus*), by the middle years of the nineteenth century. In the later years of its existence it was confined to Bering Island and neighbouring islets, but formerly it may have had a wider distribution. This was a big, flightless bird which had the handicap of being good to eat. It was probably exterminated by seal- and otter-hunters, though foxes may have hastened the end.

The Seychelles

Three species of land bird are known to have disappeared from the Seychelles Islands, which lie in the heart of the Indian Ocean north-east of Madagascar.

One of them, the CHESTNUT-FLANKED WHITE-EYE (*Zosterops semiflava*) is known from only a few specimens and was apparently confined to tiny Marianne Island. As a forest bird it probably became extinct when the forests were cleared.

Like so many other small islands, the Seychelles have lost their parrot, the SEYCHELLES PARROT (*Psittacula eupatria wardi*); it was extinct by about the end of the nineteenth century. The probable cause was persecution, triggered off by the parrot's fondness for ripening maize.

The Tristan d'Acunha Coot

This bird, *Gallinula nesiotis nesiotis*, was indigenous to the island of Tristan d'Acunha, which lies in the south Atlantic, on about the same latitude as Cape-town. It was a smallish bird, about 10 in. long, and not unlike the European Moorhen. Undoubtedly it succumbed primarily to the attacks of pigs, rats, cats and dogs introduced by sealers and also when permanent human settlement began in 1817, but some were also killed by the islanders for food. An allied sub-species, the GOUGH ISLAND COOT (*Gallinula nesiotis comeri*), still survives on uninhabited Gough Island, 200 miles to the south.

The West Indies

Parrots predominate in the list of lost birds of the West Indies. They fell not only to direct human interference but also to the destruction of their forest habitat to make way for cultivation. In many instances that happened in the early eighteenth century, with the result that some of the species are known only from a few specimens, from drawings and descriptions or from excavated bones. Three of the species were members of the genus *Amazona*. They were the GUADELOUPE PARROT (*Amazona violacea*), the MARTINIQUE PARROT (*Amazona martinicana*) and the CULEBRA PARROT (*Amazona vittata graciliceps*). They belonged respectively to the islands from which they take their name. Related species survive on Dominica, St Lucia and St Vincent, while the Culebra bird was a sub-species of a species still found on Puerto Rico.

The *Amazona* parrots were relatively small, compared to the Macaws of the larger West Indian islands. The CUBAN RED MACAW (*Ara tricolor*) was reported by early Spanish explorers as being as big as a chicken. It survived in forest swamps in Cuba until well into the nineteenth century and probably became extinct, through human interference, in the 1880s. The specific name *tricolor* refers to its brilliant red, yellow and blue coloration. A similar bird but rather differently coloured (it apparently lacked any blue feathers) was the GUADELOUPE MACAW (*Ara guadelou-pensis*). Its existence is conjectured or established from paintings and descriptions, no skins having survived.

Jamaica, too, is thought to have possessed a red Macaw, the JAMAICAN MACAW (*Ara gossei*), which had disappeared before the end of the eighteenth century. The existence of two other Jamaican Macaws—the JAMAICAN YELLOW-AND-BLUE MA-CAW (*Ara araurana*) and the JAMAICAN GREEN-AND-YELLOW MACAW (*Ara mili-taris*)—has been deduced from eye-witness descriptions of the seventeenth and eighteenth centuries, but the evidence is not above suspicion.

Conures are small, green, long-tailed parrots, of which three species are still quite plentiful on the larger West Indian islands. A fourth, the PUERTO RICAN CONURE (*Aratinga chloroptera maugei*), seems to have become extinct on Puerto Rico towards the end of the nineteenth century with, once again, the destruction of forests as the probable chief contributory cause.

Jamaica's lost birds include a Rail, the JAMAICAN WOOD RAIL (*Amaurolimnas concolor concolor*), and a Nightjar, the JAMAICAN NIGHTHAWK (*Siphonoris ameri-canus americanus*). The Wood Rail was not a small bird, its length being about 10 in., and it had the normal rail habit of skulking in swamps and among the vegetation by streams. Its demise was probably brought about by cats, rats and other predatory creatures, including particularly the very destructive mongoose. A nearly allied sub-species still exists, however, on the mainland of Central America. The Jamaican Nighthawk seems to have been exterminated before the mongoose was introduced to the island in 1872, so probably rats were to blame; it was apparently never very numerous or widespread. An allied species, the HISPANI-OLAN NIGHTHAWK (*Siphonorhis brewsteri*), still exists precariously in Haiti and the Dominican Republic.

What happened to certain West Indian Wrens is something of a mystery. The species is *Troglodytes musculus*, and of it four sub-species still inhabit the respective islands where they evolved. The races on Dominica and Grenada are quite com-mon, those on St Lucia and St Vincent much less so. But the MARTINIQUE WREN (*Troglodytes musculus martinicensis*) and the GUADELOUPE WREN (*Troglodytes musculus guadeloupensis*) have become extinct. Cats, rats and the mongoose are usually blamed for their disappearance, but these predators are found on the other islands as well. Dominica is perhaps less densely populated and less intensively cultivated than most of its neighbours, which may have some bearing on the matter. Another unexplained demise is that of the ST KITTS BULLFINCH (*Loxigilla portoricensis grandis*), a sub-species of a type still found on Puerto Rico. There are other somewhat similar species on other West Indian islands and all seem to have achieved a satisfactory status. The responsibility is usually allocated to the introduction of an African monkey, which presumably interfered with the birds' nests, though other small passerine birds have managed to survive on the island.

Two sub-species of the American Burrowing Owls have been exterminated on the West Indian islands where they were indigenous. One, the ANTIGUAN BURROWING OWL (*Speotyto cunicularia amaura*), was found not only on Antigua but also on Nevis and St Kitts. The other, the MARIE GALANTE BURROWING OWL (*Speotyto cunicularia guadeloupensis*), was confined to tiny Marie Galante Island. They seem to have become extinct in the 1880s or 1890s, and their disappearance is linked with the introduction of the mongoose about that time. In their long nesting-tunnels in the sandy soil they would have been easy prey for the mongoose.

Guadalupe Island

The Guadalupe Island in question is not the French island in the West Indies but the Mexican island which lies about 200 miles west of Lower California. It is a mountainous island of some 120 square miles and was formerly well wooded with cypress and pines and possessing in places a dense cover of sage brush. For many years the island has been devastated by an immense herd of feral goats which have progressively destroyed the vegetation and robbed several bird species of their habitats. In consequence, the GUADALUPE WREN (*Thryomanes bewickii brevicauda*), the GUADALUPE WOODPECKER OR FLICKER (*Colaptes cafer rufipileus*), and the GUADALUPE TOWHEE (*Pipilo erythrophthalmus consobrinus*) have become extinct. The Wren, which was a sub-species of a species common on the American mainland, was last seen in 1901. Predation by cats may have been a contributory factor to its extinction, and to that of the Woodpecker and the Towhee. Both of these, too, were sub-species of North American birds.

The history of the extinct GUADALUPE CARACARA (*Polyborus lutosus*) is rather different. The hawk, which is a large one, was deliberately exterminated by the peasants who had charge of the herds of goats, on the grounds (probably correct) that the Caracaras fed on young kids. The last record dates from 1900.

The cats which gave the *coup de grace* to the small passerine birds of Guadalupe are also blamed for the eradication of the GUADALUPE PETREL (*Oceanodroma macrodactyla*). They are known to have preyed on the birds unmercifully as they entered and left their nesting burrows. The last live specimen was reported in 1911.

The lost birds of North America

The extinct species of North America have foundered for very different reasons from those we have been considering. Far from having to contend with the perils naturally associated with a small population in a restricted habitat, the American casualties had a whole vast continent to range over, and in most instances their numbers were enormous. They perished through the destruction of their habitats as the tide of human settlement surged westwards across the continent, coupled with the ruthless onslaught of men with guns. The irretrievable casualties are the Passenger Pigeon, the Carolina Parakeet, the Heath-hen, and the Labrador Duck, but many other species reached such a low ebb (e.g. the Eskimo Curlew and the

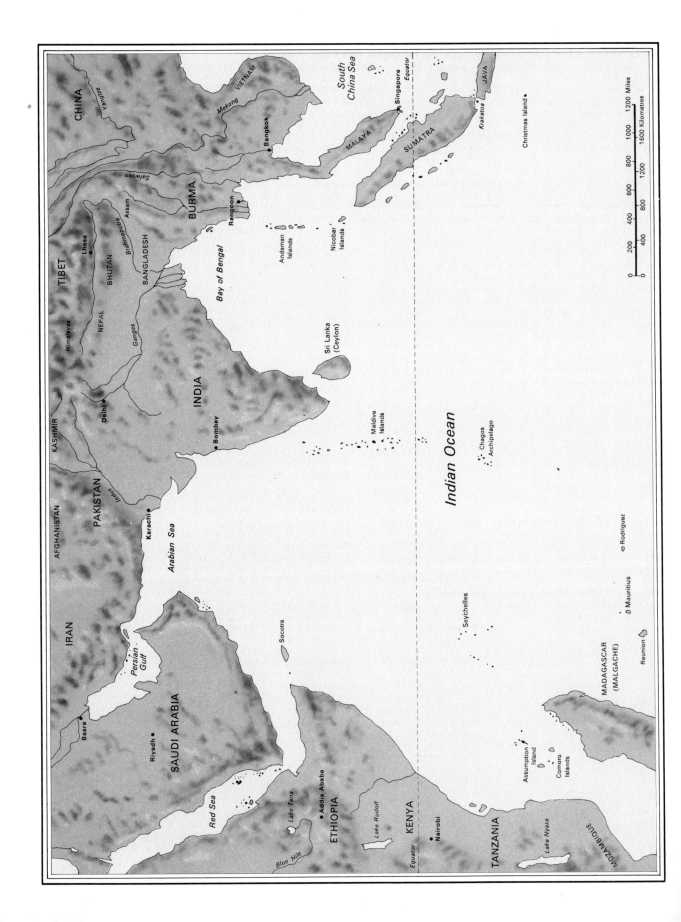

Hudsonian Godwit) that they were thought to be extinct, while the status of a number of others—such as the Ivory-billed Woodpecker, the Everglade Kite and the Whooping Crane—remains precarious.

Saddest and most disgraceful of the American obituaries is that of the PASSEN-GER PIGEON (*Ectopistes migratorius*). The story is so well known that only a summary of the salient facts need be given here. When the European settlement of North America began the Passenger Pigeon must have been one of the most numerous species of bird in the world. Its habitat was the forest country between the Atlantic Ocean and the Great Plains. Although it was essentially migratory, travelling in prodigious flocks, its summer and winter ranges sometimes over-lapped, for it is known to have wintered as far north as the New England states. Usually, however, it went farther south, to the states bordering the Gulf of Mexico. It was highly gregarious at all seasons, nesting in immense colonies and migrating in apparently endless flocks that darkened the sky as they passed, hour after hour. Many estimates have been made and stories told to illustrate the size of the migrating flocks. The early American naturalist, Alexander Wilson, calculated that a flock he saw in Kentucky in or about the year 1808 consisted of at least 2,230,000,000 birds. In 1813 Audubon, watching a migration also in Kentucky, recorded a flock that was passing overhead continuously for three days and esti-mated their numbers at 1,000,000,000 birds every three hours. As late as 1878, within about 20 years of the species' final extinction, an estimated 1,000,000,000 birds were killed at one of the last communal nesting sites, at Petoskey, Michigan.

When these vast flocks stopped to roost for the night their numbers were so great that often large trees collapsed under their weight. Sometimes when they de-scended to drink at lakes many were drowned through others landing on their backs. The passage of the flocks overhead was like that of a heavy storm. Not only was the sky darkened but the air-currents, as the birds flew past at as much as 60 m.p.h., reduced the temperature by several degrees, while their droppings fell like hail. In their nesting habits they were equally gregarious. In the chosen area, which often covered several hundred square miles, every tall tree was occupied by nests, sometimes as many as a hundred in a tree. The floor of the forest became carpeted with droppings, and the casualty-rate among young birds falling from the nests was enormous.

It seems incredible that a species which existed in such numbers should ever have been exterminated; indeed, one of the reasons for its final demise was that no-one seems to have realised that such a disaster was possible. The methods of mass slaughter used against the pigeons make depressing and often horrifying reading. At first the European settlers adopted the Red Indian procedure of collecting the fat squabs from the ground beneath the nests, which provided ample for their needs. As these young birds represented a surplus which would have been sacri-ficed anyway, no harm was done to the species. Later, of course, guns were used and sometimes it was even possible, when the flocks were flying low, to knock down hundreds of birds with long sticks. Serious trouble began to threaten when professional hunters took over. Their role was to gather large consignments of birds for shipment to the growing cities, a task facilitated after about 1850 by the rapid development of the railway network. In the second half of the nineteenth century some 5,000 hunters or trappers were engaged in the trade. As early as 1805 Audubon saw in the port of New York City ships loaded to capacity with the carcases of pigeons killed near the Hudson River, and later in the century the slaughter rate was greatly accelerated.

Besides guns and the collecting of helpless squabs, nets and decoys were widely used. Trees holding many nests were felled to get at the squabs; fires of sulphur were lit under trees to asphyxiate the birds and cause them to tumble down; grain soaked in alcohol was used as bait, to make adult birds drunk so that they could be collected. Even the colossal numbers of the Passenger Pigeon were no match for such an onslaught.

Of course, it was not to be expected that the Passenger Pigeon could sustain its enormous population once the United States became more densely settled by Man. Many of the forests which the birds had used for roosting and nesting were cleared to make way for cultivation. Subsequently the pigeons proved bad neighbours for farmers. They ate seed-corn at seedtime and ripening grain at harvest, and it took only a short time for such huge flocks to clear a field. So a measure of self-preservation as well as the desire for an easy profit entered into the campaign.

The end came with extraordinary suddenness. The species had disappeared from New England by the middle of the nineteenth century, the last communal nesting occurring in Massachusetts in 1851. In the 1870s, as already noted, a vast nesting-area in Michigan was able to yield a toll of 1,000 million birds in a single year, and in the same decade comparable colonies existed in Wisconsin, Minnesota and some other central states. As late as 1893 a St Louis game-dealer is said to have received a shipment of birds from Arkansas. But before the end of the century the bird was extinct in the wild. The last authentic record is of a bird taken in Wisconsin in 1899. Although rewards were offered for any wild birds located from 1909 onwards there were no takers, and the last Passenger Pigeon the world was ever to see died in Cincinnati Zoo in 1914. A moral to this melancholy history is that no species can ever be considered entirely safe, no matter how great its population. Every bird species can be considered 'at risk'. When Man really puts his mind to it he is extraordinarily efficient at mass destruction.

One wonders, however, about the possibility of some inherent weakness in the Passenger Pigeon. Its very sociability and gregariousness seem to have contributed to its undoing. The advantages of assembling in large flocks can be illustrated by numerous examples from the wild. The big game of Africa, for instance, seek safety from predators, such as lions and hyenas, by gathering in enormous herds. Fish congregate in shoals, and many bird species assemble in large flocks for migration. The Passenger Pigeon seems to have experienced peak years for population, asso-ciated with food supply, much as many northern species such as the Crossbill, the Waxwing and, among mammals, the Lemming, still do. As their chief foods were acorns and other fruits and berries, the habit of assembling in vast flocks wherever food happened to be plentiful would be a natural development. The little Quelea birds of Africa, which experience similar population cycles, do the same, to the detriment of farmers who grow the grain on which they feed.

But the tragedy of the Passenger Pigeon is that it failed to adapt. The European Wood Pigeon (*Columba palumbus*), which has very similar propensities, has done so successfully. It too eats acorns, berries, grain and a wide range of vegetable foods. It collects in large flocks to go raiding and, when given the opportunity, engages in communal nesting: many conifer forests have their colonies of Wood Pigeons. But many suburban gardens also have their single nests, and Wood

Pigeons are among the commonest birds in Britain and elsewhere, even in urban areas. They are an example of successful adaptation, which the Passenger Pigeon could not achieve. Perhaps it was not given sufficient time; perhaps the onslaught was too sudden; but when that has been taken into account there is still the fact to be faced that dispersed nesting by the Passenger Pigeon was unsuccessful. After the big communal nestings had been broken up in New England, the birds continued to nest in small numbers or singly for 30 years or so, but in the absence of opportunity for gregarious assembly they could not sustain their population, which dwindled and eventually died out. It seems that the huge flock-nestings provided a stimulus without which the species could not survive.

The CAROLINA PARAKEET (*Conuropsis carolinensis carolinensis*) followed a course to oblivion roughly parallel to that of the Passenger Pigeon. Like the Pigeons, the Carolina Parakeets were gregarious birds. They assembled in large flocks, roosted together in hollow trees and nested communally. Their social consciousness was well developed, and one of the factors in their extermination was their habit of returning to try to succour flock-mates who had fallen dead or wounded to the ground; they could then be shot easily. These Parrots were not, however, migratory. They were the only indigenous Parrots of the North American continent, and even those which lived as far north as New York and Wisconsin did not move south to escape the winter. Although they did not achieve such colossal numbers as the Passenger Pigeons they were abundant and widespread, and the possibility of their ever becoming extinct does not seem to have occurred to anyone until it was too late.

In one respect the Carolina Parakeet was popular with farmers. Its favourite food was the burrs of the cocklebur (a composite plant of the genus *Xanthium*), which tended to stick in the fleeces of sheep, decreasing their value and rendering shearing difficult. Their good offices in consuming burrs were, however, more than outweighed by the havoc they wrought in fruit orchards. Although they had no great fondness for apples they would descend on an orchard and strip it entirely of fruit, snipping off the apples and leaving them littering the ground. They did the same with plantations of peaches, oranges, grapes and other fruit, clearing the trees or vines before the fruit had ripened. At other times they turned their attention to crops of ripening grain or to grain already stacked. Such behaviour could, of course, not be tolerated by hard-working farmers, who shot the birds wholesale. Another factor in their decline was their popularity as cage-birds. Vast numbers were caught and sold for this purpose, including many to Europe, where they were very popular. Between 1880 and 1900, too, a vogue developed in ladies' hats ornamented with brilliantly coloured bird-feathers, and countless Parakeets were sacrificed on the altar of millinery.

Like the Passenger Pigeon, the Carolina Parakeet bred fairly freely in captivity, and there should have been little difficulty in perpetuating the species in this way once its existence in the wild became threatened. It is true that captive Passenger Pigeons became infertile through inbreeding, but that was a hazard which could have been avoided by intelligent planning. As with the Passenger Pigeon, it seems that the bird was so familiar and common that no-one realised the danger of extinction. The last undisputed specimen of the Carolina Parakeet died in Cincinnati Zoo in September, 1914—by coincidence in the same month and in the same place as the last Passenger Pigeon. Occasional sightings of wild birds were reported from Florida and South Carolina in the 1920s and 1930s, but the possibility that these may have been escaped specimens of some other species has to be taken into account. Beyond doubt, the Carolina Parakeet has long been extinct.

The HEATH-HEN (*Tympanuchus cupido cupido*) is usually regarded as another American species which has slipped into the limbo of extinct birds, and so it is. In this instance, however, it is not a complete species which has foundered, but a sub-species. *Tympanuchus cupido* has other sub-species in the GREATER PRAIRIE CHICKEN or PINNATED GROUSE (*Tympanuchus cupido pinnatus*) and in ATTWATER'S PRAIRIE CHICKEN (*Tympanuchus cupido attwateri*), both of which survive, though the latter somewhat precariously. Heath-hens and Prairie Chicken were or are handsome birds of the Grouse Family and hence popular game-birds. At one time the Heath-hen was found, in some abundance, in all the New England states, south to Virginia. For the early settlers it provided a useful addition to the larder. In spite of laws, the earliest dating from 1791, to protect the birds or at least to regulate the shooting, the Heath-hen rapidly declined in numbers. Quite early in the nineteenth century it was confined to the island of Martha's Vineyard, off the coast of Massachusetts, where a survey in 1890 revealed a population of about 200 birds.

In 1908, when the numbers had further diminished, a reserve of 1,600 acres was created to preserve them. It proved so successful that by 1915 the population had grown to about 2,000. Then disaster struck. It began with a bush-fire in the reserve in the summer of 1916, followed by a very severe winter, an irruption of Goshawks which preyed on the birds, and finally an epidemic of Blackhead, a disease of domestic poultry. Numbers were reduced to 13 in the mid-1920s, and the last bird died in 1932. It seems that similar factors were responsible for the extinction of the Heath-hen on mainland America earlier. Bush-fires are an example of the destruction of habitat, in which the spread of cultivation also played a part. The predators which preyed on this ground-nesting species included domestic and feral cats. And the bird was certainly susceptible to diseases which affect domestic poultry.

In the final stages, the Heath-hens of Martha's Vineyard illustrated the hazards attendant on a small population in a restricted area. Any natural catastrophe can do irreparable damage. A dispersal of population, so that disaster in one place can be corrected by reinforcements from another, is essential.

A fourth species lost to the United States, the LABRADOR DUCK (*Camptorhynchus labradorius*), has a much less well-documented history than the others under consideration. The bird is known to have frequented the coasts of New England and eastern Canada in winter and is supposed to have bred farther north, perhaps in Labrador, though its breeding haunts were never discovered. By the middle of the nineteenth century its occasional appearances on market-stalls in New York had ceased, and the last bird, a specimen in Long Island Sound, was seen in 1875. The reason for its demise is not known. Shooting may have contributed to it, and so may Indian expeditions to collect eggs and feathers in the eighteenth century. There is even a suggestion that it may have been one of the first victims of pollution, through a consequent decline in the numbers of shell-fish on the New England coast.

Some lists of America's extinct birds include two other names. One is the GIANT CANADA GOOSE (*Branta canadensis maxima*), a large sub-species of the still common Canada Goose. It is said to have lived in the prairie states and sometimes to have attained a great size, up to 15 or 18 lb. Doubt has been expressed, however, as to whether these birds were ever more than large specimens of the typical race.

The other is the ESKIMO CURLEW (*Numenius borealis*), whose history is on similar lines to those of the Passenger Pigeon and the Carolina Parakeet. Against all probability, however, small numbers of this species seem to have survived, so it gains a place in another chapter (*see* p. 118).

The Great Auk   The Great Auk (*Alca impennis*) and the Dodo are often regarded as epitomes of all the extinct fauna of the world. They serve as classic examples of the way in which species can be exterminated by Man. Both, however, belong to a period of history now growing remote from us. The Dodo of Mauritius was extinct before the end of the seventeenth century, while the last Great Auk of which definite evidence exists was killed off Iceland in 1844.

Much of the history of the Great Auk has been compiled from archaeological evidence. The birds seem to have been an important part of the diet of maritime tribes of prehistoric men at least as far back as 7000 B.C. Excavated middens reveal that several thousands of years ago they were widespread off the coasts of temperate North America, Iceland, the British Isles and Scandinavia and that in many places they were abundant. They continued to be plentiful until the sixteenth or seventeenth centuries by which time sailors, now accustomed to ocean voyages, were taking a heavy toll of them. For the Great Auk was easy prey. Although in its element in the sea, where it could swim faster than the fastest boat could move and where it could stay under water for several minutes, it was flightless. It was therefore unable to reach ledges on precipitous cliffs, inaccessible to men, and was confined to flat, low-lying rocks and beaches on to which it could jump. In this respect it resembled the Penguins of the southern hemisphere, and indeed many old chronicles refer to it as a Penguin. It was a large bird, standing some 30 in. high. On shore it was ungainly and it seems to have been lacking in intelligence, if by intelligence we understand the perspicacity to evade men bent on killing it.

Like many other sea-birds, it nested in colonies on suitable rocky islets. Several of these were off Iceland, an important one being destroyed by a volcanic eruption in 1830; the island of St Kilda was another. Probably the most densely populated breeding-site was tiny Funk Island, off the north-east coast of Newfoundland. From this base the bird swam out to fish off the Grand Banks, and it could well be that Bristol ships, and perhaps those of other nations of western Europe, were fishing there before the official discovery of America by Columbus in 1492 and were using the presence of the Auks as an indication that they had arrived.

By the middle of the sixteenth century or soon afterwards Funk Island was a regular provisioning station for ships. In 1578 at least 400 transatlantic vessels, of English, French and Spanish nationality, put in at Funk Island to replenish their supplies of fresh meat, meaning Great Auk carcases. Two hundred years later the birds were still numerous enough for commercial exploitation. The attraction then seems to have been their feathers, perhaps for use in stuffing pillows and mattresses. A shore-base was established on the little island and boilers erected, into which the carcases were thrown to loosen their feathers. As no other fuel was available, other carcases were employed to make the fires: being rich in oil, they burned well. This trade began in about 1785. How long it lasted is not known, but Great Auks had been exterminated on Funk Island by about 1840. The islets off

41

Iceland, and perhaps St Kilda, were now the last refuges of the species, but even there it was subject to persecution. By the 1830s ornithologists belatedly became aware that the Great Auk was in danger of extinction, but the realisation did the bird no good, for collectors of eggs and skins began to offer high prices for the survivors.

The rest of the story is a melancholy list of last occurrences. Two birds were captured in the Orkneys in 1812. One was caught on St Kilda in 1821 but escaped. There is an account of another captured there in 1840 by a crofter who kept it for three days and then, suspecting that it might be a witch responsible for a recent storm, killed it. One arrived in Waterford Harbour in 1834 and was promptly collected for a museum specimen. The End was written by the beating to death of two Great Auks found on a ledge on Eldey Island, off Iceland, in 1844, although there was a sight record for 1852. This was of a bird seen off the Grand Banks of Newfoundland, and as the observer was a Colonel Drummond-Hay who became the first president of the British Ornithologists' Union it is likely to have been correctly identified. In the history of the Great Auk there are no other possible contributory causes for its demise than the greed and ruthlessness of Man. The volcanic eruption of 1830 may have hastened the end, which would, however, have been inevitable.

The Emus of Australia

Australia, the home of the Emu, has lost three of the sub-species which used to inhabit the offshore islands. They were the TASMANIAN EMU (*Dromaeius novaehollandiae diemenensis*), the KING ISLAND EMU (*Dromaeius novaehollandiae minor*) and the KANGAROO ISLAND EMU (*Dromaeius novaehollandiae diemenianus*). Kangaroo Island is a rather large island (1,970 square miles) off the coast of South Australia; King Island a rather smaller one in the Bass Straits between Victoria and Tasmania.

The King Island Emu may hardly merit inclusion in this book, for it became extinct in prehistoric times and is known only from bones. The Tasmanian Emu lasted long enough to see the first European settlement of Tasmania but was extinct by the early decades of the nineteenth century. One suggestion is that the early settlers hunted it to extinction, but the truth of the matter is not known. On the other hand, human beings could hardly have been responsible for the extermination of the Kangaroo Island Emu, which was extinct when settlement began in 1836. Yet it had been abundant when the island was discovered in 1802. What happened in the intervening 34 years? Occasional sealers could have taken a toll, but they could not have eliminated the entire population of such a large area. A disastrous forest-fire has been suggested, but it is, of course, not known whether such an event occurred.

The disappearance of these three sub-species provides yet another set of illustrations of the vulnerability of birds confined to island habitats.

Premature Obituaries

A few species have in recent years been rediscovered after having been pronounced extinct. They are: the MOLOKAI THRUSH (*Phaeornis obscurus rutha*), a bird of the Hawaiian island of Molokai, thought to have become extinct in the 1920s or 1930s;

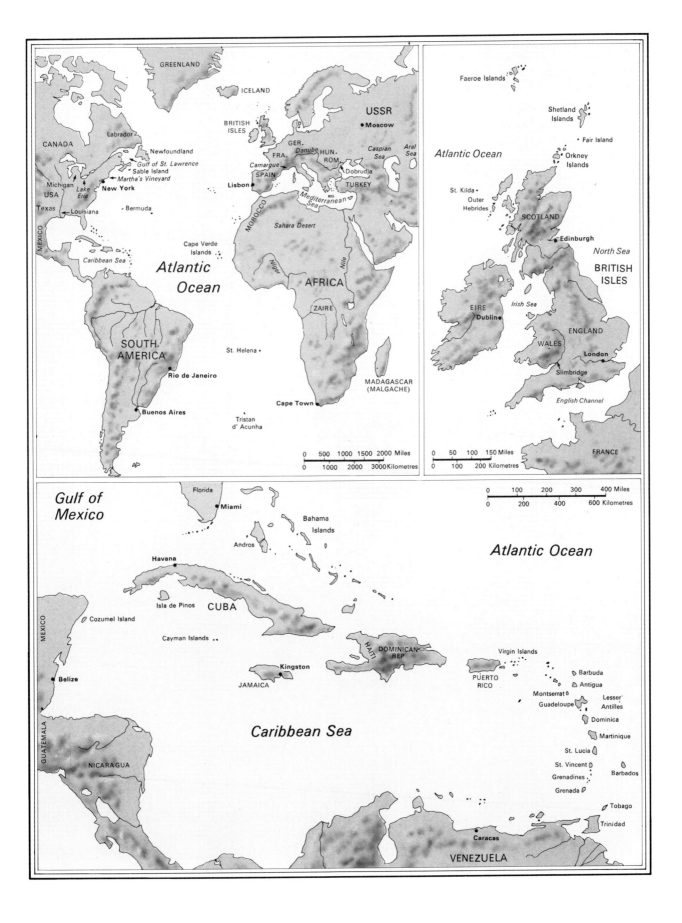

the BLEWITT'S OWL (*Athene blewitti*), an Indian species; the LONG-LEGGED WAR-
BLER (*Trichocichla rufa*), a bird of Fiji.

The BARRED-WINGED RAIL (*Nesoclopeus poeciloptera*) lived in swamp country
on Fiji but was thought to have been exterminated by the imported mongoose.

Raven (f). Once common in
Britain, but now restricted to
remote mountainous districts.
Photo. G. H. E. Young

Birds with Restricted Ranges

It would seem axiomatic that the more restricted the range of a species the more vulnerable it is. A population concentrated into a few square miles is bound to be more at risk than one with a wider dispersal. A natural disaster, such as a volcanic eruption or a typhoon, or human interference—whether by direct predation or the introduction of other predators or the destruction of habitat—can quickly eliminate a substantial proportion of a population. The extreme example is the case of the Stephens Island Wren, which lived on a small island off the north coast of New Zealand's South Island. It is said to have been unable to fly and to have scuttled about among the rocks at twilight. It is known only from specimens killed by the resident lighthouse-keeper's cat in 1894. Apparently in that year the single cat extirpated the entire population.

In 1963 a hurricane which howled across the small island of Laysan, at the western end of the Hawaiian archipelago, swept away a large proportion of the rare Laysan Teal and reduced its population from 688 (according to a count made in 1961) to approximately 200. The fact that the Laysan Teal is so reluctant a flier as to be virtually flightless doubtless contributed to the disaster. Laysan is an island of only 709 acres, much of which area is occupied by a salt lagoon, in the scrub and marshes around which the Teal nests. Its total population can therefore never have been very large, thus enabling a single catastrophe to make a disproportionate impact on it.

The colonisation of Oceanic Islands

The immense reaches of ocean are no deterrent to migrating birds. We expect that to be so with pelagic species, such as the petrels and shearwaters which spend most of their time at sea, but land-birds too make astonishing trans-oceanic journeys. For instance, the Lesser Golden Plover (*Pluvialis dominica*) after nesting in Alaska and north-western Canada, flies more than 2,000 miles over an island-less sea to winter in Hawaii. From New Zealand the Long-tailed Cuckoo (*Urodynamis taitensis*) migrates in the southern winter to Fiji and Samoa, a journey of nearly 2,000 miles. Sightings from ships indicate that the Greenland Wheatear (*Oenanthe oenanthe leucorrhoa*) sometimes chooses to make the long ocean crossing direct from Greenland to the Iberian peninsula or even Africa, rather than take the more circuitous island-hopping route via Iceland and the British Isles. On their northward migrations in spring large numbers of birds prefer to fly straight across the Mediterranean in the Old World and the Gulf of Mexico in the New rather than spend time following the land bridges.

These habitual long-distance travellers are, however, not the ones which primarily concern us when we study the colonisation of remote islands. Birds which take for granted trans-ocean flights of 2,000 miles and more are not going to feel themselves trapped when they alight on an island 1,000 miles from the nearest land; after a rest they will take to the air again. The colonisers of the oceanic islands are land-birds which are normally sedentary but which have been picked up by great winds and tossed on to islands far from their normal range. Having no well-developed migratory instinct, they tend to settle down and make the best of what they find. That, though, is likely to offer much less variety than they are accustomed to in their homeland. The vegetation and insect-life of oceanic islands, whether volcanic or coral in origin, has had to get there via immense tracts of ocean. Seeds may have drifted in on ocean currents or have been carried on the feet of sea-birds; insects may have adopted similar modes of travel or have been airborne. The farther the island lies from the base of the colonisers, the fewer of them will reach it.

When land-birds arrive on a distant island which has already been colonised by plants and insects (including spiders) they will therefore find the available food-supply much more restricted than in the more extensive habitat from which they came. There is evidence that many more birds land on such islands than ever manage to establish a breeding population. Those that do remain and survive may expect to have to adapt themselves. Their diet will probably be less varied and may call for specialist physical changes. Thus in the Galápagos Islands Darwin's Large-billed Ground Finch (*Geospiza magnirostris*) evolved a large, strong beak which enabled it to crack the hard shells of seeds which other birds could not tackle. On the other hand, the colonisers of remote islands generally find themselves in a haven remarkably free from predators. Unless aided by Man, there is virtually no way by which mammals can get there. Nor is there a resident population of predatory birds, for such islands are normally too small to support one.

Freed from fear, island birds tend to develop habits which would be lethal on a mainland. Many lose the power of flight, allowing even their wings to become atrophied. A natural corollary of that development is that they nest on the ground. Because a rapidly-increasing population would play havoc with the island's resources, they are inclined to adopt the form of birth-control which consists of laying only one egg per year. Early explorers have testified to the birds of previously unvisited islands being extraordinarily tame and trusting, an endearing flaw which contributed to the downfall of such species as the Dodo and Solitaire.

Rare birds of the Galápagos Islands

Remote in the vast Pacific Ocean, the Galápagos Islands lie approximately 600 miles west of mainland Ecuador and 1,000 miles south-west of Central America. The 13 to 16 islands (the number depends on opinion as to the demarcation-line between an island and an islet) and some 50 or 60 islets and rocks have a total area of about 3,000 square miles and are sprinkled over some 23,000 square miles of ocean. Most of them are of volcanic origin, and conventional estimates of their age is between two million and three million years, though some authorities think they are much older. Although they rise from a rock platform which is 1,000 ft or so above the level of the ocean bed, it is doubtful whether they were ever connected by a land-bridge with the mainland. Deep ocean gulfs separate them from the shores

Large Tree Finch (f), one of the Galapagos Islands finches, the evolution of which so interested Darwin. *Photo. Eric Hosking*

47

of South and Central America. Their fauna and flora must therefore have arrived by air and water. Those which were waterborne could have come on one of two main ocean currents which wash the shores of the islands. One is the warm Panamanian Current flowing down from the north, the other the cold mighty Humboldt Current which, after sweeping from the Antarctic northwards along the South American coast, fans out westwards into the central Pacific. Today, as in past ages, flotsam is still occasionally washed ashore on the islands, bearing a cargo of seeds, insects, spiders and even an occasional small mammal. The chief source is probably Central America, with its abundant tropical life.

The first Europeans to visit the Galápagos were probably a party of Spaniards, which included Tomas de Berlanga, Bishop of Panama, who discovered them by accident in 1535. However, it is thought that the Incas of Peru made voyages there in the previous century, though nothing is certain. Once European ships began to sail the Pacific, the islands became the haunt of buccaneers. No serious attempt at settlement was made until 1832, but goats were released on some of the islands towards the end of the seventeenth century, and later dogs were introduced to kill off a superfluity of goats. The unique wild life of the islands was seriously exploited, and much of it brought to the edge of extinction.

The *Beagle*, with its cargo of scientists including Charles Darwin, arrived in the Galápagos in 1835, when the permanent settlement had been established for only a few years. Already the extermination of some of the indigenous species was well advanced, the tortoises, seals and land iguanas being specially exploited. Darwin, however, was interested in the birds, and especially in the group of finches which now bear his name—Darwin's Ground Finches. It was here that Darwin acquired much of the evidence which enabled him to formulate his theory of the Origin of Species. He found that there were 13 species of ground finch resident in the Galápagos, each concentrated on one or a few islands and each differing from the rest in relatively minor details. All were undistinguished brown or black finches, superficially resembling each other, but some had short, stumpy beaks for cracking hard seeds, some had long, slender bills for extracting nectar from cactus flowers, while others had other distinctive features. Darwin concluded that all had descended from a common ancestor and that isolation for many millennia had caused them to evolve differently. We may see the idea taking shape in Darwin's mind from his chronicle published in *The Voyage of the Beagle*. He writes:

The remaining land birds form a most singular group of finches, related to each other in the structure of their beaks, short tails, form of body, and plumage. There are thirteen species, which Mr. Gould has divided into four sub-groups. All these species are peculiar to this archipelago....

The most curious fact is the perfect gradation in the size of the beaks in the different groups of *Geospiza*, from one as large as that of a hawfinch to that of a chaffinch, and even to that of a warbler.... Instead of there being only one intermediate species, there are no less than six species with insensibly graduated beaks.... The beak of *Cactornis* is somewhat like that of a starling; and that of the fourth sub-group, *Camarhynchus*, is slightly parrot-shaped. Seeing this gradation and diversity of structure in one small, intimately related group of birds, one might really fancy that from an original paucity of birds in this archipelago one species had been taken and modified for different ends.

The Ground Finches are still there on the Galápagos, as well as a number of other interesting species which Darwin saw. He records that on the islands he found 26 species of land bird, of which all but one were peculiar to the archipelago. They

Red-breasted Goose

Collared Dove

Greater Prairie Chicken

Golden Eagle

consisted of, in addition to the finches, a hawk, two owls, a wren, three tyrant flycatchers, a dove, a swallow and three species of mocking-bird.

We now, of course, have more information about the Galápagos birds. Four species of mocking-birds have been identified, namely, the Galápagos Mocking-bird (*Nesomimus parvulus*), Chatham Island Mocking-bird (*Nesomimus melanotis*), Hood Island Mocking-bird (*Nesomimus macdonaldi*) and Charles Island Mocking-bird (*Nesomimus trifasciatus*). They are a fascinating group—exceedingly tame, inquisitive, active and extrovert. Evidently they are descended from a common ancestor, but because of their weak flight there is virtually no communication between the islands, so each of the island species has evolved separately. One of the chief differences is in size, the Hood Island birds being much larger than the others.

The dove is the Galápagos Ground Dove (*Nesopelia galapagoensis*), an attractive little reddish-brown bird speckled with cream. The Galápagos Hawk (*Buteo galapagoensis*) is really a species of Buzzard, nearly related to the North American Swainson's Hawk. Among its favourite foods are the newly hatched babies of the iguanas and tortoises, themselves enjoying a highly precarious status. The Galápagos Barn Owl (*Tyto alba punctatissima*) and the Galápagos Short-eared Owl (*Asio flammeus galapagoensis*) are local sub-specific races of species which have an almost worldwide distribution. The Barn Owl is smaller and darker than the typical race, the Short-eared Owl shows small points of difference.

Galápagos birds include several marine species, among them the Flightless Cormorant (*Nannopterus harrisi*), the Galápagos Penguin (*Spheniscus mendiculus*) and the Waved Albatross (*Diomedes exulans irrorata*); also a freshwater species, the Galápagos Green Heron (*Butorides sundevalli*).

Most of the indigenous bird species of the Galápagos have managed to survive, though some by the narrowest of margins. The Galápagos Hawk, which seems to have been fairly common on all the islands until the 1920s, was almost exterminated by the 1960s, surviving for the most part only on the smaller uninhabited islands. Their decline coincided with the increasing settlement of the islands and was largely due to the shooting of the birds by chicken-farmers. An Ecuadorian law of 1959 granted them total protection, though, as everyone knows, passing a law is easier than enforcing it. The Flightless Cormorant is now probably represented by 1,000 individuals or less. Apart from its inability to fly its weakness has been a misplaced trust in Man. It now seems to be confined to two islands, Albemarle and Narborough.

Although the Waved Albatross wanders far and wide over the Pacific it has only one nesting-place in the world—Hood Island in the Galápagos. With a total population of probably around 3,000, it is not in immediate danger, but with such a restricted nesting-area it must be vulnerable, especially as it is by no means a prolific breeder. Apparently it does not start breeding until it is five years old or more; it lays one egg per year and may nest only once every two years.

The islands have their own species of crake, the Galápagos Crake (*Laterellus spilonotus*), and two species of gull, the Lava Gull (*Larus fuliginosus*) and the Swallow-tailed Gull (*Creagrus furcatus*). Both have breeding populations of reasonable size, though confined to the archipelago. Other sea-birds, with a more extensive geographical range, such as boobies, frigate-birds and petrels, are abundant. There is also a little warbler, the Galápagos Yellow Warbler (*Dendroica petechia aureolo*), which specialises in catching the tiny fiddler crabs on the beaches. And the remarkable Camarhynchus or Woodpecker Finch (*Camarhynchus pallidus*), which is one of the few birds that have mastered the use of a tool. Like woodpeckers, it preys on insects and larvae in decaying timber but it lacks the woodpecker's specialised beak. So instead, it digs out the grubs by means of a sharp thorn or twig held in its bill, dropping the tool and grabbing the insect as soon as it appears.

All of Darwin's Ground Finches, with the likely exception of a sub-species of the Large-billed Ground Finch (*Geospiza magnirostris magnirostris*) which may be extinct, still live on the Galápagos. Having survived the vicissitudes of the past few centuries there is no reason to suppose they are in immediate danger, but their restricted habitat and paucity of numbers necessarily make the future somewhat precarious. Like all wild life on the islands, they are now protected by Ecuador's conservation laws, which in 1959 designated the entire archipelago a national park. Moreover, the regulations can be monitored, to some extent, by the Charles Darwin Foundation, set up by UNESCO, which has a research station on Indefatigable Island. Both the station and the Ecuadorian Government are, however, hampered by shortage of funds.

The conservation campaign was initiated in the nick of time. Apart from the natural pressures caused by increasing settlement on the islands, modern Man has proved no less destructive of wild life than his ancestors of buccaneering days. In the 1940s men of the United States Navy completely cleared the small island of South Seymour of land iguanas and tortoises and nearly eliminated the marine iguanas, all of which were abundant there before a naval base was established in 1942. Even conservation activities are accompanied by hazards. A campaign to reduce the prolific rat population by poison backfired when it was found that the poison was killing off Galápagos hawks, which were feeding on the rat carcases. And there are still far too many feral goats roaming the islands.

Now that the unique nature of the Galápagos fauna is becoming more widely known and the fantastic, unearthly scenery of the islands better appreciated, the Ecuadorian Government is hoping that tourism will grow. This should help conservation, for it would be manifestly unwise to destroy the creatures which tourists come to see. Any large influx of tourists would, however, need to be carefully regulated.

The rare birds of Hawaii

On pages 19–23 is recorded the melancholy catalogue of native birds of the Hawaiian islands which have been swept into oblivion since Captain Cook landed there in 1778. This section is a continuation of the story, for in a number of instances the demarcation line between total extinction and extreme rarity is decidedly vague. Many of the birds in question inhabit dense rain-forests on the upper slopes of Hawaii's great mountains, habitats which lend themselves to concealment. Several species have been thought to be extinct and then, after many years, have been identified again.

The MAUI AKEPA (*Loxops coccinea ochracea*) is an example. It was first described in 1894, but since the first decade of the twentieth century nothing was heard of the species, which was therefore thought to be extinct. In 1950, however, a naturalist found a party of three at an altitude of 2,500 feet on Maui's Mount Haleakala.

The MOLOKAI ALAUWAHIO (*Loxops maculata flammea*). Whether this sub-

Small Ground Finch, another of Darwin's finches from the Galapagos. *Photo. Eric Hosking*

species has followed the Lanai Alauwahio (*Loxops maculata montana*) into oblivion is not known. Like the Lanai bird, it was still quite common early in the twentieth century, and the indigenous mountain-forest habitat which it favoured still exists, though reduced in area. Four other races of the Alauwahio still survive. They are the KAUAI ALAUWAHIO (*Loxops maculata bairdi*), the MAUI ALAUWAHIO (*Loxops maculata newtoni*), the HAWAIIAN (*Loxops maculata mana*) and the OAHU ALAUWAHIO (*Loxops maculata maculata*). All were common and are now rare, the Oahu race especially so. They are insect-eating birds which haunt the forests of the native koa trees (a type of acacia).

Two other races of the AKEPA are now present on the islands of Hawaii and Kauai. Though in greatly reduced numbers from their former abundant status, they are apparently in no immediate danger. They are the HAWAIIAN AKEPA (*Loxops coccinea coccinea*) and the KAUAI AKEPA (*Loxops coccinea caerulierostris*).

51

Both are birds of the mountain forests, at altitudes of from 2,000 ft upwards.

The KAUAI AKIALOA (*Hemignathus procerus*) is probably the sole surviving race of Akialoa, those living on Hawaii, Lanai and Oahu having become extinct. A nectar-feeding species, it lives in mountain-forest country and has been recorded on only a handful of occasions in recent years, none of them since 1965. The KAUI NUKUPUU (*Hemignathus lucidus hanapepe*) is an example of a species, thought to be extinct, which has demonstrated in recent years that, as Mark Twain said, the reports of its demise had been exaggerated. After being unrecorded for more than 60 years it was reported on several occasions in the 1960s from the Alakai Swamp, last refuge of a number of rare species some 4,000 ft up on Kauai's mountain plateau. The AKIAPOLAUU or HAWAIIAN NUKUPUU (*Hemignathus wilsoni*) is a nearly related species which survives, though in small numbers, in the mountain forests of Hawaii proper, having been driven to the higher altitudes from its former lowland haunts by the spread of cattle-rearing and cultivation.

MAUI PARROTBILL (*Pseudonestor xanthrophrys*) The status of this species is uncertain. Its last refuge has been the upper slopes of Mount Haleakala, on Maui, but whether a small population still survives or become extinct is unknown. It is regarded as an extreme example of specialisation, having evolved a large, hooked bill for the purpose of extracting beetle-grubs from under the bark of the koa (acacia) trees, now scarce in the area.

OU (*Psittirostra psittacea*) Formerly found on most of the main Hawaiian islands, the Ou, a fruit-eating species, is now confined to Hawaii proper and, possibly, Kauai. It is a bird without distinct sub-species for, being fairly strong on the wing, it moved from island to island, thus preventing the evolution of separate races.

PALILA (*Psittirostra bailleui*) A Canary-like bird, the Palila was apparently once widespread on Hawaii island but has now retreated to the upper edges of the forests on the mountains of Mauna Kea and Mauna Loa. It is now very rare, but latest reports indicate that it is holding its own.

CRESTED HONEYCREEPER (*Palmeria dolei*) Reports in the 1960s indicate that this beautiful bird survives high on the mountains of Maui, though it has long been extinct in its other former habitat, Molokai. A nectar-feeding and insect-eating species, it superficially resembles a small and fragile starling, though with a more striking pattern of pink, red and white plumage on a blackish background.

The IIWI (*Vestiaris coccinea*) perhaps hardly qualifies for inclusion in this chapter, for there are strong populations on Hawaii and Kauai. It is, however, now very scarce on Maui and Oahu and has become extinct on Lanai and Molokai, so even now, when it is afforded the protection of the Hawaii National Park, it may be considered a bird at risk.

KAUAI OO (*Moho braccatus*) As recorded on pp. 22–3, four out of the five species of Honeyeater (*Meliphagidae*) indigenous to the Hawaiian islands have become extinct. The Kauai Oo, now so rare that perhaps only two specimens are still alive, is confined to the high forests in the heart of the mountainous island of Kauai and particularly to those around the Alakai Swamp.

LAYSAN FINCH (*Psittirostra cantans*) In spite of its name, the Laysan Finch is a honeycreeper of the genus *Psittirostra*. On its coral islet it once came near to extinction but has now recovered and is reported to be quite plentiful. The island of Nihoa, westernmost of the main Hawaiian group, possesses a sub-species of the Laysan Finch, which, after a period of decline, is now apparently well established. Some of the birds introduced to Midway Island, however, died out.

NIHOA MILLERBIRD (*Acrocephalus kingi*) Page 23 contains an account of the Laysan Millerbird, now extinct. An allied species, the Nihoa Millerbird, occupies an extremely restricted habitat on the small Hawaiian island of Nihoa. Resembling the European Reed-warbler in appearance and habits, the Millerbird is a reed-haunting species confined to a locality of less than 150 acres; its total population is estimated at between 100 and 200 birds. It must obviously be regarded as highly vulnerable, even though its nesting area is a wildlife reserve.

The doom of the Hawaiian Honeycreepers

What is the explanation of the appalling casualty-rate of the Hawaiian Honey-creepers? There can be no doubt that these little birds with their strange, musical and vowel-ridden names were a fragile and vulnerable company. As species and sub-species they had been on the islands for a very long time. Their storm-blown ancestors were probably dropped there a million or so years ago. That hazardous voyage seems to have been enough for them for, finding congenial habitats in the dense forests of primitive Hawaii, few of them went adventuring again.

The Ou was one of the few species that moved fairly freely between the islands. Most became entirely sedentary and thus had every chance to develop specialised characteristics. As we have seen, with most species each island had evolved its own race.

Their evolution seems to have been largely determined by their food and so to have been characterised by the shape of their bills. Some became almost exclusively seed-eaters and developed stout, heavy bills for the purpose of cracking open hard-shelled seeds. Some even tended to confine their attentions to certain types of seed or fruit, such as those of the koa (or acacia) or the Freycinetia. Some were insectivorous, and others were nectar-feeders. None had any weapons of offence or defence, and almost all seem, in the comparative absence of predators, to have been tame and trusting. Let us consider the dangerous limitations that result from these developments. In most instances, each race or species of bird is confined to one island. Often it is confined to only part of the island, such as a certain altitude-zone or the forests in which its favoured trees grow. Its numbers are therefore, at the best, severely limited. Physically, it is small, defenceless and unaccustomed to the presence of predators.

This all adds up to extreme vulnerability, whether to climatic or man-made stresses. An example of climatic disaster can be found in the history of the Laysan Apapane (*see* page 23), the last specimens of which were blown out to sea by a violent storm. Before that, however, the population had been greatly reduced by the action of imported rabbits, which fed on the grasses which provided cover for the birds. Environmental stresses appear to have affected a number of Hawaiian species before the advent of European man, for the earliest reports on some of them indicate their rarity.

It is thought that the impact made by the Polynesians, who may have colonised the islands as early as the sixth century A.D. and who comprised the population in pre-European times, was not great. Indirectly they affected wild life by periodic burning of forests, but most of the islands were well forested when Europeans first saw them. Direct interference with such small birds as honeycreepers was naturally limited, though the Polynesians did develop a vogue for feather cloaks, which were highly prized. In the making of these cloaks it is said that the skins of five or six of the most colourful species were used, notably the black-and-yellow Mamo, the black-and-yellow Oo, the green-and-yellow Ou, the red-and-black Iiwi and the crimson Apapane, and many hundreds must have been slaughtered for the purpose. On the other hand, the feather cloaks were traditionally the attributes of Hawaiian royalty, and strong taboos existed against anyone else acquiring them. It was after the taboo was lifted, towards the end of the nineteenth century, that most of the honeycreepers met their doom, though even then it is doubtful whether direct action by men with shotguns was a major factor. And there is the awkward fact that the Apapane, in spite of its feathers being still popular for making cloaks, is still plentiful.

The primary causes for the decline and demise of so many of the honeycreepers are probably (a) the increased human settlement of the islands, resulting in the destruction of the forests to make room for agriculture; and (b) the introduction of those satellites of European civilisation—cats and rats. Most of the lowlands are now occupied by sugar-cane and pineapple plantations and other crops, as well as by urban development. The surviving honeycreepers have retreated uphill and are now found mostly in the forest-zone on the rugged mountains, from about 2,500 ft upwards. As for the introduction of alien mammals, one that may have been responsible for some problems was the mongoose, imported from Jamaica in 1883. One further suggestion is that an epidemic disease, bird pox, introduced through the agency of domestic poultry and of mosquitoes, took a heavy toll of native birds. The idea is interesting but awaits further investigation.

Other Hawaiian birds which have been brought to the edge of extinction, though some have now recovered and are on the upgrade, are a Crow, a Gallinule, a Hawk, a Thrush, a Duck, a Teal and the Hawaiian Goose or Néné.

The HAWAIIAN GOOSE or NENE (*Branta sandvicensis*) is today familiar to visitors to wildfowl collections in many parts of the world. Those who tempt the tame and handsome little geese to eat from an outstretched hand might be surprised to learn that less than 40 years ago the species was on the verge of extinction, being reduced to a total population of only 50 birds anywhere in the world. Before the coming of Europeans to Hawaii the population of Nénés is thought to have been pretty stable at around 25,000. It is true that the native Hawaiians went hunting the geese in the craters of the volcanoes, where they assembled when moulting, but this seems to have amounted to nothing more than an annual culling of surplus birds. European settlement soon took its toll and by 1850, about 70 years after the archipelago had been discovered, the geese had retreated to the mountain tops, where they maintained a precarious existence, much harried by sportsmen. What European and American sportsmen failed for a long time to realise was that the Néné nested in what was for them the middle of the traditional shooting season.

Nénés were introduced to private collections in Europe at various times during the nineteenth century and some successfully bred, but no sustained breeding-programme was undertaken and the European population died out. An enlightened Hawaiian landowner, Herbert C. Shipman, established a captive flock on Hawaii island in 1918 and kept it going for more than 30 years. Sir Peter Scott's celebrated venture to rescue the Néné from oblivion by breeding a stock in captivity for ultimate return to the wild began at Slimbridge, England, in 1950, when two birds were brought there from Hawaii. Next year, when they both started to lay eggs and so revealed themselves as females, they were joined by a stud gander from Hawaii, named Kamehameha. This prepotent bird sired a succession of progeny for the next 12 years and at his death in 1963 had 230 descendants. Some of these had been returned to Hawaii, where the Board of Agriculture was building up its own stock.

Since then the Néné has become thoroughly re-established not only on Hawaii, where it has extensive sanctuaries on the lava-slopes of the great volcanoes, but also on Maui, where it had been completely exterminated. In addition, breeding stocks of Néné are kept in a score of wildfowl collections in Europe, well dispersed so that new stock should be readily available should any disaster strike the wild birds of Hawaii in the future. The rescue of the Néné from what appeared to be certain extinction is one of the best success stories of conservation in the present century and an example of what can be done by adopting an intelligent and well-sustained programme.

The HAWAIIAN CROW (*Corvus tropicus*) would seem to be an unexpected candidate for extinction, in view of the general adaptability of the Crow family and their abundance in most countries. Until the end of the nineteenth century the species was common on the comparatively dry south-western side of the main island of Hawaii and its decrease has been due almost entirely to persecution coupled with the clearance of land for agriculture. Crows are seldom popular with farmers, and the Hawaiian farmers seem to have been especially effective in the war they waged against them. At one time, in the early 1960s, the population was believed to be down to 50 birds or less, but the situation is thought now to have improved a little.

HAWAIIAN HAWK (*Buteo solitarius*) is, like the Hawaiian Crow, confined to the island of Hawaii. A diminutive buzzard, it is now strictly protected and is probably holding its own, though in the past it has been severely persecuted. Its numbers are low, probably no more than a hundred or two.

HAWAIIAN GALLINULE (*Gallinula chloropus sandvicensis*), a bird very similar to the European Moorhen, was once widespread and fairly numerous on all the Hawaiian islands but has now been exterminated from Hawaii and Maui. On Oahu, Molokai and Kauai it survives in small numbers, but the total population is probably only a few hundreds. The clearance of land (including swamps) for cultivation and the activities of cats, rats and other introduced predators have been responsible for the decline, rather than direct interference by Man.

The disaster which struck the LAYSAN TEAL (*Anas laysanensis*), in the form of a hurricane in 1963, has already been mentioned. After the storm, the population was down to about 200, but fortunately in 1957 and 1958 steps had been taken to establish the species elsewhere, both in the United States and at Slimbridge, England. The species proved quite amenable to breeding in captivity, and in the very year of the hurricane 55 young birds were reared at Slimbridge. The species is now

Flightless Cormorants engaged in courtship display (often referred to as the 'snake dance') on Fernandina Island, Galapagos. *Photo. Eric Hosking*

well distributed in zoos and wildfowl collections around the world, and the population on Laysan could easily be reinforced should another natural disaster occur.

Hawaii has another rare duck, the HAWAIIAN DUCK (*Anas platyrhynchos wyvilliana*), which is a specialised sub-species of the Common Mallard, than which it is smaller and less brightly coloured. Owing to the draining of swamps, the activities of predators and some shooting, the population fell to a very low ebb in the 1950s and early 1960s, when probably it was down to 200 or 300. It is no longer found on Hawaii Island, Maui and Molokai but survives in small numbers on Oahu, Nihau and Kauai. Here again steps have been taken to safeguard the species by building up a population in zoos and collections elsewhere, but the exercise has been less successful than those concerned with the Néné and the Laysan Teal, for the Hawaiian Duck does not breed so freely in captivity.

On page 23 details are given of two sub-species of Hawaiian Thrushes which have become extinct. Both were sub-species, or island races, of the typical HAWAIIAN THRUSH (*Phaeornis obscurus*). The thrushes of Oahu and Lanai have gone, but those of Kauai (*Phaeornis obscurus myadestina*) and Hawaii island (*Phaeornis obscurus obscurus*) survive, the latter being not uncommon in certain mountain habitats. There is also a smaller Thrush, the KAUAI THRUSH (*Phaeornis palmeri*), which is regarded as a separate species. Known also as the Small Omao, it is now extremely rare in two forest localities on Kauai.

As already noted, the Mascarene Islands (Mauritius, Réunion and Rodriguez) feature prominently in the chapter on 'Failures'. Indeed, so thorough has been the work of extermination of indigenous species that very few are left. It is estimated that when the islands were first discovered by Europeans Mauritius had some 19 species of resident land and freshwater birds, Réunion 13 and Rodriguez nine. All but one of these species were exclusive to the islands, and very few of them have survived.

The Mascarene Islands

One which is now in distinct danger, having a probable population of only about 24, is the MAURITIUS PINK PIGEON (*Nesoenas mayeri*). The MAURITIUS KESTREL (*Falco punctatus*) also survives by the slenderest of margins: in 1978 the total population was thought to be down to nine; two of them were in captivity, in the hope that they would breed. At the beginning of the present century it was still fairly common and well distributed throughout the island, but a dramatic reduction in numbers has been brought about by shooting (and to a lesser extent by the destruction of habitat). Inaccurate observation a long time ago bestowed on this bird an unfortunate name—*mangeur-de-poules*—'chicken-eater', and the undeserved reputation has doubtless had as much as anything to do with its demise.

The MAURITIUS PARAKEET (*Psittacula krameri echo*) is thought to survive in small numbers in the forests of the island, though some authorities think it is probably extinct. The same may apply to the RODRIGUEZ PARAKEET (*Psittacula exsul*) which has not been seen for many years but which may still just possibly survive on offshore islets.

A population of the OLIVACEOUS BULBUL (*Hypsipetes borbonicus*) was almost wiped out on Réunion by a cyclone in 1948, but it eventually recovered and is said to be now not uncommon in the forests. A sub-species, *Hypsipetes borbonicus olivaceus*, which lives on Mauritius, is very much rarer, probably because on

Mauritius the forest habitat which it favours has been much more extensively destroyed than on Réunion.

Rodriguez has its own Warbler, the RODRIGUEZ WARBLER (*Bebrornis roderi-canus*), of which it is thought that less than 20 birds survive, though the species may be extinct.

Birds at risk in the Seychelles

North and north-east of Madagascar scores of tiny islands and sandbanks are sprinkled over a shallow section of the Indian Ocean. The four largest, which are mountainous, well-watered and permanently settled by humans, form the Seychelles group (total area, about 87 square miles). They have 17 species and sub-species of land and freshwater birds, of which 14 are exclusive to them. All of them must therefore have a rather slender hold on viability, though some seem not to be immediately threatened. One, the SEYCHELLES WARBLER (*Bebrornis sechellensis*), which is nearly related to the Rodriguez Warbler, gave cause for anxiety a few years ago but has now staged a remarkable recovery. An undistinguished little bird, not unlike the European Willow-warbler, it was thought to have a total population of less than 50. The Seychelles Warbler is confined to the rocky islet of Cousin, which has an area of only 60 acres, and re-establishment on another island of the group would be highly desirable. The recent increase in population has been due chiefly to the protection of the indigenous vegetation through the intervention of the International Council for Bird Preservation.

The Warbler must therefore have one of the most restricted habitats on earth. While there is no reason to think that the population is declining, obviously a natural disaster such as a cyclone or a fire might well extirpate the species. One has only to remember the Stephens Island Wren, apparently wiped out by a single cat, to appreciate the danger. At present there are no cats or rats on the islet, and probably the best conservation measure that can be taken is to ensure that they and all other predators remain absent.

Another Seychelles species confined to one small island, in this instance the hilly island of La Digue (area four square miles), is the SEYCHELLES PARADISE FLY-CATCHER (*Terpsiphone corvina*). This beautiful little bird, nearly related to the Paradise Flycatchers of mainland Africa, has a population of about 70 in its tiny habitat, which still has plenty of dense cover to which it can retreat. Also it has the salutary habit of building its nest towards the end of very slender twigs which will not support the weight of cats or rats. So it may survive for quite a time yet, but it does have to share its island with an increasing human population, which, while it does not apparently interfere deliberately with the birds, is more or less indifferent to their welfare. Formerly it was found on several other islands of the group.

Not long ago the SEYCHELLES MAGPIE ROBIN (*Copsychus sechellarum*) was thought to be extinct. It now probably survives on the small island of Frégate, where in the late 1960s its numbers were down to between ten and 20 birds. Formerly it was fairly widespread throughout most of the Seychelles but was gradually exterminated by domestic predators, by rats and by small boys. Energetic steps have been taken to protect the birds on Frégate, including the elimination of much of a thriving cat-population, but whether this will be enough remains to be seen. In the 1930s the bird was introduced to the island of Alphonse, some 250 miles south-west of the main group, but it failed to establish itself.

The numerous African family of Weaver-birds (*Ploceidae*) is represented on the Seychelles by the SEYCHELLES FODY (*Foudia sechellarum*). Formerly found on several other islands it is now confined to three small ones, Frégate, Cousin and Cousine. The reasons for its decline are the destruction of its habitat to make room for agriculture (which includes coconut plantations) and the depredations of introduced rats and cats. The total population is now probably down to a few hundred. The disappearance of the SEYCHELLES TURTLE-DOVE (*Streptopelia picturata rostrata*) is due to somewhat different causes. This bird is a sub-species of the typical race which inhabits Madagascar, and at some time individuals from Madagascar were introduced, via Mauritius, to the Seychelles, where they have interbred with the local race, thus tending to eliminate the differences between the two. That is a pity, for the coloration of the Seychelles birds is much brighter and richer than that of the birds from Madagascar. At present, while Turtle-Doves are fairly well distributed in the islands, representatives of the Seychelles type are found only on the tiny islands of Cousin and Cousine, and even there interbreeding may occur.

The SEYCHELLES LESSER VASA PARROT (*Coracopsis nigra barklyi*) is restricted to one small valley of one small island, Praslin (which has a total area of only about 12 square miles). It seems to be confined to the vestiges of the indigenous palm forest, where, however, it is still present in quite good numbers. In this cramped area the birds are effectively protected, and they are popular enough to be depicted on a Seychelles postage stamp. In a family of brilliant coloration they are unusual in having black, or rather very dark brown, plumage.

The SEYCHELLES OWL (*Otus insularis*) was for several decades earlier this century thought to be extinct but has subsequently been found, though in very small numbers, in a mountainous area of Mahé. A bird of approximately the size of the European Little Owl though with prominent ear-tufts, it seems to have been driven into these last fastnesses partly by the destruction of its habitat. However, some responsibility may be attached to competition with the introduced South African Barn Owl, which flourishes. The Barn Owls may in addition be responsible for the decline of the SEYCHELLES KESTREL (*Falco araea*), with which it apparently competes for nesting sites and, being a more aggressive bird, usually wins. Like so many other island species, the Seychelles Kestrel is also too tame and trusting for its own good; birds are often killed by small boys. The species is now confined to the island of Mahé, where it is fairly plentiful. It frequents the neighbourhood of human settlements and feeds chiefly on lizards. A move is afoot to transfer some of the birds to other islands of the group, where they were formerly resident.

The Boobies of Christmas Island

Christmas Island, a tropical island some 250 miles south of Java and now administered by the Australian Government, is the last known nesting-place of the ABBOTT'S BOOBY (*Sula abbotti*), a bird of the Gannet family. In the 1940s the total population was estimated at little more than 1,000, but the latest survey suggests a total of 8–10,000. In spite of this encouraging trend the species, restricted to an island of 64 square miles and even there only to part of it, must be regarded as vulnerable. Unlike other members of the family, it nests not on the ground but high up in tall trees. Once it had a second nesting locality, the island of Assumption on the other side of the Indian Ocean, but the birds were eventually driven away by the wholesale exploitation of the island's guano deposits. The same activities have been occurring on Christmas Island, but the groves in which the birds nest are under the official protection of the Australian Government, and as long as that state of affairs prevails the species should be safe.

The Narcondam Hornbill

Narcondam is a small island of the Andaman Group, some 200 miles south of the Irrawaddy Delta in Burma. It lies nearly 100 miles east of the main archipelago and so its fauna may have evolved in some isolation, though one might expect a bird as strong on the wing as a Hornbill to circulate fairly freely. The reason for including the NARCONDAM HORNBILL (*Aceros narcondami*) in the list of very rare birds is that Narcondam has been so little visited by ornithologists that not much is known about it. There may be a very small population, but there may be more than is at present apparent, concealing themselves in the dense forests which clothe the island. It may even be found on some of the other islands of the group.

Birds at risk in the Pacific Islands

The small scattered islands of the broad Pacific provide habitats so restricted that the species in them are automatically vulnerable. The list of obituaries is heavily weighted with Pacific species. Reference back to Lord Howe Island (page 27) will show that this lonely island, 300 miles east of Australia, has lost eight out of its 12 indigenous species of land-birds since its discovery in 1788. Their place has been taken by introduced birds (including several European species) and storm-blown wanderers which have managed to establish themselves. Of the endemic species which survive one which would seem to be the most vulnerable is the LORD HOWE ISLAND RAIL (*Tricholimnas sylvestris*). Indeed, in view of the melancholy list of Rails extinguished on other small Pacific Islands, the survival of this species is quite remarkable. The bird is now apparently restricted to mountainous localities in the southern part of the island (a very limited range, for the entire island is only about seven miles long by one wide), where it is seldom interfered with by men but is subject to the depredations of rats and pigs. Its exact status at present is uncertain, but the latest reports suggest that its population has sunk as low as 20 individuals.

The obituary list of the Chatham Islands (pp. 26–7) carries four names. Besides Chatham Island proper and Pitt Island (the second largest of the group), the archipelago has a small island, Mangare, which comprises a hill 940 ft high and about a mile in diameter, South-east Island (two square miles) and several rocks and islets. One of these last is Little Mangare, a rock some 50 yds off Mangare, with about an acre of tangled vegetation on its summit. This acre of bush was the last refuge of the CHATHAM ISLAND ROBIN (*Petroica traversi*), which thus must have had the most restricted habitat on earth. This little bird, very like the European Robin in appearance and habits but sooty-black in colour, has survived on Little Mangare for 70 years or so. Its islet remains free from rats and cats, which apparently exterminated it on Mangare and perhaps on some of the other islands, and access is difficult. The species was, of course, protected, and there were plans to re-introduce it to Mangare and perhaps some of the other islands when suitable bush habitats can be provided. By 1976, however, the population of Little Mangare had sunk to only four breeding pairs, due largely to the deterioration in quality of its habitat, and the programme for re-establishing the bird on other islands had to be considerably advanced. The planting of trees on the neighbouring

Mangare Island for the purpose of creating a suitable habitat for the transplanted Robins, had been proceeding since 1973, but although ideally the new trees should have been ten years old before the experiment was made, the transfer had to be effected in 1976 and 1977. The entire Robin population was, in fact, moved to Mangare and consisted in 1977 of three pairs and one surplus male.

South-east Island was the only known habitat of the CHATHAM ISLAND SNIPE (*Coenocorypha aucklandica iredalei*), a sub-species of the New Zealand Snipe, until it was re-introduced to Mangare Island where it increased and spread rapidly. Other sub-species occur on other South Pacific Islands.

The same island is the only known nesting-locality for the now very rare NEW ZEALAND SHORE PLOVER (*Thinornis novaeseelandiae*), a species once found on both North and South Islands, New Zealand. In the Chatham Islands it formerly bred on all the islands but was apparently eliminated from the larger ones by rats, which have so far been unable to reach South-east Island. As the species is ground-nesting it would be highly vulnerable to introduced predators. Attempts to re-establish the species on other islands of the group have proved unsuccessful.

Besides the two extinct species recorded for the Auckland Islands, which lie 200 miles south of New Zealand's South Island, three other sub-species which inhabit this windswept archipelago are now rare. The AUCKLAND ISLAND SNIPE (*Coenocorypha aucklandica aucklandica*) is now restricted to two of the smaller islands, as is also the AUCKLAND ISLAND ROBIN (*Petroica macrocephala marrineri*). As its name implies, this latter bird is nearly related to the Chatham Island Robin. The third bird, the AUCKLAND ISLAND FLIGHTLESS TEAL (*Anas aucklandica aucklandica*), is the type of which the New Zealand Brown Teal (*Anas aucklandica chlorotis*), itself now a rarity, is a sub-species. At some remote period certain Teal evidently found their way to the Auckland Islands and there settled down to evolve into a new species, one of the characteristics of which is that, due doubtless to the absence of predators, it is flightless. This development served them badly when European ships began to visit the islands and leave their usual residue of rats and cats. The bird is now confined to some of the smaller islands, at present not infested with predators, where fortunately it seems to be fairly plentiful.

Even more remote Campbell Island, which lies about 150 miles south-east of the Aucklands, also has a race of flightless Teal, the CAMPBELL ISLAND FLIGHTLESS TEAL (*Anas aucklandica nesiotis*). It shows only slight differences from the Auckland Island race but, as both sub-species are flightless and are separated from each other by 150 miles of stormy sea, it is likely that they evolved separately. Campbell Island (43 square miles) is covered with scrub and tussocky grass and, as it has no permanent human inhabitants, accurate information about its fauna is scarce. The numbers of the Flightless Teal are, however, probably very small.

Some 600 miles south-east of New Zealand and about midway between Campbell Island and the Chatham Islands, the Antipodes, a group of small, gale-lashed islands with no trees and no human inhabitants, have, somewhat surprisingly, two types of Parrot. One is the ANTIPODES KARARIKI (*Cyanoramphus unicolor*); the other, the smaller of the two, REISCHEK'S KARARIKI (*Cyanoramphus novaezelandiae hochstetteri*), a race of the New Zealand Karariki, or Red-crowned Parakeet. Well acclimatised to the harsh environment, they seem to be in no danger apart from the risk inherent in a habitat of no more than 24 square miles. The two appear to agree quite well together and are not in competition. Another race of the

New Zealand Karariki, the NORFOLK ISLAND KARARIKI (*Cyanoramphus novaeze-landiae cookii*), is restricted to Norfolk Island (*see* p. 28). In contrast to the Antipodes race, the Norfolk Island birds have to adapt to the presence of a permanent human population with its satellite cats and rats, and to a regular tourist influx. Although there is little current information about it, the population is probably low.

The Kermadec Islands, some 550 miles north-east of New Zealand, have yet another race of the New Zealand Karariki, the KERMADEC ISLAND KARARIKI (*Cyanoramphus novaezelandiae cyanurus*). Though once thought to be extinct, it survives apparently in quite good numbers, though it now has to share its habitat of 11 square miles with a handful of human settlers.

The five main islands of Fiji, though in atlases they appear little more than dots in the immensity of the Pacific Ocean, are really quite large, the biggest, Viti Levu, having an area of 4,053 square miles; around them are sprinkled hundreds of smaller islands and rocks. The main islands are mountainous and heavily forested, though now large areas of the lowlands have been cleared for cultivation.

The archipelago has 22 endemic species and sub-species of land and freshwater birds, some of which are now rare. The European impact came later than in many Pacific islands, largely owing to the fearsome reputation of the cannibal islanders, which kept whalers and traders away. After 1874, when Fiji was taken over by the British at the islanders' request, development was rapid, the population was vastly increased by immigration (chiefly from India), and the introduction of cats, rats and mongooses made life difficult for some of the native birds, most of which survive in the rugged mountain districts. Fiji has three species of Dove which will bear watching. They are: the ORANGE DOVE (*Ptilinopus victor*); the YELLOW-BELLIED DOVE (*Ptilinopus luteoventris*); the LAYARD'S DOVE (*Ptilinopus layardi*), all of which are found on some of the major islands as well as the smaller ones.

There are also three Parrots or Lorikeets: *Vini amabilis*, *Phygis solitarius* and *Prosopeia personata*. The last-named is sometimes known as the YELLOW-BREASTED MUSK PARROT and may be in danger because of its depredations in fruit plantations, which earn it a charge of gunshot whenever possible.

Other Fijian species possibly on the danger list are: the FIJIAN FANTAIL (*Rhidi-pura personata*), a flycatcher belonging to the same family as the Penduline Tits (it is apparently confined to the large island of Kandavu); and two WREN-WARB-LERS *Lamprolia victoriae victoriae* and *Lamprolia victoriae kleinschmidti*), of the Australasian family *Maluridae*: the former is restricted to the island of Taviuni.

Some 600 miles north-east of Fiji the much smaller archipelago of Samoa possesses a remarkable avian survival in the TOOTH-BILLED PIGEON (*Didunculus strigirostris*). Related to the Dodo of Mauritius, this species seemed doomed to follow it to extinction but has been reprieved and is not now on the danger list. It is restricted to the main island of the group, Savaii, which has an area of 703 square miles, and Opolu (430 square miles). The Tooth-billed Pigeon has one inestimable advantage over the Dodo, it can fly strongly.

2,000 miles of ocean separate Samoa from the scattered groups of islands in the eastern Pacific, the largest of which are the Society Islands, which include the important island of Tahiti (600 square miles). To the east lie the Tuamotu Archipe-lago and, beyond that, lonely Pitcairn Island. To the west, sprinkled over an equally vast expanse of ocean, are the Cook Islands, the chief of which is Rarotonga. Reference is made on page 31 to certain species which have become extinct on Tahiti. The following species are confined to certain small islands and, although not known to be at present in danger, must by reason of their restricted habitats be considered at risk.

About midway between Fiji and Samoa, in the Tongaa group of islands, the island volcano of Niuafo'ou possesses a rare species of Megapode, the PRIT-CHARD'S MEGAPODE (*Megapodius pritchardi*), isolated from other members of the Megapode family by thousands of miles of ocean. The bird is reputed to have adapted the habits of the Megapode tribe to its unusual environment, for instead of preparing mounds of decaying vegetation to incubate its eggs it is said to bury the eggs in hot ashes from the still-active volcano. Its population must necessarily be small and is subject to the dangers of volcanic eruptions as well as the normal hazards of small islands, but the species is believed to be holding its own.

The sections on the birds of Hawaii contain references to the Nihoa Millerbird (very rare) and the Laysan Millerbird (extinct). These are birds of the genus *Acrocephalus*, the European examples of which include the Reed-Warbler, and other species are found in other Pacific islands. *Acrocephalus caffra* is found on Tahiti, the neighbouring island of Moorea and on several of the islands of the Marquesas Group. *Acrocephalus atypha* is found on certain islands of the Tua-motu Archipelago. *Acrocephalus vaughni* is restricted to Henderson Island, a small and lonely island lying east of Pitcairn.

Henderson Island also has a Parrot (*Vini stepheni*), a Fruit Pigeon (*Ptilinopus huttoni*), and *Nesophylax ater*. A Kingfisher (*Halcyon venerata*) which is found on Tahiti also occurs of some of the Tuamotus, but another Kingfisher (*Halcyon tuta*) is apparently restricted to a group of three small volcanic islands, the Leewards, about 60 miles west of Tahiti.

In addition to the land-birds of the Pacific, certain sea-birds, notably Petrels, belong in this chapter. Petrels, of course, spend most of their lives at sea but are obliged to nest on land and usually do so in colonies on small islands. The nesting season is obviously the one at which they are most vulnerable, especially as they are ground-nesting birds and therefore at risk from prowling vermin. Because they are on land for only a short period each year and are then mainly nocturnal, it has proved difficult to pinpoint the nesting-localities of some species, and for some there is still exploration to be undertaken. MURPHY'S PETREL (*Pterodroma ultima*) is now known to nest on the tiny island of Oeno, north of Pitcairn. The MAS AFUERA PETREL (*Pterodroma masafuerae*) has been found breeding on a small island, Mas Afuera, of the Juan Fernandez group, 500 miles west of Chile. It is now thought that this Petrel may be identical with others, taken out of the breeding season near Japan, which are labelled STEJNEGER'S PETREL (*Pterodroma longiros-tris*). Another Petrel, the FIJI PETREL (*Pterodroma macgillivrayi*), was certainly breeding on Fiji 100 years ago, when a fledgling was taken there, but it has not been identified since; however, it may still be nesting there. BECK'S PETREL (*Ptero-droma rostrata becki*) is known from two specimens from the region of the Solomon Islands, but its nesting-locality has not yet been discovered. PYCROFT'S PETREL (*Pterodroma pycrofti*) has been found nesting on some small islands off North Island, New Zealand.

Similar considerations apply to the Albatrosses, three of which could feature before long on the danger list and one of which certainly is. This is the SHORT-

Brown-capped Weaver
Photo. Eric Hosking

Avocets changing over at nest
Photo. Eric Hosking

Galapagos Penguin
Photo. Eric Hosking

TAILED ALBATROSS or STELLER'S ALBATROSS (*Diomedes albatrus*), which once bred on a number of small islands in the western Pacific but is now restricted to the one island of Torishima (the name of which means 'the island of birds'). Torishima is the southernmost but one of the 'Seven Isles of Izu' which are strung out southwards from Tokyo Bay and link up with the Bonin Islands. From 1887 onwards Torishima was settled by fowlers and feather-hunters, who took an enormous toll of nesting albatrosses and brought them to the edge of extinction. The massacre was of almost the same proportions as that of the Passenger Pigeon and other extinct species, amounting, it is estimated, to half-a-million birds in 17 years. By 1933 the total population of the Short-tailed Albatross was down to less than 100. The war interrupted attempts to establish a conservation programme, and when it was over the Albatross seemed to have disappeared. In 1953/4, however, about ten pairs were back, and since then the population has been building up again, though not without setbacks. Torishima happens to have an active volcano, which from time to time takes a toll of the nesting birds, while Sea-eagles prey on the chicks. In 1973, 52 pairs were nesting on Torishima, which is now a national monument, and it was thought that others might be present on other islands.

The Bonin Islands have an endemic passerine species in the WHITE-EYED WARBLER-BABBLER (*Hapalopteron familiare*), a little yellow bird which has become extinct on the main islands but survives on several of the others. On the Japanese island of Okinawa, in the Riu-Kiu group, an indigenous woodpecker, the OKINAWA WOODPECKER (*Sapheopipo noguchi*), may yet survive, though it has been reported on only a few occasions since the war. Its habitat is a dense forest at the northern end of the island, where it could exist without being detected for a long time.

The western Pacific between Japan and New Guinea is sprinkled with a multitude of tiny islands, many of which have never been adequately explored for wild life. The group nearest Japan, situated some 700 or 800 miles south of the Bonins, comprise some of the larger islands, including Guam (200 square miles), Saipan and Tinian (70 square miles), and are collectively known as the Marianas. They possess several interesting and rare species of birds. It is assumed that the LA PEROUSE'S MEGAPODE or MARIANA ISLANDS MEGAPODE (*Megapodius laperouse*) is still surviving on some of the outlying islands, particularly on those with no human inhabitants. On the larger ones it has been exterminated by domestic animals, by being killed for food and by the destruction of its habitat, these islands now being devoted largely to the growing of sugar-cane. The PALAU ISLANDS MEGAPODE (*Megapodius laperouse senex*), found on the Palau Islands, south-west of the Marianas, is a sub-species of the Mariana Island type. Here, too, the birds have been extirpated on the larger and more densely populated islands but may survive on the outlying ones. It is suggested that the total population is probably less than 100.

The Megapodes are an Australian family of large birds, deriving their name from their habit of building large mounds of earth and vegetation as a kind of incubator for hatching their eggs. Another rare member of it is the BRUIJN'S BRUSH-TURKEY (*Aepypodius bruijnii*), which lives in a mountain-forest region of New Guinea and has not been reported since the early 1940s.

Among the smaller birds of the Marianas the TINIAN MONARCH (*Monarcha takatsukasae*) must be reckoned as dangerously rare. It is supposed to be restricted to the island of Tinian, from which there are no recent reports of its status. South of the Marianas extend the even more scattered group of islands, mostly coralline but a few volcanic, known as the Carolines. Truk, Ponape and Yap are the chief ones. Each of these main islands has its own species of GREAT WHITE-EYE, members of the *Zosteropidae* family. All seem to be extremely rare. The TRUK GREAT WHITE-EYE (*Rukia ruki*) and the PONAPE GREAT WHITE-EYE (*Rukia sanfordi*) appear to be birds of mountain forests and are evidently very secretive. There is a fourth species, the PALAU GREAT WHITE-EYE (*Rukia palauensis*), which is restricted to the islands of Babelthuap and Peleliu in the Palau Islands and is equally rare.

A new investigation of the birds of the multitudinous islands of the Pacific is overdue. When undertaken it could well reveal more species to be added to the catalogue of birds at risk.

CEBU BLACK SHAMA (*Copsychus niger cebensis*) This sub-species of a species which is fairly widespread in several islands of the Philippines, is confined to the island of Cebu and indeed to the very limited area of original forest on that island. It has proved less able to adapt to change than other Shamas on the Philippines and its population therefore declines as the forests are cleared for cultivation. A re-afforestation programme may help it, but its prospects at present are not very rosy.

ROTHSCHILD'S STARLING (*Leucopsar rothschildi*) A restricted area on the island of Bali, Indonesia, is the home of the Rothschild's Starling, a near relation of the Mynahs. Although fairly plentiful in its narrow habitat until quite recently, its numbers have been severely reduced by (a) destruction of the forests in which it lives, and (b) the activities of bird-catchers. Rothschild's Starling is an attractive bird, white with dark eyestripe, wing-tips and tail-tip, and so is a popular acquisition for zoos and aviaries. Fortunately it has shown it can breed in captivity, so it should manage to escape extinction, but there is a case for curbing the trade in trapped birds.

From the viewpoint of the ornithologist, the most interesting of the oceanic islands of the Atlantic is the Tristan d'Acunha group, with which is usually associated Gough Island, though it lies 200 miles farther south. Tristan d'Acunha is situated about midway between Africa and South America and in approximately the same latitude as Capetown and Buenos Aires. The main group of small islands consists of Tristan itself, Nightingale Islands (of which there are three) and Inaccessible Island, with a total area of 45 square miles. The group is volcanic, and in 1961 a volcano on the main island erupted, causing the island to be evacuated for two years. The highest peak on Tristan is 6,760 ft and is often covered with snow, though at the lower altitudes the climate is mild. In the ravines and gullies which score the mountainsides, dense, tangled vegetation and tussocky grass provide good cover for the resident land-birds. Gough Island (40 square miles) is a haunt of sea-elephants and penguins and has guano deposits. Tristan has a human population of several hundred, Gough has no permanent inhabitants except for the personnel of a weather station. Tristan and its near neighbours have four resident species of land-birds; Gough two others.

Rare birds of the Atlantic Islands

TRISTAN GROSBEAK (*Nesospiza wilkinsi*) is found only on Nightingale Islands,

66

while a sub-species (*Nesospiza wilkinsi dunnei*) lives only on Inaccessible Island. The fact that these two sub-species have evolved separately indicates that they are extremely sedentary, indulging in no interchange between the islands, though so close together. There they have lived throughout geological ages, one confined to an area of not more than one square mile, the other, only about 15 miles away, to a habitat of perhaps twice that size, and yet never meeting. In the course of time they have developed distinctive characteristics, the Inaccessible Island birds being smaller and yellower than those on Nightingale Islands. The populations of both sub-species are very small, that of the Nightingale Islands race being probably rather less than 100 birds, that of the Inaccessible Island birds rather more. Both islands are uninhabited by humans and, what is even more important, by rats. At the moment the Grosbeak seems safe, but the situation could radically alter if once rats got ashore.

TRISTAN FINCH (*Nesopiza acunhae*) is also split into two distinct sub-species, one on Inaccessible Island and the other (*Nesopiza acunhae questi*) on Nightingale Islands. Again the species is not represented on Tristan's main island, probably because if ever the birds (of whatever sub-species) were there they have been exterminated long ago by rats, cats, pigs and other introduced animals. The Tristan Finch is a ground-nesting species and therefore highly vulnerable. On Inaccessible Island the finches are not uncommon, but there is little available information on the Nightingale Island birds.

TRISTAN STARCHY (*Nesocichla eremita*), a species of thrush, has no fewer than three distinct sub-species, the typical race on the main island and sub-species on Nightingale Islands (*Nesocichla eremita procax*) and Inaccessible Island (*Nesocichla eremita gordoni*). All are ground-nesting birds and so are vulnerable to animal predators, but in spite of the presence of cats, dogs and rats on the main island they contrive to hold their own. In the tussocky grass of all the islands they are fairly common.

The other land species peculiar to Tristan is the TRISTAN RAIL (*Atlantisea rogersi*), a flightless bird found only on Inaccessible Island. A small, secretive brown bird it survives probably through the absence of rats and other predators on its island home. Gough Island has its own species or sub-species of Rail or Coot, the GOUGH ISLAND COOT (*Gallinula nesiotis comeri*), which is a sub-species of the TRISTAN COOT (*Gallinula nesiotis nesiotis*) now extinct (*see* page 33). It also has a Bunting, the GOUGH BUNTING (*Rowettia goughensis*), which apparently is not related to the Tristan finches and grosbeaks. It is thought to have originated with South American birds, no doubt carried over the ocean by storms, whereas the Tristan species are believed to have an African origin. Though restricted in habitat, it is not particularly rare.

St Helena, another volcanic island of about the same size as Tristan but 1,500 miles farther north, has no indigenous land-birds but one shore-bird, the ST HELENA PLOVER (*Charadrius sanctae-helenae*). It seems to be in no danger. The Cape Verde Islands, 350 miles west of the westernmost point of Africa, have a species of Lark, the RAZA ISLAND LARK (*Alauda razae*), which is to be found on only one small island of the group, Raza Island (three square miles). It appears to be nearly related to the European Sky-lark, from which it differs chiefly in having a very much larger and stronger bill. Whether it was once distributed over the entire group of islands or whether it has always enjoyed this extremely restricted habitat is not known. There is little recent information about its status.

On the other side of the Atlantic Bermuda, which is situated nearly 1,000 miles from the American coast, in the same latitude as Georgia, has a remarkable chronicle of conservation in the story of the Cahow. The CAHOW (*Pterodroma cahow*), a kind of petrel, bred in immense numbers on the islands until their discovery by Europeans in the sixteenth century. In 1609 Bermuda was settled by the British, but unfortunately the black rat was introduced, inadvertently, at the same time and soon began to compete with the human population. By the winter of 1614/15 the islanders were facing famine to the extent that the Governor adopted the expedient of sending '150 persons of the most ancient sick and weake into Coopers Iland, ther to be relieved by the comeigne in of the sea birds, especially the Cahowes'. Such a toll was taken of the birds by the hungry settlers that they were almost exterminated. In 1616 the Governor, alarmed at the massacre, issued a proclamation 'against the spoyle and havock of the Cahowes', to be followed in 1621/22 by a law to protect the birds during the nesting season—one of the first bird-protection laws ever enacted.

All this did the Cahows little good, and the species was thought to have been extinct for about 300 years when one was unexpectedly identified in 1916. Further individual records in the 1930s and 1940s prompted the despatch of an expedition in 1951 to locate any breeding-sites of the Cahow that might still exist. On rocky islets around the main group seven Cahow nests were found. It was immediately realised that these surviving Cahows had a problem. The birds start nesting in January, using natural holes among the rocks. When they had access to the larger islands they dug their own burrows in the soft earth, but on the rocks to which they have been banished there is insufficient soil. They return to their nests at night and are at sea during the day. In March the White-tailed Tropic-birds arrive to nest. They find the holes which had been used by generations of their ancestors now occupied by Cahows. But, being diurnal birds, they are active when the Cahows are away at sea. They speedily evict the young to make way for their own eggs.

An answer was devised by Bermuda's conservation officer. The Tropic-birds are larger than the Cahows. He therefore designed a baffle to be placed in front of nesting-holes, with an entrance just big enough to permit the Cahow to pass while keeping the Tropic-bird out. The scheme worked quite well. In 1961 a painstaking census revealed 18 Cahow nests; the population has since risen to 26 nesting pairs in 1976. But the increase was not as great as it should have been, in view of the success of the protection measures. Recent investigations have shown that the fertility of the eggs has been affected by pesticides (for a discussion of which *see* page 136).

In general, prospects for the Cahows are now rosy. In addition to the baffles, artificial nesting-burrows are now constructed for them. Moreover, the Government has designated as a conservation-area an island of 15 acres (Nonsuch Island) which has soft, deep soil into which the Cahows can easily burrow. Wardens keep the sanctuaries free from rats and other predators, and theoretically there is no limit to the expansion of the population. Provided the pesticide problem can be overcome.

The IPSWICH SPARROW (*Passerculus princeps*) would be more correctly named the Sable Island Bunting because it is more nearly related to the European Buntings than to the Sparrows and, though named after the town of Ipswich in Massachusetts, it nests only on Sable Island, some 90 miles off the coast of Nova Scotia. Unfortunately Sable Island is being steadily eaten away by the sea, and with the reduction in its habitat the total population of Ipswich Sparrows when a count was made in the early 1960s was only 58. The species is migratory and therefore obviously needs protection in its winter quarters as well. Though some reserves have been established in wintering areas on the east coast of the United States, they cannot yet be said to be completely adequate, and the Ipswich Sparrow must still be regarded as a bird at risk.

In the British Isles the lonely and now uninhabited island of St Kilda, 60 miles west of the outermost Hebrides, has its own species of Wren, the ST KILDA WREN (*Troglodytes hirtensis*). This little bird is rather larger, more barred and less rufous in colour than the typical Wren of mainland Britain. The species can hardly be considered at risk, for it is believed that several hundred pairs breed regularly on the extremely precipitous and rugged cliffs of the small islands of the St Kilda group. On the other hand, the entire group comprises only just over 2,000 acres, so the St Kilda Wren must count as one of the world's rare birds.

Although the St Kilda Wren is the only distinct species of Wren, apart from the typical Common Wren (*Troglodytes troglodytes*) found in the British Isles and the adjacent northern isles, there are several island sub-species. The Shetlands have one in the SHETLAND WREN (*Troglodytes troglodytes zetlandicus*), which in general is considerably darker than the mainland race. The HEBRIDEAN WREN (*Troglodytes troglodytes hebridensis*) occupies an intermediate position between the Shetland and mainland races, as does also the FAIR ISLE WREN (*Troglodytes troglodytes fridariensis*), which occupies the tiny island of Fair Isle, midway between Shetland and Orkney. The total population of the Fair Isle Wren is thought to be less than 100, but its future is pretty secure, for the whole island is a nature reserve, with a resident warden. There are also Wren sub-species in the Faeroes (*Troglodytes troglodytes borealis*) and Iceland (*Troglodytes troglodytes islandicus*).

Other Island Wrens

Wrens, being small and relatively sedentary birds capable of maintaining a viable population in a restricted area, are especially inclined to evolve island races. In addition to the variations on the Common Wren in the smaller islands of the British Isles, other sub-species occur on the other side of the world, in the North Pacific. The Pribiloff Islands, in the Bering Sea, have a sub-species of the Common European Wren, the PRIBILOFF ISLANDS WREN (*Troglodytes troglodytes alascensis*). Another race of the same species is *Troglodytes troglodytes orii*, found only on the tiny Borodino Islands, 250 miles or so east of Okinawa, in the western Pacific. In Europe, Corsica and Sardinia have a separate race, *Troglodytes troglodytes koenigi*, while Cyprus has *Troglodytes troglodytes cypriotes*.

The American House Wren (*Troglodytes aedon*) has no fewer than 31 sub-species, many restricted to small islands. Those of which the populations are so low as to be in danger of extinction are: the ST VINCENT HOUSE WREN (*Troglodytes aedon musicus*), which is confined to the West Indian island of St Vincent, where it is now very scarce; the ST LUCIA HOUSE WREN (*Troglodytes aedon mesoleucus*), which is so scarce that it may be extinct and, if it survives, is restricted to only one locality on the West Indian island of St Lucia; the MARTINIQUE HOUSE WREN (*Troglodytes aedon martinicensis*) seems to have been extinct since 1886; and the GUADELOUPE HOUSE WREN (*Troglodytes aedon guadeloupensis*) probably since 1914.

On the other hand, the TOBAGO HOUSE WREN (*Troglodytes aedon tobagensis*) and the DOMINICA HOUSE WREN (*Troglodytes aedon rufescens*) are still plentiful on their respective islands, while on Grenada the GRENADA HOUSE WREN (*Troglodytes aedon grenadensis*), though not abundant, is still widespread. Why Wrens have been exterminated on some of the West Indian islands and not on others remains a mystery. One suggestion is that the Wrens have suffered most on the islands to which the mongoose has been introduced, but in all probability the attitude of the human inhabitants has much to do with their status.

Among other House Wrens of this species which are confined to small islands are the COZUMEL HOUSE WREN (*Troglodytes aedon beani*) which lives on the island of Cozumel off the coast of Yucatan, Mexico; the COIBA HOUSE WREN (*Troglodytes aedon carychrous*), on the island of Coiba which lies off the Pacific coast of the Isthmus of Panama; and the CLARION HOUSE WREN (*Troglodytes aedon tanneri*), whose home is on tiny Clarion Island, the outermost of the lonely Revilla Gigedo group, some 600 miles west of the Mexican mainland. As noted on page 35, the island of Guadalupe, off Lower California, once had a wren (*Thryomanes bewickii brevicauda*) which is now probably extinct.

A Wren which, although it lives on a large island—Cuba—is restricted to a very small part of it is the ZAPATA WREN (*Thryomanes* or *Ferminia cerverai*). It is found only in an area of about five square miles in the Zapata Swamp, where, however, it seems to be reasonably common.

The Zapata Swamp in Cuba is the home of another rare bird, the ZAPATA RAIL (*Cyanolimnas cerverai*), a small rail that is so unlike any other that it has been given a genus of its own. It is restricted to a very small area of dense scrub with some grassland, which makes it very difficult to establish the status of this naturally secretive bird. Its population is, however, bound to be small.

Rare birds of the West Indies

South of Cuba the Cayman Islands have or had their own species of Thrush, the GRAND CAYMAN THRUSH (*Turdus ravidus*), a bird very like the European Blackbird, but grey rather than black, with a white rump and red bill and feet. Although this bird may just possibly survive, the likelihood is that it is extinct. It is non-migratory and confined to Grand Cayman, the larger of the two islands, where it lives or lived in forest country. These small islands, with a total area of about 100 square miles, have two races of Parrot, sub-species of the Cuban Parrot. The GRAND CAYMAN PARROT (*Amazona leucocephala caymanensis*) is confined to Grand Cayman, the LITTLE CAYMAN PARROT (*Amazona leucocephala hesterna*), to Little Cayman and the islet of Cayman Brac. Another sub-species of the Cuban Parrot, the BAHAMA PARROT (*Amazona leucocephala bahamensis*), is now reasonably plentiful only on the Bahamian island of Great Inagua, though formerly well distributed throughout most of the Bahamas.

Amazona Parrots of one species or another were once found on virtually all the islands of the West Indies. On the larger islands a satisfactory population is, in most instances, maintained; on the smaller ones the local species is often reduced to a tenuous foothold in the wilder, remoter regions, and some (see previous chapter) have become extinct. There are some exceptions to the wellbeing of species even on the larger islands. The PUERTO RICAN PARROT (*Amazona vittata*) now survives in only a few undeveloped localities, one of which, fortunately, has been designated a National Forest. The total population has recently been estimated at 18 pairs.

The situation on the islands of the Lesser Antilles is strangely patchy. Taking the larger islands from north to south, Guadeloupe lost its indigenous parrot long ago, probably in the eighteenth century, but Dominica, the next island, still has two species. These are the IMPERIAL PARROT (*Amazona imperialis*), a bird of impressive size and magnificence, and the RED-NECKED PARROT (*Amazona arausiaca*). The Imperial Parrot (with a population of about 150 birds) now seems to be confined to the forested mountains in the centre of the island, the Red-necked (with a probable population of less than 300) to the lower slopes. Though both are in no immediate danger of extermination they are subject to considerable persecution by traps and guns, while their forest habitat is being continually whittled away.

Martinique, the next island to the south, is another which lost its indigenous Parrot a century or two ago, but its near neighbour, St Lucia, still retains the ST LUCIA PARROT (*Amazona versicolor*). Here too, however, the bird is now restricted to the central mountains and is probably declining in numbers fairly rapidly; A recent estimate of its population was 125. Still moving south, St Vincent, a smaller island, has the ST VINCENT PARROT (*Amazona guildingi*) which seems to be holding its own reasonably well, though its numbers are necessarily small, and although there is much illegal collecting of live specimens for export.

Trinidad, Tobago and the other islands fringing the Venezuelan coast share in the South American species of Amazona Parrots, though there are some sub-species, not rare. In general the pressure on the surviving Amazona Parrots, especially in the Lesser Antilles, comes partly from the clearance of their habitat to make way for cultivation, but even more from trapping and shooting. There is still quite a strong demand for parrots as cage-birds, and the West Indian Amazonas are attractive and colourful species. Unfortunately, most of them do not breed at all freely in captivity. At present few islands give their rare birds active protection.

Several species and sub-species of Mocking-birds indigenous to the Lesser Antilles have become rare almost to the point of extinction. One is the BROWN TREMBLER (*Cinclocerthia ruficauda*). The northern sub-species, *Cinclocerthia ruficauda pavida* now has its strongholds on the islands of Saba, Nevis and Montserrat, where it is not uncommon; but the MARTINIQUE BROWN TREMBLER (*Cinclocerthia ruficauda gutturalis*) has become extremely rare. Also restricted to Martinique and St Lucia is the WHITE-BREASTED THRESHER (*Ramphocinclus brachyurus*), of which each island has a sub-species. The Martinique race was thought to be extinct, but a few have been found there during the past two decades. The St Lucia sub-species, too, has only a very precarious hold on life. Ground-nesting birds, they are highly vulnerable to prowling predators.

Of the numerous birds of the Pigeon family which inhabit the West Indies, the GRENADA DOVE (*Leptotila wellsi*), which is confined to the island of Grenada, is unexpectedly rare. For several decades in the middle of the present century it was considered extinct, but it turned up again in the 1960s and is thought to be still in existence. An undistinguished little dove, it may have suffered from competition by more robust species. The grey-and-white SEMPER'S WARBLER (*Leucopeza semperi*) is another extremely rare West Indian bird, restricted to the island of St Lucia, where it has been seen only very infrequently in recent years. Its habitat is the dense undergrowth of mountain forests, where of course it is not easy to detect.

A West Indian species with a curious history is the PUERTO RICAN WHIP-POOR-WILL or NIGHTJAR (*Caprimulgus noctitherus*). At first it was known only from fossil bones excavated from caves on Puerto Rico, which were thought to belong to some species long extinct. Then living birds were discovered which evidently belonged to the same species. So few of them were recorded, however, that it was thought they had become extinct, until in the early 1960s they were found in an evidently thriving colony in the north of the island. The species must be reckoned as decidedly rare but probably not in danger of extinction, though its exact status has not yet been fully determined.

Two other types of Nightjar have become rare in their West Indian habitats. One is BREWSTER'S NIGHTHAWK (*Siphonorhis brewsteri*) which has a few very limited habitats on the island of Hispaniola (the republics of Haiti and San Domingo); the other, the ST LUCIA NIGHTHAWK (*Caprimulgus rufus otiosus*), which is confined to St Lucia and is apparently uncommon there. A Jamaican species, the JAMAICAN NIGHTHAWK (*Siphonorhis americanus americanus*), may just possibly survive but is perhaps more likely to be extinct. It has not been seen for over 100 years.

Precipitous cliffs in Haiti are the only known breeding site of the BLACK-CAPPED PETREL or DIABLOTIN (*Pterodroma hasitata*), a bird which was once widespread throughout much of the Caribbean but was later feared to be extinct. The colony is said to hold at least 4,000 breeding birds. Just possibly there may be other smaller colonies on islands of the Lesser Antilles, where once it nested in strength. Its near-demise was due to human persecution by hungry islanders who regarded it as a delicacy, and later to predation by the introduced mongoose.

Small Island rarities in New Zealand

Once apparently widespread in North Island, New Zealand, the STITCHBIRD (*Notiomystis cincta*), a species of honeyeater, is now confined to Little Barrier Island, a refuge of some 7,000 acres at the entrance to the Hauraki Gulf. The island has been a bird sanctuary since 1896, thus enabling the Stitchbird to stage a recovery from a point very near extinction. Its population is thought to be increasing but is probably not more than about 100 birds.

The SADDLEBACK (*Philesturnus carunculatus*) is a kind of Wattle-bird once well distributed in New Zealand but now restricted to a few small areas. The species is divided into two sub-species, one for the North Island, the other for the South. Until very recently the North Island race was confined to Hen Island (1,775 acres) near the entrance to the Hauraki Gulf, but it has now been introduced to one or two other small islands in the vicinity. The South Island Saddlebacks have been similarly restricted to two small islands—Solomon and Big South Cape Islands, off Stewart Island—but, as they were threatened by rats there, steps have been taken to get them established on other suitable islands around the coast.

Some rare birds of Madagascar

A bird not unlike the American Road-runner in appearance, the LONG-TAILED GROUND ROLLER (*Uratelornis chimaera*) has a restricted range in scrubby grassland near the coast of south-western Madagascar. It has now apparently become very rare, owing to continual human encroachment on its habitat.

The MADAGASCAR TEAL (*Anas bernieri*), whose home is or was a very restricted area of lakes and swamps in Madagascar, has not been seen since 1930 and may be extinct. The reason for its decline is not known but is probably connected with human interference with its habitat. It is a small brown teal, undistinguised save for a white wing-bar.

Continental birds with very Restricted Habitats

Not all birds with very restricted habitats are found on small islands. Some of them occupy specialised territory in the heart of continents. In many instances their present range is simply the vestigial remains of what was once a much wider distribution. It represents the last refuge to which they have been driven by adverse conditions. In a few instances, however, the habitat seems to be naturally restricted, with no evidence that it has ever been much larger.

An example is the GIANT PIED-BILLED GREBE (*Podilymbus gigas*), which is found only on Lake Atitlan, at an altitude of 5,000 ft in the highlands of Guatemala. Its total population is thought to be about 250 birds. The lake has been declared a sanctuary for wildfowl but, at least until recently, control has not been very strict, and the birds are still shot from time to time. The Giant Pied-billed Grebe is virtually flightless, as are two other similar Grebes, the SHORT-WINGED GREBE (*Rollandia microptera*) and the TACZANOWSKY'S GREBE (*Podiceps taczanowskii*), each of which inhabits a mountain lake in South America.

An African bird with a very restricted range in the heart of the continent is the TEITA OLIVE THRUSH (*Turdus helleri*), which has a forest habitat said to be not more than about 1,000 acres on the Teita Hills, in southern Kenya. Its territory consists of islands of forest, all at about or over the 5,000-ft contour, left after prolonged felling. Presumably when there was more intact forest it had a wider range and larger numbers, though it was probably never very widespread or common. It is now decidedly scarce.

Allied to the other Touracos, which are noisy, pigeon-sized birds of the East African forests and include some quite common species, PRINCE RUSPOLI'S TURACO (*Tauraco ruspolii*) is apparently restricted to an area of about ten square miles of juniper woods in the highlands of southern Ethiopia. As the district is seldom visited, little is known about the species and its status. This attractive bird is brilliantly coloured, with bright green head and breast shading to deep blue on back and tail, while the primary wing-feathers and the nape of the neck are bright red and the crest white.

The DAPPLED BULBUL (*Phyllastrephus orostruthus*), a thrush-like bird of tropical forests, is found, as far as is known, only in two isolated and restricted mountain districts 700 miles apart in East Africa. As the forms found in these localities are sufficiently distinct to be classified as sub-species, it is unlikely that any population exists between them. One of the 'islands' is a forest in the Usumbara Mountains of northern Tanzania; the other a table-topped massif known as the Namuli Mountain, in northern Mozambique. Only a few specimens have ever been identified, but the situation is complicated by the habit of several similar species choosing to forage together.

The fierce droughts that desiccate the heart of Australia probably have much to do with the scarcity of some of the bird species erratically reported there. In that vast, austere, rugged region they move about in search of swamps and water-holes that have not dried up, and the coincidence of the birds and travelling naturalists in the same locality is not very frequent. One of the rarest species, the EYREAN GRASS WREN (*Amytornis goyderi*), has been recorded on only three occasions—one in 1875, then in 1931, and again in 1961. At various times in the intervening periods it has been assumed to be extinct. The region where it has been found is north of the extensive inland sea known as Lake Eyre, which itself dries up from time to time. In all there are eight species of Grass-Wren, none of them common though none quite as rare as the Eyrean Grass Wren. All live in the hot heart of Australia.

Of the Grass Parakeets of Australia some species, notably the familiar Budgerigar, are still abundant, while others are in no danger. A few, however, have become perhaps dangerously rare.

The SPLENDID or SCARLET-CHESTED PARAKEET (*Neophema splendida*) is a brilliantly coloured but shy bird of the Australian plains in the western parts of South Australia and the Nullabor Plain in Western Australia. It has lost much of its former range to land reclamation for farming, but the remote districts where it still lives are not often visited by ornithologists and its true status is not known.

The BEAUTIFUL PARAKEET (*Psephotus pulcherrimus*) lives in a restricted territory along the Darling River and its tributaries where Queensland meets New South Wales. Earlier in the present century it was thought to be extinct, and although now it seems reasonably safe its numbers are probably very small. This is a species which nests in the towering nests of termites. Another very rare species which chooses the same nesting habitat is the PARADISE PARAKEET (*Psephotus chrysopterygius*), of which two sub-species are found in the country draining into the Gulf of Carpentaria, in the north of Australia. In the late 1960s the population of one of the sub-species was thought to be as low as about 250, and it had been harried by professional bird-catchers in spite of laws for its protection.

The ORANGE-BELLIED PARAKEET (*Neophema chrysogaster*), once feared extinct, is thought now to have passed the danger point and be on the road to recovery. It nests in Tasmania, particularly on uninhabited islands off the south coast, and migrates to mainland Australia in winter. A bird primarily of savannah country, it nests in hollow trees.

Somewhat different is the story of the EVERGLADE KITE (*Rostrhamus sociabilis plumbeus*), now more or less confined to the Loxahatchee Wildlife Refuge in a corner of Lake Okeechobee, Florida. This bird was once widely distributed throughout Florida but since the beginning of the present century its habitat has been steadily reduced by the draining of swamps to make way for cultivation. The Everglade Kite feeds almost exclusively on giant freshwater snails (*Pomecea*) which live in these amphibious localities, and its down-curved bill has a very sharp point designed for extracting the snails from their shells. By 1965 the total population had sunk to about ten birds, and although there has been some recovery since then the situation is still precarious. One element is the abnormally low fertility rate noted in the eggs. This may be due to pesticides or it may be due to inbreeding. Shortage of food is unlikely to be a factor, as ample supplies of snails are still to be found in Florida. If the Everglade Kite can once get itself well established in the Everglades National Park, its future should be much more stable.

Even the extinction of the Everglade Kite would not, however, eliminate the species. The Florida birds are the northern race or sub-species of a species distributed throughout Central and South America as far south as the La Plata river of

Kirtland's Warbler (m).
Photo. G. Ronald Austing

Argentina. The Cuban sub-species has become rather rare in recent years for similar reasons, namely, the draining of marshlands.

A curious phenomenon is presented by certain bird species which have a very restricted breeding-area and a similarly restricted wintering-area but occur on migration between the two. One of the most notable and most publicised is the KIRTLAND'S WARBLER (*Dendroica kirtlandi*), a handsome grey and yellow bird, restricted in summer to the Jack Pine area of the State of Michigan, and in that territory to stands of Jack Pines (*Pinus banksiana*) between six and 18 ft high. At this stage the trees produce the kind of thickets favoured by the Warblers for nesting and are especially prone to do so in the process of natural regeneration after forest fires. The birds spend the winter only in the Bahamas and there probably only on certain islands.

When the remarkable life-style of the Kirtland's Warbler became known, determined steps to protect the species were taken in Michigan. Several thousands of acres were set aside as nesting reserves, in which controlled burning of jack pines

75

was organised, to ensure a succession of suitable nesting-sites. Annual counts of singing males are taken, which reveal a present population of about 400 breeding birds. In the 1940s and 1950s it was discovered that about 55 per cent of Warbler nests were parasitised by the Brown-headed Cowbird (*Molothrus ater*). When in the 1960s the percentage rose to over 70 a campaign was mounted to trap the Cowbirds and remove them from the Warbler territory. This has been attended by limited beneficial results. There is now a suggestion, so far unsubstantiated, that a small population of Kirtland's Warblers may also exist in similar Jack Pine country across the Canadian border in Ontario. In the Bahamas the birds may be at increasing risk through the growth of the human population and the development of the islands as holiday resorts.

Two other American birds with extremely restricted habitats are the CAPE SABLE SEASIDE SPARROW (*Ammospiza mirabilis*) and the DUSKY SEASIDE SPARROW (*Ammospiza nigrescens*). The Cape Sable from which the former species takes its name is the south-western tip of Florida, a marshy area included in the Everglades National Park. The species was discovered and named as recently as 1919 and is probably now represented by no more than 500 birds, if that. It has lost some of its territory by land drainage and has been much harassed by fires, droughts and hurricanes. The bird is non-migratory. Two hundred miles or so farther north, on the east coast of Florida, the Dusky Seaside Sparrow occupies a small pocket of territory which, it so happens, was chosen as the site for developing space rockets, its name being altered from Cape Canaveral to Cape Kennedy. At first the influx of scientists, technicians and all their equipment seems to have benefited the birds, largely because, as in other similar areas, the general public was rigidly excluded and urban development, other than that directly concerned with the space project, banned. Since then, however, marsh drainage and measures to reduce the mosquito population have had adverse effects. In short, the environment has been drastically changed, and it remains to be seen to what extent the Sparrow will be able to adapt. The present population is probably less than 500 birds.

While some Humming-birds have a wide distribution (the Ruby-throated Humming-bird (*Archilochus colubris*) nests from southern Canada southwards to the Gulf States), others have very restricted habitats. Some are confined to certain altitudes on tropical mountains or to certain mountain craters. So little is known about many of them, however, that it is difficult to say with certainty that any particular species is rare. As recently as 1959 the Hooded Vizor-bearer (*Augastes lumachellus*), a species reputed to have been extinct for 50 years, was discovered flourishing in a mountain district of north-eastern Brazil. And new species and sub-species are still found and identified from time to time.

Environmental Changes

Reiterating what has been stated in the first chapter, continuing change is a feature of the natural order. Nothing is static. Species are continually having to adapt themselves to changes in the environment and have had to do so since the earliest days of life on earth. Those which are unable to do so perish.

Considerable adaptation must have been required of species to survive the Ice Ages. In the more immediate geological past the north polar ice cap expanded and contracted several times, its glaciers penetrating into the heart of Eurasia and America. Some authorities think that at present we are in an interim period between two Ice Ages, that the ice will return and more adaptation will be needed. During the period of recorded history the deserts of Africa and the Near East have been growing, and still are. The sands of the Sahara creep southwards at an average rate of several miles per year. Life in vast areas of the tropics depends on the regular recurrence of monsoon rains, and when these fail the countryside deteriorates into temporary desert. In the heart of Australia rains occur only sporadically. The normal condition of much of the interior of that continent is therefore hot and arid desert, to which, however, the occasional visitation by heavy rain brings about a miraculous resurgence of life. Even more dramatic are the earthquakes, volcanic eruptions, hurricanes and other natural upheavals which make a spectacular impact on the environment of limited areas. The second chapter gives instances of species and sub-species which, confined to small islands, have been wiped out by such events.

While the rhythmic advance and retreat of the ice, the desiccation of the former grasslands of the Sahara, the occurrence of monsoon rains and the incidence of earthquakes, eruptions, typhoons and the like are beyond the control of Man, most other changes in the environment have been effected by him. Even the extensions of deserts have, within historical times at least, been largely due to the activities of his domestic animals, notably goats. The unwise agricultural exploitation of the American prairies nearly resulted, in the 1930s, in the creation of a similar desert—a dust-bowl.

The very numbers of the human race are in themselves a problem of increasing severity. It took Man until the year A.D. 1500 to reach a world population of 1,000 million; 400 years later the 2,000-million mark was achieved. But only another 50 years were required to add the next 1,000 million. The present world population is estimated at over 4,000 million, and the likelihood is that by the end of the century it will have topped 7,000 million. Such a population explosion, caused primarily by Man being more efficient at death control than at birth control, naturally has a cataclysmic impact on other species. Even apart from direct interference by Man, the consequential changes in environment demand an increasingly rapid rate of adaptation. It is sometimes forgotten, too, that in addition to his own needs Man has a host of dependent domestic animals to provide for. Translated into terms of food production, those animals would represent the equivalent of a further 15,000 million people.

Mass-production of humans and animals on such a scale obviously demands the mass-production of food. A natural consequence is the development of monoculture on an immense scale. For efficient growing and harvesting crops of a single-plant variety, such as wheat, maize or rice, occupy enormous areas, to the exclusion of everything else. The term 'deserts of wheat' has been applied to the arable lands which were once the American and Canadian prairies, and from the point of view of most of the other species of plants and animals which used to inhabit them they *are* deserts.

For several thousands of years some men have tended to cluster in densely peopled settlements, over the past few hundred years, and especially in the present century, the trend has accelerated until now probably the bulk of mankind is domiciled in vast urban sprawls. Associated with this growth of city-life are the needs of industry. More and more land is, from the point of view of other species, sterilised by the activities of miners, builders and an increasing range of industries, while urban man demands more and more space for recreation. In fact, Man is everywhere, exploiting everything, possessing everything: he is to be found on the most remote islands, in the harsh wastes of Antarctica, tapping oil beneath the burning deserts, climbing to the tops of the highest mountains, and now penetrating into the ocean deeps. For other species there is no escape from Man. They must either come to terms with him or perish.

BIRDS OF SWAMP AND FEN As Britain was one of the first countries to be overtaken by the industrial revolution and the consequent growth of great manufacturing cities, and as it has also long been parcelled out among agricultural villages and has a high population density, it can be considered a convenient unit for a brief study of the relationship between birds and men.

Within historical times it has lost very few bird species, and some of those which disappeared temporarily have returned in recent years. At the dawn of history it seems that the Pelican (*Pelecanus onocrotalus*) was fairly plentiful on the undrained marshes of Somerset; and while the Great Auk (*Alca impennis*) has, of course, gone beyond recall, as recounted on pp. 41–2, it lingered until early in the nineteenth century. The Kite which swarmed over London's rubbish dumps in Tudor times has now been banished to the remotest districts of Wales, though there is a suggestion that the Kites of London and other cities were not the Red Kite (*Milvus milvus*) of Wales but the Black Kite (*Milvus migrans*), still common in much of Europe and often found in the vicinity of towns.

The environmental change which caused the greatest trauma to the bird-life of Britain was the drainage of swamps and fens, and especially the reclamation of the extensive Fenland of the eastern midlands in the counties of Cambridgeshire, Huntingdonshire, Lincolnshire, Norfolk, Bedfordshire and Suffolk. Beginning in earnest in the seventeenth century, a succession of ambitious schemes made avail-

Birds and men in Britain

Avocet: this bird has re-colonised certain areas of eastern England in recent years. *Photo. Eric Hosking*

able a vast area of fertile soil for cultivation but deprived an immense number of marsh-birds of their habitat. The chief species banished from Britain by this upheaval (though some managed to maintain a precarious foothold in other parts of the country, and others have since returned) were the Black Tern (*Chlidonias niger*), the Ruff (*Philomachus pugnax*), the Avocet (*Recurvirostra avosetta*), Savi's Warbler (*Locustella luscinoides*), the Crane (*Grus grus*), the Spoonbill (*Platalea leucorodia*), the Black-tailed Godwit (*Limosa limosa*), the Marsh Harrier (*Circus aeruginosus*) and the Bearded Tit (*Panurus biarmicus*). Other species of which records are fragmentary, such as the Spotted Crake (*Porzana porzana*) and Baillon's Crake (*Porzana pusilla intermedia*), may have been similarly affected.

Of the Black Tern a sixteenth-century writer comments: 'Throughout the whole summer at which time it breeds, it makes such an unconscionable noise that by its unrestrained clamour it almost deafens those who live by lakes and marshes.' As late as 1818 it was still breeding 'in myriads' at Upton, near Acle in Norfolk, and was plentiful at Crowland Wash in Lincolnshire in 1832. It probably ceased to nest regularly in what remained of the Fens by about 1840.

The Ruff, which was banished from the British list of breeding-birds at about the same time, was once so abundant that 'they were caught in nets in great numbers and fatted on bread and milk, hempseed, boiled wheat and sugar'. When fat enough for the table, their heads were cut off with a pair of scissors.

The Crane was an early casualty. In his *Historia Avium* (1544) William Turner states: 'Cranes breed in England in marshy places, I myself having often seen their pipers'—the 'pipers' being young cranes. Breeding in England probably ceased by about the end of the same century, but the birds continued to visit their old haunts on migration or in winter, though in ever-diminishing numbers, for the next century or two. The species now occurs only as a very rare vagrant, though it still nests in Scandinavia and the Baltic countries.

One of the strongholds of the Spoonbill was evidently the vicinity of the Thames in and near London, where it nested with Herons in tall trees, contrary to its more usual habit in the Netherlands, where it nests in reed-beds. In his book *London's Natural History* R. S. R. Fitter quotes a document which states that 'in 1523 the Bishop of London sued one of his tenants who had broken into his park and taken herons and "shovelers", as spoonbills were then called, which were nesting in trees there'. Though London clearly became too congested for them, Spoonbills were nesting on the Duke of Norfolk's estate in West Sussex in 1570 and in Pembrokeshire in or about 1602. Sir Thomas Browne in his book *Account of the Birds found in Norfolk* (1678) wrote that 'they formerly built in the heronry at Claxton and Reedham, now at Trimley, in Suffolk. They came in March and are shot by fowlers, not for their meat, but for the handsomeness of the same.' Like a number of other Fenland species, the Spoonbill has found a northern refuge in Holland, the Dutch having adopted an enlightened attitude towards their marshland birds much earlier than the British. The Dutch reserves are, however, an isolated outpost of a species whose main territory is now in south-eastern Europe.

The Avocet was absent from the list of British breeding birds for just over a century. Owing chiefly to land drainage but also to indiscriminate shooting it had become rare by the beginning of the nineteenth century, and the last breeding record was for Romney Marsh in 1843. In 1947 two small colonies established themselves on marshy Havergate Island on the Suffolk coast where, carefully

Ipswich Sparrow
Photo. Bill Wilson
(National Audubon Society
Coll./Photo. Researchers Inc.)

Cape Sable Sparrow
Photo. Ron Willocks
(National Audubon Society
Coll./Photo. Researchers Inc.)

protected, the birds nest regularly and in increasing numbers, some having spread to the neighbouring counties of Essex and Norfolk. The Avocet is one of the marshland species which has for long found a safe refuge in Holland, from which the revived British population doubtless originated.

Another bird of the Dutch marshland sanctuaries, the Black-winged Stilt (*Himantopus himantopus*), has also bred in eastern England on a few occasions in recent years. Although there is no documentary evidence that it once nested in the Fens it was probably revisiting ancient lost territory. Black-tailed Godwits, which have also found a haven in Holland, undoubtedly once nested in many marshy districts in eastern England and also in Scotland. This bird used to appear in great numbers on passage as far as west Cornwall. Despite the destruction of most of its former breeding-haunts, it never completely abandoned the British Isles. Every now and then a nesting pair would be reported, and in recent years these occurrences have become more frequent.

Most of the marsh-birds that frequented the amphibious wastes of the Fens before they were drained did so in large numbers, being mainly species that engaged in communal nesting. An exception was the secretive Savi's Warbler, which apparently was never very common. The destruction of the reed-beds which it favoured resulted in its total extinction as a breeding species, but fortunately it is migratory and since a more enlightened attitude has prevailed a few pairs have returned to nest.

Although the Bearded Tit lost much of its habitat when the Fens were drained it had other territory where it managed to survive. In his *British Ornithology* (1811–1812) G. Graves indicated that it was plentiful for almost the entire length of the Thames, from its estuary as far inland as Oxford. Though now very much restricted in its range it still nests in Norfolk, Devon, Dorset, Suffolk and perhaps other counties. The population may be reinforced from time to time by immigrants from the reed-beds of Holland.

The drainage of the Fens and of other marshland regions in Britain severely depleted the population of Marsh Harriers, and their destruction was undoubtedly hastened by the fact that they were hawks and therefore shot at sight. However, they never became entirely extinct. A small population survived, notably in the Broads of eastern Norfolk and in the wilder parts of Scotland and Wales. The population of this species, too, is probably replenished from time to time by immigration from Holland.

The booming of the Bittern (*Botaurus stellaris*) was once a familiar sound over wide areas of England—wherever, indeed, there were undrained swamps and fens. Numerous allusions in the poetry of past centuries imply that it was a sound which every countryman would know. Every county natural history is replete with records of Bitterns, mostly obituary notices, for they were written when the species was becoming rare and when the normal fate of a rarity was to be shot by the nearest man with a gun. The last indisputable record of the Bittern nesting in England in the nineteenth century was for 1868, after which the species could be reckoned extinct in that country. In 1911, however, it was again found to be nesting in Norfolk, and over the past 40 years its numbers have steadily increased. It now nests in most of the eastern counties and in some elsewhere; indeed, in some localities it is present in considerable numbers.

Noisy Scrub-bird
Matthew Hillier

In primeval times forest trees were the natural vegetation of most of Britain. Even 1,000 years ago it was said that a squirrel could travel across the country from sea to sea without setting foot on the ground. Oak and hazel were probably the dominant trees over much of England and Wales, with lime and elm also abundant. In Scotland their place was taken by pine and birch. Villages grew up in forest clearings, some of them later evolving into towns while others remain little changed to this very day. The fields of each village were gradually extended until they linked up with those of the next and the greater part of the country became a network of enclosures. Royal policy, however, formulated by monarchs who loved hunting and needed venison to keep their tables supplied with meat, determined that enormous areas should remain in their primitive state. Some of these 'chases'—notably the New Forest—still do so. They are not entirely wooded but include, in addition to forest, much heath and moorland with streams and bogs.

By the end of the fifteenth century most of the forests were being utilised, largely by the techniques of pollarding and coppicing, each section in turn being enclosed for a few years to allow natural regeneration of the trees unchecked by the activities of grazing or browsing animals. During the Middle Ages many of the forests were gradually denuded by tree-felling for ship-building, house-building and charcoal-burning. As England became involved more and more in European wars and in world-wide trade, so the demands for ship-timber grew heavier so that, although charcoal was largely superseded by coal, the forests continued to be progressively diminished. By the nineteenth century most of the surviving woodlands had been incorporated into private estates and were valued chiefly as game preserves, notably for pheasants. As such many were maintained in a more or less efficient manner by their owners, but the Government, by now accustomed to obtaining most of its supplies of timber from abroad, took little interest in forestry. The exigencies of the two great wars of the twentieth century made further inroads into the depleted forests, and it is only since the end of World War Two that the Forestry Commission, established in 1919, has made real headway in the creation of new commercial forests. Unlike the indigenous forests, however, these new ones are predominantly of conifers, which is what commerce demands.

It is against this background that the changing fortunes of the woodland species of birds must be set. Whether the destruction of its forest habitat has been the prime factor in the extinction or decline of any species is, however, doubtful. No doubt it has been a contributory cause, but direct persecution by Man has played a more important role, particularly where hawks and falcons are concerned.

The GOSHAWK (*Accipter gentilis*) is a forest species which may have been a widespread indigenous bird when Britain was covered with woodland. No-one knows whether it was really indigenous because when throughout the Middle Ages it was among the noble birds of the chase, reserved for the gentry, many individuals were imported from continental Europe. From time to time in the present century breeding has been recorded, but whether by genuinely wild birds or by birds escaped from captivity is impossible to determine.

The remnants of the great Caledonian Forest are the home of the turkey-sized CAPERCAILLIE (*Tetrao urogallus*), but the stock is not indigenous. The Scottish population of Capercaillies was exterminated by the ruthless felling of the ancient pine forests in the eighteenth century, coupled with uncontrolled shooting. The last birds of the Scottish race were killed in 1771, those in Ireland, where they were also

Griffon Vulture: still found in mountain districts of southern Europe, but has suffered from eating poisoned-bait set for wolves. *Photo. Dr Alan Beaumont* indigenous, about 1760. Towards the middle of the nineteenth century attempts, finally successful, were made to reintroduce the species by importing stock from Sweden and the present population, well-established though with a sporadic distribution, is descended from these birds. As the Scottish and Irish birds had been cut off from contact with the European population for several millennia, and the species is not migratory, it seems likely that they had developed sub-specific characteristics, in which case the sub-species must be reckoned as extinct races.

The BRITISH BLACK GROUSE (*Lyrurus tetrix britannicus*) has certainly developed sub-specific features to distinguish it from the Continental type, but these can be studied and identified, for the British race is not extinct. The Black Grouse frequents wooded country adjacent to moorland and has declined with the destruction of much of this type of habitat. It is now confined to suitable country in Scotland, northern England, parts of Wales and the Welsh border counties, and Exmoor, but was formerly found in East Anglia and much of midland England, as well as in Sussex and the New Forest.

On pages 75-6 an account is given of the rare Kirtland's Warbler which has a very limited range in the state of Michigan, where it is restricted to stands of jack pines from six to 18 ft high. Before men took a hand, acceptable conditions for nesting-sites were provided as an aftermath of forest fires. So the Kirtland's Warblers were to be found nesting wherever, in a total area of 100 by 85 miles, jack pines were recovering from a forest fire which had occurred six to 13 years earlier. The species was first identified in its winter quarters in the Bahamas and on migration in 1879 and subsequent years, and the numbers recovered there between 1880 and 1900 indicate that it was much more plentiful than it is now. What probably happened is that in those years there was an increase in the area of jack pines regenerating after the first onslaught of timber-fellers; the population seems now to have stabilised at about 500 pairs.

Parallel fluctuations may be noted in the bird populations of woods in the process of regeneration in other parts of the world. In Britain, where many new forests are being created and where the first plantations made by the Forestry Commission are now ripe for felling and replanting, an interesting sequence of events occurs. In many instances, conifers are planted on land formerly occupied by deciduous trees, which would in itself trigger off a series of changes, but others occur whenever a forest is renewed. In the ancient forests of Britain and other countries of northern Europe the big trees were rather thinly distributed, at about 20 per acre. This allowed space for much secondary growth, the lesser trees being chiefly holly, hawthorn and, most plentiful of all, hazel. Beneath these, again, a vigorous jungle of lesser plants such as bracken, bramble, honeysuckle, briar, woodland thistles and mercury, flourished. When Man started to exploit the forest, it became customary to cut the underwood regularly, usually at intervals of about eight years. In cutting the useful hazel the woodmen also cleared away the encumbering weeds, leaving the floor of the forest swept clean.

In an efficiently managed forest such as this a varied company of woodland birds found congenial habitats. Some tended to circulate in the higher-tree canopy; some in the intermediate levels; some, such as woodpeckers and tree creepers, on the trunks of the trees; some on the woodland floor. Some preferred the newly cleared areas, some those in which the undergrowth was several years old. The bird population thus tended to shift from one part of a forest to another, in response to the timber-cutting programme. When such a forest is switched to the growing of thickly planted conifers, an entirely different habitat at first develops. While the trees are small a dense growth of weeds, especially coarse grasses, springs up around them. The birds of the open woodland move away and their place is taken by seed-eating birds, especially finches. The thick grass cover also proves an ideal breeding-ground for woodland mice and voles, which in turn triggers off a population-increase in hawks and owls. Then, as the conifers grow tall, the former woodland birds begin to return though some, such as tits and goldcrests, like the new surroundings better than others. Hawks and owls, if not deliberately eliminated by Man, often remain more plentiful than they had previously been; wood pigeons, which like to nest in tall conifers, become abundant.

So the bird population of a woodland area changes its character in response to changes in the forest itself. An essential feature of the cycle is the existence, in the same general area, of congenial habitats to which birds temporarily ousted can retreat. In the variegated pattern of the British landscape there is no shortage of such havens, but the situation is different in newly settled or newly exploited countries, such as the United States in the nineteenth century and the tropical forests of Africa and Asia today, where the clearing of forests, without replanting, was or is conducted on a grand scale. Most serious of all is the clearing of forests on small islands which offer no alternative habitats for the dispossessed birds. The list of extinct and endangered species is thus disproportionately weighted with birds from islands which have lost their forests.

Birds of farmland and open country

In Britain, as in most highly developed countries, a large proportion of the land is devoted to agriculture, which usually means monoculture. The countryside is comprised of blocks of land, some large and some small, each devoted to the growing of only one crop and divided from its neighbours by fences or hedges. Arable crops, such as wheat, oats, barley, kale and potatoes, require seasonal cultivations and other operations, such as harvesting, in the course of which every square yard of ground is subjected to the passage of heavy machinery. At other seasons, however, the land is left more or less undisturbed. The wet, mild climate of Britain results in much of the country being occupied by grassland which, however, is utilised as thoroughly and efficiently as the arable crops. Some is cut for hay or silage, and much more is intensively grazed by cattle and sheep. The open fields of Britain are thus excellent foraging-grounds for birds but offer limited opportunities for nesting. Very many species, such as starlings, blackbirds, thrushes, finches, rooks and buntings, find much of their food in the fields but nest in adjacent trees or hedges. Some ground-nesting species, however, still manage to nest successfully in the open fields, outstanding examples being the Lapwing, the Sky-Lark and the Corn Bunting. Here we are concerned with certain species which have *not* been able to adapt themselves.

One which gave up the struggle a century or two ago is the GREAT BUSTARD (*Otis tarda*). Five hundred years ago this magnificent bird nested on open heaths and downs in many parts of Britain, especially the chalk downs of Wiltshire, Hampshire, Dorset, Sussex, Lincolnshire and Yorkshire, and the heaths of Norfolk and Suffolk. These open spaces were then largely uncultivated and were

inhabited only by sheep and shepherds. In autumn the birds collected in large flocks, preparatory to migration. The Bustard was one of the first British birds to be afforded legal protection, for a law of Henry VIII (1534) protected the eggs 'upon paine of imprisonment for one yeare, and to lose and forfeit for every egge of any Bustarde so taken or distroid xx pence, the one moietie thereof to be to the King our Soveraigne lorde, and the other halfe to him that will sue for the same in forme aforesaide'. Legislation did the species no good in the end, however, for by the end of the eighteenth century it had become very scarce. The last pairs known to have nested did so in Norfolk in 1830 and in Suffolk in 1832. Occasional birds continued to put in an appearance in winter and on migration. William Chafin records seeing a flock of 25 on the downs between Andover and Salisbury in November 1851, and somewhat similar influxes were reported in the winters of 1870–71, 1879–80 and 1890–91, but no further attempts at nesting have ever been recorded.

Beyond doubt the increase in human population and the extension of cultivation to former wastelands had much to do with the Bustard's decline, but the invention of firearms was certainly a contributory factor. From early times the Bustard was considered a game-bird, and guns proved far more efficient than hawks and arrows. When in decline the birds were mercilessly harried, and their eggs, being large and wholesome, were considered a prize by anyone who could find them. Even could it have been given the protection afforded to rare species in our present tolerant age, it is doubtful whether the Bustard would have survived as a breeding species. The fate of its smaller relation, the STONE-CURLEW (*Burhinus oedicnemus*), suggests otherwise. The former range of the Stone-curlew was roughly the same as that of the Great Bustard. When in the 1920s and 1930s much of the downland areas of southern England were derelict the birds were widely distributed and not uncommon, their favourite nesting-sites being, apparently, on former arable land left uncultivated without having been sown to grass. Flocks of 50 to 100 used to assemble in autumn preparatory to migration. Such assemblies are now features of the past. Nowhere does the Stone-curlew nest in sufficient numbers to produce flocks of autumn birds. In Wiltshire, which was one of its strongholds, probably less than ten pairs now nest, and these on Ministry of Defence land, which is never ploughed.

The decline of the Stone-curlew must be attributed almost entirely to the spread of cultivation. It has never been reckoned a game-bird and since its decline began it has not been subjected to any persecution. Evidently it simply cannot adapt itself to the disturbance created by cultivation and the presence of men. Comprehensible though this may seem, it has to be set against the success of the Lapwing (*Vanellus vanellus*), a bird of very similar habits and behaviour, which continues to flourish. Probably the fact that the Stone-curlew is, in Britain, on the fringe of its natural range is a cogent factor. It is still quite common in arid, open country throughout most of southern Europe and the Middle East.

Another bird which has disappeared from its former downland haunts is the WHEATEAR (*Oenanthe oenanthe*). The sole reason is the destruction of its nesting-sites, namely, rabbit-holes. Rabbits became excessively plentiful on abandoned farmland on the chalk downs and sandy heaths of southern England in the first half of the present century, and their surplus holes provided ideal nesting-sites for Wheatears. When the land was reclaimed for agriculture these amenities naturally

Stone Curlew: has become scarce in Britain and other western European countries from the effect of agriculture on its nesting-sites. *Photo. G. H. E. Young* disappeared, their departure being hastened by the onslaught of the rabbit disease, myxomatosis. As a result, Wheatears now occur in these areas only on migration, passing on to nest in more congenial territory farther north.

The decline of the CORNCRAKE (*Crex crex*) presents a more complex problem. Until about the end of the nineteenth century this bird was abundant throughout most of England, its harsh, strident calls being as familiar in spring as the notes of the Cuckoo. It is a ground-nesting species, particularly addicted to fields of tall grasses. Its decline was sudden and almost total in the last decade of the nineteenth century and the first two of the twentieth. In most of Britain it is now a scarce bird of passage, occurring chiefly in late summer and autumn, though it continues to nest in the western parts of Scotland and Ireland. Changes in agricultural practice are usually blamed for its disappearance. One theory is that it followed the introduction of the mechanical grass-cutter, which destroyed the nests. Perhaps more likely is the introduction of new varieties of grass, which are ready for mowing earlier than the old July-harvested meadow grasses. Even that, however, is not an entirely satisfactory explanation, for the bird has vanished from certain places, such as the wetland meadows of central Somerset, where the old type of permanent pastures is still dominant. Although the species is still widespread throughout much of continental Europe its numbers have decreased there, too, though not uniformly.

The CIRL BUNTING (*Emberiza cirlus*) is another species which in Britain is at the northern limit of its range. As a breeding species it is found only in the southern half of England and a few localities in Wales. Earlier in the present century it seems to have been much commoner than now, especially on the chalk and limestone downs. The author's personal observation is that in winter it used to congregate with other finches and buntings in rickyards, picking up the weed-seeds left from newly-threshed corn ricks. Threshing was formerly a winter-long task, performed by travelling threshing-gear powered by steam-engines, so the birds could follow the thresher from place to place within a limited area and be assured of a reasonably plentiful food supply throughout the winter. Now the combine-harvester scatters weed-seeds and stray grains of corn over the entire fields, where for a time they offer a good supply of food but are then ploughed in. The consequent dearth of seeds in late winter may account for the decline of the shy Cirl Bunting which, unlike the more plentiful Yellow Hammers and Chaffinches, cannot seem to adapt itself to a more suburban type of life.

Unlike the preceding species the DARTFORD WARBLER (*Sylvia undata dartfordiensis*) is, although a bird of open heathland, more or less unaffected by agricultural operations. It is, however, right on the northern limit of its geographical range and is found in only a few suitable places in the southern counties of England, notably in southern Hampshire, Dorset and Surrey. Its haunts are heathland well interspersed with gorse, a type of country formerly much more plentiful than it is now, in the days before large areas of common land remained unclaimed by the plough. The Dartford Warbler was nesting on Hampstead Heath, Finchley and other places near London just over 100 years ago and takes its name from Dartford, in Kent, another site long since abandoned. Building development and the invasion of its nesting-areas by hordes of humans have, as well as the extension of agriculture, played their part in the decline of the Dartford Warbler. In its surviving territory it is from time to time much harassed by heath fires, and every

Wheatear: has lost many of its former nesting-sites to the plough. *Photo. G. H. Young*

88

Cirl Bunting (m). This has become increasingly rare as a British breeding bird through destruction of its nesting-sites. *Photo. G. H. E. Young*

really severe winter threatens to make it extinct. So far, however, it has managed to stage some remarkable recoveries, although its status remains precarious. In continental Europe it is found in western France and much of Italy, Spain and Portugal.

The draining of swamps, fens and wetlands in general to make available new land for agriculture has become a world-wide phenomenon over the past few centuries, with the result that the displacement of bird species through the destruction of habitat, noted in Britain, has been often repeated. In Europe interest is at present centred in south-eastern countries, where some of the largest areas of primeval marshland survive. The Dobrudja, at the mouth of the Danube in Romania, is marvellously rich in bird species but large-scale exploitation of the reeds is causing some disturbance, despite the establishment of government reserves. Among the species whose numbers have diminished, though they may not yet be at risk, are the Dalmatian Pelican (*Pelecanus crispus*), the White Pelican (*Pelecanus onocro-*

Wetland drainage in Europe and elsewhere

Dartford Warbler, a rare British bird very vulnerable to destruction of its habitat by heath fires. *Photo. G. H. E. Young*

90

talus), the Great White Egret (*Egretta alba*), the Pygmy Cormorant (*Phalacrocorax pygmeus*), the Spoonbill (*Platalea leucorodia*), the Glossy Ibis (*Plegadis falcinellus*), and the Ruddy Shelduck (*Tadorna ferruginea*).

The same state of affairs prevails in Asia. There the Japanese Crested Ibis (*Nipponia nippon*) has been pushed to the verge of extinction by the destruction of forested wetlands in Japan and the adjacent Asiatic mainland. The only known nesting-colony is on the small Sado Island off Honshu, though there may possibly be others in remote parts of Manchuria or the Russian territories by the Ussuri river. On Sado Island a programme of supplementary feeding has been initiated in the 1,000-hectare reserve created for the protection of the species. As with most rare species, shooting contributed to the decline brought on by habitat destruction, but the bird is now strictly protected in Japan and is indeed considered a national monument.

Little is known at present about the status of the Giant Ibis (*Thaumatibis gigantea*), a bird of the Mekong delta and the lower reaches of the Mekong river in Vietnam and of marshland in Cambodia and Laos. Its habitat has doubtless been disturbed by war and diminished by drainage-schemes, and its population is thought to be low. Another large and beautiful bird of eastern Asia is the Japanese Crane (*Grus japonensis*) which features frequently in Japanese art but is now very rare. It has one known Japanese breeding-colony on the island of Hokkaido and another by Lake Khanka, in eastern Siberia, the total population being probably not more than a few hundreds.

Across the Pacific, the Hawaiian Mallard or Koloa (*Anas platyrhyncha wyvilliana*) came near to extinction through the drainage of the wetlands of Hawaii, coupled with hunting, which eliminated it from many of the Hawaiian islands. Another Hawaiian bird which has suffered severely through the draining of wetlands for growing sugar-cane is the Hawaiian Gallinule (*Gallinula chloropus sandvicensis*), a sub-species of the common European Moorhen. It seems now to be confined to the islands of Oahu, Kauai and Molokai, with a total population down to probably a few hundred. Unlike European Gallinules, it does not take at all kindly to suburban life and so is dependent on the retention of its remaining marshland habitats.

In the U.S.A., mention has already been made (on page 74) of the Everglade Kite (*Rostrhamus sociabilis plumbeus*) which formerly bred throughout most of Florida but is now confined, through the draining of the marshes, to a small sanctuary in the Everglades National Park. Its status is precarious. In the same district the Florida Sandhill Crane (*Grus canadensis pratensis*) finds one of its last refuges, small numbers being also present in the breeding season in Georgia and Mississippi. The Sandhill Crane has six sub-species, of which two, the Lesser and the Greater, are abundant. The Florida race probably has a total population of 2–3,000 and is not in any great danger, its nesting-sites in recognised reserves being safe from any further disturbance through drainage. Of the Cuban race, however, little is known, and it may be in difficulties.

As related on page 76, the Dusky Seaside Sparrow (*Ammospiza nigrescens*) and the Cape Sable Sparrow (*Ammospiza mirabilis*) have both suffered a restriction of habitat through the draining of marshlands on the coasts of Florida. Encroachment on their surviving haunts still continues, though conservationists are trying to get the trend reversed.

While in Britain a compromise on land-use has been reached and the area under forests is actually increasing, in much of the world—and particularly in the tropics—forests are being subjected to an intense and sustained onslaught which is playing havoc with the habitats of many forms of wild life. Probably more species of birds are at risk today through forest destruction than from any other single cause. Tropical forests are not, like those of temperate regions, stands of predominantly one or two species of tree but usually contain specimens of scores, perhaps hundreds of species. Timber-fellers tend to be selective, choosing the forest giants which tower hundreds of feet above the lesser growth, but in extracting their prey they create chaos all around. In general, wild life cannot cope with the upheaval but retreats into fastnesses so far undisturbed. When such species have no more havens available they are indeed at risk.

Birds of prey are notoriously targets for men with guns, and the great Monkey-eating Eagle (*Pithecophaga jefferyi*) of the Philippines is no exception, but of equal importance in its regrettable decline is the destruction of its forest habitat. The forests of the Philippines are rapidly disappearing as lumbermen penetrate deeper into their primeval fastnesses in quest of commercial timber, while peasants nibble away ceaselessly at their margins to claim more land for agriculture. This huge eagle, one of the largest of all birds of prey, soars over the forest canopy to swoop down from time to time to snatch a monkey or some other mammal from the tree-tops. Though present in a number of the larger islands of the archipelago until fairly recently, it is now probably confined to the island of Mindanao, where its total population may be down to less than 100.

It would be a reasonable assumption that if any Pheasants are on the danger-list they are there because of human persecution. Although uncontrolled shooting of these large and edible birds is undoubtedly a factor in their decline, it seems the destruction of their forest habitat is of greater importance. Pheasants are birds of forest fringes, and the attack on their environment has been severe and sustained. The natural home of most Pheasants is the mountain ranges of inland Asia. It extends from the Caucasus in the west to the mountains of Vietnam in the east, and some species are restricted to high altitudes, of from 9,000 to 16,000 ft. Isolated species are found in the mountains of Taiwan and some of the Philippines. Although little known to western civilisation, these regions have been increasingly exploited during the present century and severe inroads made into their forests. Of the 48 known species of Pheasant (all but one of which belong to this part of the world) about one-third are in imminent danger. Some authorities put the number of species at risk at 14, others at 16 or 17. All are magnificent birds with gorgeous plumage—their extinction would be a great loss. Fortunately many of them will breed in captivity, and with some species the number of birds in zoos is probably greater than that of birds in the wild.

A score or two specimens of the Imperial Pheasant (*Lophura imperialis*) now living in zoological collections in Europe and America are all descended from one pair sent to France in the 1920s. Their natural home is a limited area of mountain-forests in central Vietnam, and nothing is known of their present status there.

Swinhoe's Pheasant (*Lophura swinhoei*) is probably more familiar to visitors to European and American zoos than to most people in its homeland, the island of Taiwan, where it is confined to the highest and wildest forests of the inland mountains. The stock has been reinforced in recent years by the introduction of a

Swinhoe's Pheasant, restricted to a few mountain forests on Taiwan. *Photo. Dr Alan Beaumont*

number of pairs bred by the Ornamental Pheasant Trust in Norfolk, England. Several hundreds of birds are now breeding in captivity.

Edwards's Pheasant (*Lophura edwardsi*) is another Vietnamese species, found in much the same restricted area as the Imperial Pheasant. Its present status there is unknown, but two or three hundred specimens in captivity in Europe are probably sufficient to keep the species viable.

The future of the Monals of China may well be more precarious, for none of them has so far bred in captivity. The two most at risk are probably the Chinese Monal (*Lophophorus lhuysi*) and the Sclater's Monal (*Lophophorus sclateri*). Both live at high altitudes in mountain-forests, up to the tree-line, the former in Szechwan and neighbouring provinces, the latter in south-eastern Tibet, Yunnan and the adjacent regions of Burma and Assam. None has been reported for many years, though admittedly these regions are not often visited by ornithologists.

The beautiful Tragopans are now among the rarest of Pheasants, and while some of them breed successfully in captivity others so far have not done so. The Cabot's Tragopan (*Tragopan caboti*), which has become very rare in its homeland in south-eastern China, largely through forest destruction, is one of those which have adapted themselves to life in zoos. The Ornamental Pheasant Trust in Norfolk, England, has a nucleus stock which should save the species from extinction.

The Blyth's Tragopan (*Tragopan blythi*) and the Western Tragopan (*Tragopan melanocephalus*), on the other hand, have no such reserves. The former is split into two sub-species, one found in Assam and Burma, the other in south-eastern Tibet and Bhutan. Both are very rare, though so few ornithologists have visited the regions that their exact status is not known. The Western Tragopan has its home at the western end of the Himalayan range, in and around Kashmir. There have been no reports of it for the past 40 years or so, though again perhaps through lack of visits by competent observers.

The Eared Pheasants of the genus *Crossoptilon* are sometimes considered to be races of one species and sometimes separate species. Following the nomenclature which classifies them as sub-species they are: the typical White Eared Pheasant (*Crossoptilon crossoptilon crossoptilon*), which is found in Szechwan and neighbouring provinces of China; the Tibetan Eared Pheasant (*Crossoptilon c. drouyni*), which lives in south-eastern Tibet and the adjacent province of Sikang; Dolan's Eared Pheasant (*Crossoptilon c. dolani*), from the mountainous province of Tsinghai, north-east of Tibet; Harman's Eared Pheasant (*Crossoptilon c. harmani*), from south-eastern Tibet. Little information is available about any of these birds, but they are thought to be scarce and decreasing in range and numbers. Small numbers of the typical race from Szechwan are believed to exist in zoological collections in various parts of the world, but they have not so far bred at all freely in captivity.

The Brown Eared Pheasant (*Crossoptilon mantchuricum*) is a related bird though recognised as a distinct species. Found in Inner Mongolia and the adjacent Chinese provinces, it has undoubtedly been affected by the large-scale forest clearance which has been in progress in recent years, though its present status is unknown. Captive stock which have bred in captivity in Europe and America for more than 100 years are a safeguard against extinction, though their numbers are thought to be only one or two hundred.

The Pheasants of the genus *Syrmaticus* are likewise birds of eastern Asia, inhabiting, like most other pheasants, the mountain-forests of the region. The Hume's Bar-tailed Pheasant (*Syrmaticus humiae*) is found in mountainous country in north-eastern India, Burma and Yunnan. Small numbers of the species live in zoos in Europe and America, and some are breeding.

The Elliot's Pheasant (*Syrmaticus ellioti*) inhabits less elevated, though still mountainous, country in the Chinese coastal provinces of Fukien and Chekiang, where it is subject to increasing pressure by the rapidly expanding human population. However, it breeds quite freely in captivity and is found in many Western zoos. The captive population is probably between 300 and 400, which should be enough to ensure its survival.

The Mikado Pheasant (*Syrmaticus mikado*) has its home in the central mountains of Taiwan, where it is subjected to increasing pressure and is thought to have declined to a dangerous level. A small nucleus of captive stock in Western collections has within the past two decades been reinforced with captured birds from Taiwan and, with that stimulus, has started to breed satisfactorily. A reserve has now been established in Taiwan, in which it is hoped that the resident stock will be reinforced by captive-bred birds brought back from the West. Similar arrangements are being planned in Palawan, the eastern-most island of the Philippines, for the eventual rehabilitation of the Palawan Peacock Pheasant (*Polyplectron emphanum*), which has become scarce in its native country through the wholesale clearance of forests during the past 30 years. Nucleus stocks exist in Europe and North America, but the species does not breed at all freely in captivity.

A family of large birds nearly related to the Pheasants are the Guans, Curassows or Chacalacas of Central America. Similarly resident in the forest-zones of the higher mountains, they are more truly arboreal than the Pheasants and not easily observed. Visits to these remote wildernesses by ornithologists being very infrequent, information about the present status of the various species of Guan is meagre, but one species at least seems to be rare and under pressure. The Indian peasant-population tends to practise the wasteful slash-and-burn technique of cultivation, which calls for the temporary clearance and then abandonment of tracts of forest, and as the population increases and new settlements are formed the pressure on the Guans' habitats becomes more and more severe. The most threatened species at present seems to be the Horned Guan (*Oreophasis derbianus*) which is found in a fairly restricted area on the borders of Guatemala and Mexico. The bird is officially protected by law, which, however, is inadequately enforced.

A group of birds obviously liable to be affected by forest clearance is the Woodpeckers. In the Ivory-billed Woodpecker (*Campephilus principalis*) the United States has an example of a splendid species which has been driven to the threshold of extinction. At the beginning of white settlement of America this Woodpecker was probably to be found in all suitable country in the southern and eastern States, from Texas to Carolina. Suitable country means forests of mature trees in river valleys, and there each pair requires a territory of about 2,000 acres, which is more than men are prepared to give it, except where special provision in the form of reserves is made. Various authorities in the 1940s and 1950s concluded that the Ivory-bill was extinct, but since then occasional records, some from unexpected localities, demonstrate that it is still alive, and there is evidence to suggest that it is not confining itself so rigidly as in the past to big, old timber trees. Its decline was doubtless hastened by irresponsible shooting by or for collectors

Black-tailed Godwit

Imperial Pheasant

Everglade Kite

Kaui Oo

who coveted specimens of this handsome and spectacular bird. A sub-species of the Ivory-billed Woodpecker which once was fairly common throughout Cuba is now either extinct or restricted to a few localities in the south-eastern part of the island.

Korea has another very large Woodpecker, the Tristram's Korean Woodpecker, or White-bellied Black Woodpecker (*Dryocopus javensis richardsi*) which must be very near extinction. Like the Ivory-billed Woodpecker, it frequents ancient forest regions with at least a sprinkling of giant trees and, like it too, it requires a spacious territory per pair. Although now fully protected and with national reserves available, it suffered considerably during the Korean War but probably even more so through the destruction of much of its forest habitat. This Woodpecker is, however, a sub-species of a species (*Dryocopus javensis*) with a wide distribution in eastern Asia, which is not endangered.

The island of Okinawa, in the Riukiu chain, is the home of the Okinawa Woodpecker (*Sapheopipo noguchii*), a medium-sized woodpecker which has become very rare. It is thought to survive in some of the remaining forests in the north of the island, but war and tree-felling have destroyed much of its former habitat.

On pages 70-71 details are given of a number of *Amazona* parrots indigenous to certain islands of the West Indies and now on the endangered list. Most of them are forest species and have declined with the destruction of the forests which once clothed many of the islands. The Puerto Rican Parrot (*Amazona vittata*) had become almost extinct by the end of the nineteenth century but managed to hang on in what is now the Luquillo National Forest, where its population is now down to about 18. The Imperial Parrot (*Amazona imperialis*) of the island of Dominica has been driven back by the woodman's axe to the remaining forests on the high mountains of the interior, where it is decidedly scarce. Much the same is true of the St Lucia Parrot (*Amazona versicolor*).

The Seychelles Lesser Vasa Parrot (*Coracopsis nigra barklyi*) is noted on page 60 as a species restricted to one small island, Praslin, in the Seychelles group. Its range is even more limited. On Praslin its population is concentrated in one valley, the Vallee de Mai, where it is associated with a certain type of palm. The exact relationship between the birds and the trees is not precisely understood, for the trees do not provide these little black parrots with their exclusive food supply.

A bird of the Cuckoo family, the Red-faced Malkoha (*Phaenicophalus pyrrhocephalus*), is threatened with extinction through the steady encroachment on its forest habitat in central Ceylon (Sri Lanka). It survives in a few vestiges of dense, tall forest in the highlands, many of its former haunts having been claimed for agriculture.

On pages 53-4 an account is given of a number of Honeycreepers and other Hawaiian species which have proved unable to adapt themselves to the modern world. In most instances the destruction of their habitat to make way for cultivation has been the prime factor. The extinct Nukupuu (*Hemignathus lucidus*) of Oahu, which was plentiful on that island until much of the forest was cleared but then completely vanished, and the Oo, which was common on Kauai when that island was covered with forests but is now confined to one small swamp forest 4,000 ft up on a mountain, may be taken as typical examples.

The south Pacific island of New Caledonia was once well populated by the Kagu (*Rhynochetos jubatus*), a handsome and anomalous species of bird related to the

Rails and Bustards. Land-reclamation has caused it to withdraw farther and farther into the interior and it now seems to be confined to a mountainous area in the south of the island. Decidedly it is a bird at risk, and it may eventually be saved from extinction by the existence of a fairly large captive population in zoos around the world. Although it breeds in captivity, the infant mortality-rate is high.

Pages 74-6 give an account of the Kirtland's Warbler (*Dendroica kirtlandi*) and its dependence on the presence of jack pines at a certain stage of growth in its nesting area. The related Golden-cheeked Warbler (*Dendroica chrysoparia*), which is also migratory, has somewhat similar requirements. Its breeding-range is a restricted area of Edwards Plateau in central southern Texas, where it favours stands of mature junipers (locally known as 'cedars'). Although its population is still large enough to indicate that it is in no immediate danger, the agricultural practice of clearing the 'cedar' stands to improve the grazing could alter the situation quite rapidly.

Considerable space has already been devoted to the Mascarene Islands and their lost or rare birds. One of the main factors in the decline of so many species has been the drastic and wholesale changes in the environment. When discovered, these islands were uninhabited by Man and clothed in dense forest. On Mauritius the forests have been almost eliminated, to be replaced by sugar-cane plantations. Réunion has not been cleared to nearly the same extent, largely because of the rugged nature of its mountains, and its forest-birds are therefore in a stronger position than those of Mauritius. An example is the Olivaceous Bulbul (*Hypsipetes borbonicus*), which manages to survive in fair numbers on Réunion but is considered to be at risk on Mauritius.

The rapid destruction of the evergreen forests of Africa will, unless checked, undoubtedly result in many more species of woodland birds being put at risk. On page 73 mention is made of the Teita Olive Thrush (*Turdas helleri*) which is now restricted to a few patches of forest in southern Kenya, near but just outside the Tsavo National Park. Formerly a much wider area was forested and therefore inhabited by this thrush, whose population has shrunk with its habitat.

Madagascar is as badly affected as any country by the ruthless exploitation of forests, with the consequence that a number of Malagasy birds are becoming scarce. Among them are the Asities or False Sunbirds, a family (*Philepittidae*) found exclusively in Madagascar. Two of the species of False Sunbird, namely the Small-billed False Sunbird (*Neodrepanis hypoxantha*) and the Wattled False Sunbird (*Neodrepanis coruscans*), are believed to be now very rare. However, as quiet little birds of the dense forest undergrowth they are difficult to observe, and little is known about them.

Australia is the home of the only two known species of the family *Atrichornithidae* or Scrub-birds, and both have become rare through the clearing of the scrub for agriculture. They are the Noisy Scrub-bird (*Atrichornis clamosus*) and the Rufous Scrub-bird (*Atrichornis rufescens*). The latter has a restricted range on the eastern slopes of the Great Dividing Range near the borders of New South Wales and Queensland. Scarce though it is, the Noisy Scrub-bird is much rarer, being found in one small area near Albany, Western Australia. For a long time it was thought to be extinct, but in 1961 a few were found, to everyone's surprise, on a mountain-slope near the town. It happened that plans were afoot to build a new town on that very site, but thanks to the intervention of ornithologists—and

ry-billed Woodpecker, now very rare
d confined to a few woodland areas of
xas. *Photo. James Tanner*

especially to Prince Philip—the site was changed and a national park established
primarily to safeguard the resurrected species.

Grassland and open country   A considerable proportion of the earth's land-surface is occupied by grassland. In
general it is an intermediate zone between forest and desert, occurring chiefly in the
interior of continents, where rainfall is low and there is a big difference in temperature between summer and winter.

In the northern hemisphere a vast tract of temperate grassland extends from the
Plain of Hungary to northern China. It is matched in America by the prairies
which occupy most of the centre of the continent. In the southern hemisphere the
areas of grassland are less extensive and more broken, but they include the pampas
of Argentina, the veldt of South Africa, and the grasslands which merge with
desert in the hot heart of Australia. In the tropics about four-million square miles

99

of Africa are savannah country—grassland interspersed with thorny trees and scrub—with an area of high-altitude grassland, resembling the plains of Europe, on the plateaux of Kenya, Tanzania and Uganda. South America has large tracts of similar country in the campos of Brazil and the llanos of Venezuela. Most of the grasslands of India were once forested and have been changed to pasture by human intervention.

The primeval grasslands of the world are thickly populated by mammals. Herbivorous animals assemble in vast herds to graze on the abundant grass and are attended by a host of satellite predators. Thus the African plains support immense herds of antelopes, zebras, giraffes, elephants and other kinds of big game, to which lions, cheetahs, hyenas and other carnivores attach themselves. In North America the place of the mixed herds was formerly occupied by the bison, of which there are thought to have been 60 million grazing the prairies before Man moved in. With them were associated herds of pronghorn antelope and numbers of smaller mammals, such as prairie-dogs and gophers. The chief predator was the wolf. The vast plains of Eurasia were the home of wild horses and asses and, in ancient times, of mammoths and aurochs. In Australia the most abundant herbivore is the kangaroo, with the carnivorous dingo in attendance. South America has the pampas deer and a number of large rodents, with an assortment of foxes and wolves to prey on them.

Associated with the assemblies of herbivorous animals are some of the world's largest birds. Africa has several species of Ostrich, Australia has its Emus, South America its Rheas, Eurasia its Bustards and Cranes, and New Zealand formerly possessed about 20 species of Moa. America lacked any comparable large bird, but its prairies had a flourishing population of Prairie Chicken and Sage Grouse. Although both birds and mammals are conspicuous in the open countryside they have the advantage that they can see danger afar off. Most of them, too, assemble in large flocks or herds, adopting the principle of safety in numbers. When danger threatens they take flight, and their environment offers them limitless opportunity for retreat.

The impact of human settlement on such a nicely-balanced ecological system can be catastrophic. The fauna of the grasslands of Eurasia had time to adapt themselves; it was here that the techniques of agriculture were developed. On the unfortunate prairies of North America the irruption of human settlers was as devastating as an earthquake. Here vast numbers of human beings, fully equipped to farm, appeared suddenly like a thundercloud in a blue sky and made a clean sweep of everything in the way; in Australia the kangaroo proved more resilient than the bison of North America. Competition by the introduced rabbit was at one time as great a problem to the indigenous population as the plough or direct persecution in the cause of sheep. Now myxomatosis has decimated the rabbits and things are easier. In Africa the challenge is still developing. Much of the larger fauna has been banished from the veldt of South Africa, and now change is threatening the big-game areas of East Africa. The flocks and herds can accommodate to life with nomadic and semi-nomadic tribes, but what happens when humans become entirely sedentary and start to partition off the open grassland with fences?

Earlier in this chapter the melancholy history of the Great Bustard in Britain is recounted. Elsewhere in Europe it is also on the decline. A recent estimate of its population is about 1,200 in central Spain and Portugal, 1,500 or so in East Germany and a larger but diminishing number in Hungary, Rumania and southern Russia. Much more serious is the plight of the Great Indian Bustard (*Choriotis nigriceps*), which was formerly well distributed on the plains of India, from the Ganges to south of Madras. Now only a scattered population survives here and there in central India, and the species is on the endangered list. Although the extension of cultivation into its former haunts is undoubtedly a major factor in its decline, such a huge bird (males sometimes attain a weight of 40 lb) is an obvious target for men with guns. In former times when it was considered a game-bird reserved for princes, game laws rigorously enforced gave it effective protection. It is still protected by law but efficient wardening is lacking, and even in established nature reserves poaching is rife. Not that nature reserves are of much use to this species which, out of the breeding-season, tends to wander far and wide. Several Bustards, including the giant Kori Bustard, are still widely distributed in tropical Africa, but their time may come.

In North America one of the most spectacular victims of the agricultural settlement of the prairies was the great Whooping Crane (*Grus americana*), which formerly nested in marshy places on the great plains throughout the northern central states and in southern Canada. Persecution by men with guns accompanied the draining of their amphibious habitats until before the end of the nineteenth century their numbers were down to an estimated 1,000 or so. A small number of birds continued to turn up in the Aransas National Wildlife Refuge on the coast of southern Texas after their autumn migration, but no nesting-site was known from 1922 till 1955, when one was discovered in the Wood Buffalo Park in northern Alberta. The surviving Whooping Crane population still shuttles between its summer home in Alberta and its winter one in Texas, in both of which it is strictly protected. Its total population is now something over 120, of which nine pairs, several of them breeding, are in captivity at Patuxent, Maryland.

Page 40 gives the sad obituary of the Heath Hen, which was the sub-species of the Prairie Chicken (*Tympanuchus cupido*) resident in the New England states and therefore the first to bear the impact of white settlement. It finally became extinct about 1932. The populations of the other sub-species have in due course been so drastically reduced that all are considered at risk, though some more than others. The Greater Prairie Chicken (*Tympanuchus c. pinnatus*), also known as the Pinnated Grouse, has been exterminated in a large part of its former range but is still present in some numbers in the northern and central prairie states. The Lesser Prairie Chicken (*Tympanuchus c. pallidicinctus*) has a range farther to the south, being found in Texas, New Mexico, Oklahoma and parts of Kansas. The most seriously threatened is the Attwater's Prairie Chicken (*Tympanuchus c. attwateri*), which formerly inhabited the coastal plain of Texas and Louisiana but is now confined to only a few nesting-localities and probably has a total population of only a few hundred. The spread of cultivation has been a prime cause of the abysmal decline of all three surviving sub-species of the Prairie Chicken, though it naturally suffers from being edible and a tempting target for guns.

In Australia one of the species which has suffered most through the transformation of former grassland to farmland is the Ground Parrot (*Pezoporus wallicus*). The reclamation of the rough coastal pastures which it frequented was often preceded by burning, a procedure which caused much mortality. Of the three sub-species into which the species is divided the western one, *Pezoporus wallicus flavi-ventris*, has been most seriously affected and is now very rare.

Earlier this century the Abbott's Booby (*Sula abbotti*) was driven away from Assumption Island, a coral island in the western Indian Ocean, by large-scale mining of guano deposits. Fortunately the bird had another base, Christmas Island on the other side of the same ocean, and here the species survives (*see* page 60). Although guano mining is carried on here as well, the island is much larger and has on its central plateau groves of tall trees on which the birds nest.

Guano mining

In the Pacific the island of Nauru, 450 miles west of the Gilbert Islands, has been pretty well devastated by mining for guano. While the phosphate deposits were being exploited the native population was evacuated to Fiji for some years, so complete was the destruction of the natural environment. How the resident birds have fared is not yet known, but one fears the worst. One which may have vanished is the island race of a species of Reed Warbler (*Acrocephalus luscinia rehsei*).

The guano islands off the coasts of Chile and Peru have also been mined on a large scale in recent years, to the detriment of the local birds, though no species is known to be at risk.

Natural changes in the environment can be either dramatic and sudden, or gradual. An example of the former category was the eruption of Krakatoa in 1883 and of Mount St Helen's in Washington State more recently, in 1980. No birds in the immediate vicinity of such a catastrophe could have survived, but it is not known that any species was exterminated or even seriously endangered by either of these events, for the reason that all those affected were able to re-colonise the devastated area, from population reservoirs outside it, when conditions were right. The hurricane which struck the tiny island of Laysan in 1963 (*see* page 45) was a more serious affair from the point of view of survival of species, for the entire population of the Laysan Teal was resident there. Probably about two-thirds of the birds were swept out to sea where they perished, for afterwards only about 200 out of nearly 700 remained. Though less fully recorded, other storms quite frequently occur in many parts of the world during the migration season and cause heavy mortality among travelling birds.

Natural changes in the environment

The rare Ipswich Sparrow provides an illustration of a bird at risk through gradual changes in its environment. The smallish island on which it lives is being steadily eroded by the sea (*see* page 69). How long it would take for the slow tides to eat away the bird's entire habitat is, of course, uncertain, but assuredly the species must at some time find itself a new home or inevitably perish.

On a far larger scale is the extension of the world's deserts. Some five or six thousand years ago the Sahara was a grassy plain grazed by innumerable herds of wild animals, much as the grasslands of East Africa are today; now it is an immense desert, more than 1,000 miles wide, and is growing wider by several miles a year. Not only do locally resident birds have to be continually retreating before the sand, but the desert is imposing an ever more formidable barrier in the path of migrating birds which nest in Europe and winter in tropical or southern Africa. In years of drought, such as occurred in the late 1970s, the numbers of certain species reaching north-western Europe in spring were seriously depleted. The Swallow (*Hirundo rustica*), Whitethroat (*Sylvia communis*), Sedge Warbler (*Acrocephalus schoenobaenas*), Garden Warbler (*Sylvia borin*) and Redstart (*Phoenicurus phoenicurus*) were especially affected.

A similar desiccation of former grasslands and an extension of deserts is apparently taking place in central Asia, notably now in the steppe-land between the Caspian and Aral Seas. Certain Grebes and other species which need inland waters are tending to spread westwards into Europe as a consequence.

The status of certain species which live in the arid and scorching centre of Australia fluctuates alarmingly according to the weather. At times, after prolonged droughts, they appear to be extinct but after the infrequent but torrential rains are miraculously resurrected. One of the most vulnerable is the Eyrean Grass Wren (*Amytornis goyderi*) which inhabits the barren country north of Lake Eyre and which takes refuge by water-holes during droughts. Other Grass-wrens live in very restricted localities in Western Australia and in a marshy region on the border between Queensland and New South Wales. Another bird of the same inhospitable region which may have been driven to extinction is the Night Parrot (*Geopsittacus occidentalis*), of which there have been no certain records for many years.

With certain other species in other parts of the world the reasons for decline are obscure though probably natural. Several New Zealand birds seem to have been rare when Europeans first visited the islands, and a change in climate has been suggested as a likely cause, though whether that is so or whether the activities of the Maoris had anything to do with the situation is uncertain. One of the species affected was the Kakapo or Owl Parrot (*Strigops habroptilus*), which was thought to survive only in forests in the wildest part of South Island and possibly in one locality in North Island. In 1960 the total population of this species was estimated to be rather less than 200; by 1975 it was down, as far as was known, to twelve birds, all of which were probably males. Unless an undiscovered reserve existed somewhere, the extinction of this species appeared imminent, but fortunately such a population was discovered in 1977 on Stewart Island.

The Takahé or Notornis (*Notornis mantelli*) was thought to be extinct for 50 years, and great jubilation attended its re-discovery by Lake Te Anau, in the Southland province of South Island, in 1948. The area in which it was found was almost immediately designated a sanctuary by the New Zealand Government, and since then the birds have been strictly protected as well as intensively studied. The present population is now estimated at around 300 birds, most of them concentrated into one colony. For the present they are safe, but they do no more than hold their own, largely because of poor reproduction and a fairly heavy adult mortality, so the future still holds a question-mark.

Every country can produce its own inexplicable fluctuations in status of local species. In Britain, for example, no convincing reason has yet been advanced for the decline during the present century of the Wryneck (*Jynx torquilla*) and the Red-backed Shrike (*Lanius collurio*), both of which have become very scarce. Both are here at the north-western limit of their range, so natural causes are doubtless at work. On the other hand, outstanding instances can be quoted of species (of which the Collared Dove is probably the most notable) which have for no obvious reason greatly increased their range, but these are dealt with later.

The Interference of Man

Introduced aliens In the previous chapters prime responsibility for the decline or extinction of a large number of species has been attributed to changes in the environment, most of them admittedly Man-induced. While that assessment of the situation is correct, in most instances important secondary factors have also been at work. Nearly always the birds at risk have had to contend not only with the destruction of much of their habitat but also with the intrusion of unfamiliar predatory species and often with deliberate persecution by Man. Besides Man himself, the most widespread and destructive species of the aliens have been the Cat, Dog, Pig, Rat and, in tropical countries, Mongoose. Dogs, cats, pigs and mongooses are deliberate introductions, rats are involuntary. The impact of alien species is most catastrophic in a restricted area, notably a small island, which offers very limited opportunities for retreat.

Many of the failures referred to earlier were of birds of small islands first visited by Europeans in the seventeenth and eighteenth centuries. As sailing-ships scoured the world in a search for seals, whales, furs, piracy and any other source of wealth, they tended to use remote islands as bases, to which they could retire for careening or provisioning. Often they turned loose on these oceanic islands a herd of pigs as an insurance against future visits. Cats and dogs were either inadvertently or deliberately left behind. Rats, unwelcome passengers on most ships, found their own way ashore, sometimes as a result of shipwreck. Ground-nesting birds were usually the first to suffer. The reason why many island species tended to develop the habit of nesting on the ground was immunity from interference. Where no carnivorous mammals existed, the ground was as safe a place as any. Over long periods of time many bird species on oceanic islands, such as the Dodos and Solitaires of the Mascarene Islands and the flightless Rails of a number of Pacific Ocean islands, not only developed the practice of ground-nesting but even lost the power of flight, their wings degenerating to atrophied appendages. The impact of alien predatory species on such birds was overwhelming and disastrous. They had no adequate defences.

The Iwo Jima Rail (*see* page 31) is thought to have been harried to extinction by introduced cats. The Kusaie Island Rail (*see* page 31) seems to have been exterminated by rats which had escaped from ships being careened there. In the Chatham Islands the local birds have been much harassed by cats and other animals. Remarkably, another very rare species, the Chatham Island Karariki (*Cyanoramphus auriceps forbesi*), a kind of parrot, also shares the bushes of Little Mangare with the Robins and is found nowhere else.

Red-backed Shrike. Has become very scarce as a British breeding species. *Photo. G. H. E. Young*

105

Pages 61–5 give accounts of a number of other Pacific species which once had a wider distribution but are now confined to a few predator-free islands or islets. They include the New Zealand Shore Plover (*Charadrius novaeseelandiae*) which, once breeding freely on the main islands of New Zealand, is now restricted to South-East Island in the Chatham group, which has not yet been invaded by rats; the Auckland Island Flightless Teal (*Anas aucklandica aucklandica*), which survives only on those smaller islands of the Auckland group which are free from rats; and the Stitchbird (*Notiomystis cincta*), a species now confined to the rat-free Little Barrier Island at the entrance to the Hauraki Gulf of New Zealand, though once it was found throughout most of North Island, New Zealand. Lord Howe Island, in the Tasman Sea, lost four of its indigenous bird species within 30 or 40 years of its first settlement in 1834. Direct interference by the human settlers, who killed them for food and also because of the damage some of them did to cultivated crops, was the chief factor in their extinction. In 1918, however, a shipwreck decanted a horde of rats on to the island, with the result that four more species were quickly exterminated. The Lord Howe Island Rail (*Tricholimnas sylvestris*) which still survives is under great pressure from both rats and pigs.

In the Tristan d'Acunha group of islands in the South Atlantic the main island has a flourishing population of rats, cats and pigs as well as humans, while the outlying Nightingale and Inaccessible Islands have none. In consequence the indigenous bird-populations of Nightingale and Inaccessible are virtually intact, whereas the main island has certainly lost one species, the Tristan d'Acunha Coot (*Gallinula nesiotis nesiotis*), and possibly others. Although rats, cats, pigs and dogs have had the most widespread and devastating effects on indigenous populations, the introduction of any alien species naturally has an upsetting effect on the local ecology, and calls for adjustments which some species are not able to make. In some instances the local birds are swamped by sheer numbers. On Laysan island, in the Hawaiian group, rabbits were introduced in 1911 and multiplied to the extent that they almost destroyed the grass cover which provided shelter and feeding-grounds for the Laysan Teal (*Anas laysanensis*) and the Laysan Finch (*Psittiorostra cantans*). In consequence, both species became rare. Recognising the danger, United States biologists began a campaign in 1923 to eliminate the rabbits. This culminated in complete success in 1926, since when the Laysan Finches have flourished exceedingly and the Laysan Teal, though experiencing setbacks from other causes, is happily removed from danger of imminent extinction.

Guadalupe, the Mexican island 200 miles off the coast of Lower California, is infested with herds of goats in such numbers that they have virtually destroyed the dense vegetation which once clothed much of the island. Deprived of their shelter, three indigenous species have become extinct (as described on page 35), while two others have disappeared through associated causes.

On the Seychelles the introduction of the South African Barn Owl (*Tyto alba*) to combat a plague of rats seems to have had an adverse effect on certain local bird species. Now that these alien owls have fulfilled their mission, at least to the extent of making the surviving rats shy and difficult to catch, they have become increasingly aggressive towards other birds of prey, notably the Seychelles Kestrel (*Falco araea*) and the Seychelles Owl (*Otus insularis*). The competition seems to be for nesting- and roosting-sites rather than for food, though the Seychelles Owl is so rare that little is known about its habits and behaviour.

In some of the West Indian islands the mongoose, introduced to control rats and snakes, has played havoc with the local bird life. Puerto Rican birds also have to contend with an introduced population of margays, which are small South American cats, arboreal and addicted to eating eggs.

The scales may be tipped against survival by the intervention of what may seem unlikely species. A classic example is that of the relationship between the Cahow (*Pterodroma cahow*) of Bermuda and the White-tailed Tropic-bird (*Phaeton lepturus*). As discussed on page 68, the problems arise through the complementary habits of the two species. However, in 1961 the Government of Bermuda designated the 15-acre Nonsuch Island a sanctuary for the Cahows. Before human settlers arrived on Bermuda the birds nested on most of the islands of the archipelago, excavating their own burrows in the soft soil. Banished from most of the islands, they managed to survive on a few rocky islets too small to hold soil and so were forced to use the rock crevices also favoured by the Tropic-birds. Nonsuch Island has plenty of soft deep earth, and ornithologists hope that its attractions will coax the Cahows away from Tropic-bird territory and thus solve the problems.

The Kirtland's Warbler (*Dendroica kirtlandi*) has been placed at some risk by increased parasitisation by the Brown-headed Cowbird (*Molothrus ater*). Here again, the ultimate responsibility rests with Man. Before the settlement of the prairies the Cowbird was not apparently found in the jack-pine area of Michigan favoured by the Kirtland's Warbler, but in the present century it has moved in to escape from pressure on its former habitat, now intensively cultivated or built over. By the early 1960s it was found that more than 70 per cent of the Warblers' nests were being parasitised by Cowbirds, which have the cuckoo habit of laying their eggs in the nests of other birds. A campaign to reduce the Cowbird population of the area was mounted but has apparently been only partially successful.

Even remote Macquarie Island, about midway between Tasmania and the shores of Antarctica, has had its problems with introduced species. In addition to dogs, cats and rats, the Weka Rail (*Gallirallus australis*) has been introduced from New Zealand. Its acclimatisation on the island doubtless had much to do with the decline of weaker and less aggressive Macquarie Island Rail (*Rallus philippensis assimilis*).

The avifauna of New Zealand itself has had to contend with an unusual influx of introduced aliens. The first human settlements here are thought to have occurred about A.D. 1000, when settlers arrived probably from eastern Polynesia. They brought with them dogs and, probably unintentionally, Polynesian rats. As these were the first carnivorous mammals to appear in New Zealand in the course of its long geological history, their impact on the native fauna must have been quite traumatic. No records, of course, survive, but it is thought that the decline and eventual demise of the Moas may have been due to rats and dogs destroying the eggs and young of these ground-nesting species rather than to direct interference by the Maoris. And the European settlement of New Zealand, which assumed considerable proportions only in the second half of the nineteenth century, was accompanied by the influx of a host of other species. In addition to the usual cats, dogs, pigs and European brown rats which have been features of European settlement in every country, the British immigrants brought with them a variety of European birds such as the blackbird, pheasant, goldfinch and starling, and a number of European mammals, including the hedgehog, stoat, weasel, deer and rabbit. From Australia wallabies and opossums were introduced, and from Asia, the Mynah bird. As a consequence of these irruptions, a number of New Zealand's native birds were driven to remote fastnesses in forests and mountains and to offshore islets, and several, including the Huia, the northern race of the New Zealand Laughing Owl, the New Zealand Quail and the Stephens Island Wren (*see* page 26) became extinct. In view of the magnitude of the invasion, it is surprising that several of the most interesting ground-nesting species, notably the Kiwi (of which there are three species) and Takahé (*Notornis*), have managed to survive. In all, 43 introduced species of birds have now become established in New Zealand, as well as eight species which have found their own way thither within historic times, mainly from Australia. Most of the new species are, however, found primarily in the new agricultural and suburban environments and do not appear to compete with the indigenous birds in what is left of the original habitats.

The ecology of Australia, too, has been vastly altered by the introduction of many European species by Man. The most traumatic introduction was, of course, that of the rabbit, of which 12 pairs were settled on a ranch in Victoria in 1859. The result is well known. Within the next few decades rabbits spread throughout practically the whole of Australia, building up a huge population which denuded grassland, competed with the commercially important sheep, and promised to increase enormously the area of the central deserts. How many of the now rare birds of the Australian grasslands were reduced to that status by the ubiquitous rabbit is not known, nor can we be sure that other birds which have never been described scientifically did not also perish. Now the fauna of Australia is having to adapt itself once again to a rabbit-population of more reasonable proportions, still trying to recover from the ravages of myxomatosis.

Elsewhere, too, Man's domestic animals have had much to do with changed ecological conditions over vast areas of our planet. In particular, goats are notorious agents for promoting the spread of deserts, their constant nibbling at everything green preventing the natural regeneration of vegetation. The steady southward advance of the Sahara and the consequent increasing hazards attending summer bird migrants to Europe has been blamed largely on excessive grazing by goats and cattle.

THE BIRDS OF PROVIDENCE One of the purest examples of killing out of necessity is provided by the onslaught of the convicts of Norfolk Island on the local Petrels (*Pterodrama solandri*). Dumped on the small and remote island and left to fend for themselves, at least for a time, they regarded the Petrels nesting there in abundance as 'Birds of Providence' and so named them. For them the birds represented the difference between food and slow starvation. They soon exterminated the Petrels, but one suspects that, under similar circumstances, most of us would have done the same.

Direct action by Man

THE FATE OF THE GREAT AUK By citizens of an age which regarded all creation as designed especially for Man's benefit, the Great Auk was regarded in much the same light. A writer of 1622 was filled with admiration for the forethought of God who had 'made the innocencie of so poor a creature ... such an admirable instrument for the sustention of man'. No doubt to many generations of men in previous centuries the Great Auk represented heaven-sent provisions, for long before Columbus opened up the sea-ways to America the inhabitants of north-western Europe were regularly exploiting it. On the coasts of Iceland, Norway, Denmark, Scotland and Ireland the bones of the Great Auk have been found in plenty in kitchen middens of several thousand years B.C. The same is true of North America as far south as Florida. The eggs also, being wholesome, must have been extensively collected, which probably accounts for the fact that the Great Auk nesting-colonies which survived into historic times were on offshore islands. When, after the re-discovery of America in 1492, seamen of many nations began to roam the world's oceans, the Great Auks of the greatest breeding station of the species, Funk Island, off the coast of Newfoundland, offered a convenient source of food for fishermen at work on the Grand Banks. Throughout the sixteenth, seventeenth and eighteenth centuries this populous colony was mercilessly exploited. The curtain rose on the final act in 1785, when some enterprising person established on Funk Island a processing-plant for utilising Great Auk feathers, presumably for stuffing mattresses and pillows. The birds were driven into pens, beaten to death with clubs and tossed into cauldrons of boiling water.

The scale of the holocaust is indicated by a writer who visited the island in 1785, when the commercial feather factory was just beginning operations. The first part of his statement concerns the provisioning of ships:

When the water is smooth they make the shallops fast by the shore, lay their gangboards from the gunwale of the boat to the rocks, and then drive as many Penguins on board as she will hold, for the wings of these birds being remarkably short they cannot fly. But it has been customary for several crews of men to live all summer on that island for the sole purpose of killing birds for the sake of their feathers. The destruction they have made is incredible. If a stop be not soon put to this practice the whole breed will be diminished to almost nothing.

He was right. Within 50 years the species was extinct.

THE ALBATROSSES The demands of the feather trade also came near to accomplishing the extinction of the Short-tailed or Steller's Albatross (*Diomedea albatrus*), one of the world's largest and most impressive birds. Towards the end of the nineteenth century the Japanese began to engage in feather-collecting on a large scale, and the Short-tailed Albatrosses, unfortunately for them, had their chief nesting-site within easy reach of Japan. Eight certain nesting-places are known to have been used on small islands in the western Pacific, and all were exploited by hunters and feather traders. In the early 1880s at least 100,000 Short-tailed Albatrosses were nesting on the volcanic island of Torishima, the southernmost of 'the Seven Isles of Izu', lying some 400 miles south of Japan. In 1887 a party of feather-collectors took up permanent residence on Torishima. Over the next 17 years they took a terrible toll of the species, accounting for 500,000 birds during the period according to one estimate, 5,000,000 birds according to another: single-minded conservationists may be tempted to regard the death of all the feather-hunters in a volcanic eruption in 1903 as an act of deserved retribution. Unfortunately not only did the volcano kill many of the Albatrosses as well but the respite was only temporary. Other feather-hunters came, and the massacre was resumed until by the late 1930s the population was considered to be extirpated. Earlier attempts by Japanese ornithologists to protect the birds had proved ineffective, but when, after the war, the surviving birds were found to be nesting on Torishima the whole island was declared a sanctuary. Another volcanic eruption in 1965 did not help the birds, but again there were survivors, and the total population (the *world* population) is now probably 50 to 60 pairs.

Two other species, the Laysan Albatross (*Diomedea immutabilis*) and the Black-footed Albatross (*Diomedea nigripes*) were similarly exploited by the Japanese during the same period, but as their nesting-grounds were much farther from Japan, in the Hawaiian islands, the impact was not quite as severe. In 1903, an eruption-year on Torishima, a party of Japanese feather-hunters made a raid on the island of Laysan, and another similar expedition in 1909 almost wiped out the Laysan Teal (*see* page 45). Since Laysan has been made a reserve, however, both species of Albatross (as well as the Teals) have recovered and are now numbered in hundreds of thousands.

THE TRUMPETER SWAN Another bird which was brought to the threshold of extinction largely through the demands of the feather trade though also from the activities of sportsmen and the draining of its natural habitats, was the Trumpeter Swan (*Cygnus buccinator*). The American counterpart of the European Whooper Swan, the Trumpeter is a magnificent bird, the males frequently weighing 25 lb or more. It nested wherever in the U.S.A., from Alaska to the mid-west prairie states, inland waters offered attractive sites, and huge numbers appeared on migration. From the earliest times it was killed for food by Indian and Eskimo tribes but was able to cope quite easily with the toll they were able to take. Its doom became imminent when the Hudson's Bay Company began, in the middle of the nineteenth century, to take an interest in its skins and feathers, and the spread of gun-toting settlers across the continent in the succeeding years more or less sealed it. By the 1880s the big migratory flocks had dwindled to a few occasional individuals and the species had ceased to breed in all but a few mid-western states.

In the first two decades of the twentieth century it was widely feared that the Trumpeter Swan was either extinct or about to become so. The species teetered on the edge of oblivion for many years. The total number of birds in America, outside Alaska, in the breeding-season of 1933, was only 69. By then, however, the tide was turning, and there has subsequently been a steady increase. From the headquarters of the species in Yellowstone National Park new nesting-sites have been established in Montana, Wyoming, Oregon, Nevada, South Dakota, Alberta and Manitoba. In 1964 it was established that swans nesting in central Alaska were definitely Trumpeters, a discovery which greatly increased the known strength of the species. At present it is estimated that at least 3,000 birds nest annually in Alaska, migrating south to Vancouver Island in winter, while a further thousand or two breed in the United States, Canada and in a few parks in Europe. The swans are now strictly protected and are provided with supplementary feeds of grain in their winter quarters. At last it has been possible to remove the Trumpeter Swan from the list of endangered species.

COVETED PLUMES The gorgeous plumage they display in the mating season has been the undoing of more than one species of bird. Among primitive peoples throughout the world brightly-coloured feathers are prized items of personal adornment, the most brilliant and rarest being often reserved for chiefs and kings. Among the Maya of Central America the feathers of the Quetzal (*Pharomachrus*

110

Trumpeter Swan—an American species
once feared almost extinct but now
recovering. *Photo. Dr Alan Beaumont*

mocino), a kind of Trogon possessing long, emerald-green plumes, were reserved for persons of the highest rank. The bird lent its name to one of the chief Mayan gods, Quetzalcoatl, and is still depicted on the flag of Guatemala. In New Zealand the Huia (*Heterolocha acutirostris*) provided white-tipped tail feathers worn by Maori chiefs and regarded as a token of mourning. The Hawaiian kings greatly valued the plumage of the glossy blue-black and yellow Mamo (*Drepanis pacifica*), a now extinct species of honeycreeper. Today some of the rarer Birds of Paradise of New Guinea and the Bismarck Archipelago are under considerable pressure through the demand for their flamboyant plumes for chief's head-dresses.

In general the beautiful birds in question were protected by that same covetousness which subjected them to an annual culling. The Guatemalan Quetzal was so highly valued that the unlicensed killing of one incurred the death penalty. Among the Maoris the taking of Huias was strictly controlled by the priests, who pronounced the bird *taboo* if the numbers seemed to be diminishing. *Taboo*, backed by superstitious awe, has been a potent force in protecting more than one species from extinction and doubtless still is. Such supernatural inhibitions, however, had little influence with Europeans, whose callous example has been quickly followed by the indigenous peoples whose lands they have settled in. Before long the Maoris, Hawaiians and others were pursuing their sacred birds with guns, in search of a quick profit through the plumes which they had learned had a good cash value. The Huia and the Mamo vanished from the earth, and there are fears that some of the Birds of Paradise may be going to same way.

At intervals from the seventeenth century onwards changing fashions in millinery created sporadic but intense demand for feathers for adorning hats. In late-Victorian times the fashion extended, indeed, for a time to mounting the entire skins of exotic birds. At the height of such phases of fashion the demand for feathers was staggering. Among the bird species worst affected were the Egrets, some of the Herons, the Great Crested Grebe and the Eider Duck. In 1902 no less than $1\frac{1}{2}$ tons of feathers of the American Egret (*Casmerodius albus egretta*) were sold to London milliners alone. The Great Crested Grebe (*Podiceps cristatus cristatus*) was brought near to extinction for the sake of its downy breast-feathers, once commercially known as 'grebe fur' and in great demand for adorning women's hats. From time immemorial eider-down has been valued for its warm, insulating properties. It is the breast-covering from the Eider Duck (*Somateria mallissima*), plucked out by the duck herself for lining her nest. At certain periods in the past the birds have been ruthlessly exploited, with no regard at all for their own welfare, but those days are happily past, and although the down is still collected commercially, in Iceland and elsewhere, the harvest is strictly controlled. The late nineteenth and early twentieth centuries saw a temporary vogue in Ostrich plumes, but the wild birds were saved to some extent by the development of Ostrich farming.

It was the Egrets which suffered most severely from the demands of milliners. Unhappily, the coveted plumes are characteristic of the breeding plumage and so had to be obtained during the nesting season. At 38 dollars an ounce, which was the price prevailing in New York in 1895, they were a prize too rich to be ignored. The resultant massacre quickly became world wide and of appalling proportions. To obtain the plumes it was necessary to kill the birds, usually by shooting. That meant the deaths not only of the parent birds but of their young, who were left to die of starvation. The catastrophe was vividly described by an Australian writer, A. H. E. Mattingly, after a visit to an Egret colony in New South Wales:

Strewn on the floating waterweed, and also on adjacent logs, were at least fifty carcases of large white and smaller plumed egrets. There were fifty birds ruthlessly destroyed, besides their young (about 200) left to die of starvation. This last fact was betokened by at least seventy carcases of nestlings, which had become so weak that their legs had refused to support them, and they had fallen from the nests into the water below, and had been miserably drowned; while, in the trees above, the remainder of the parentless young ones could be seen staggering in their nests, some of them falling with a splash into the water, as their waning strength left them too exhausted to hold up any longer, while others simply stretched out of the nest and so expired. Others, again, were seen trying in vain to attract the attention of passing egrets, which were flying with food in their bills to feed their own young, and it was a pitiful sight indeed to see these starvelings with outstretched necks and gaping bills imploring the passing birds to feed them.

The scene was duplicated in America, Europe, Asia and indeed in virtually every country in the world, for almost any bird with bright or white feathers was a target for the feather-hunters. Two of the species which suffered most were the Great Egret (*Casmerodius albus*) and the Snowy Egret (*Leucophoyx thula*), mainly because their nesting-places in Florida and other states on the Gulf of Mexico were so readily accessible. After a few years many of the abundant heronries on the Gulf coast were devastated and abandoned, and the continuing holocaust was so scandalous that several states, including Florida and Texas, were moved to pass laws prohibiting the slaughter. So great were the rewards of illegal shooting, however, and so difficult was the enforcement of the laws, that the latter made little difference. Campaigns to influence public opinion were conducted, and the tide at last turned in 1905, when most of America's state ornithological societies merged to form a national Audubon Society. One of the first acts of this new society was to appoint wardens to ensure, as far as possible, that existing laws were obeyed. In that same year one of the newly-appointed wardens was shot dead in Florida by the captain of a schooner which he caught loading up with dead egrets. The agitation which followed was largely responsible for a law, passed in 1906, making illegal the use of the feathers of wild birds in the millinery trade. Other nations duly followed with similar legislation, with the result that millinery fashions soon changed and the worst was over.

Five million birds annually is an estimate of the toll during the peak of the craze. In America the Great and Snowy Egrets were saved from extinction by the enlightened attitude of certain landowners who set aside private sanctuaries in the worst-affected states. In Europe, although the numbers of Egrets and Herons declined dramatically, no species was entirely eliminated. In eastern Asia the Chinese Egret (*Egretta eulophotes*) was the victim of such intensive and sustained persecution, possibly still continued today, that its survival is doubtful. A few pairs may still nest on mainland China and in Korea, but little is known of its present status. Another species put at risk by the plume trade, though now it is also under heavy pressure from introduced aliens, from hunters and from the destruction of its habitat, is the Kagu (*Rhynochetos jubatus*) of New Caledonia. A handsome bird with grey and white plumage, it is virtually flightless and so highly vulnerable. Captive specimens offer the chief hope of survival for the species.

An offshoot of the plume-trade was the demand for the quill-feathers of the huge Californian Condor (*Gymnogyps californianus*) for carrying gold-dust during the

Californian gold rush. It is said that a full-sized quill would hold just ten cubic centimetres of gold and that hundreds of Condors were killed solely to obtain these quill feathers. Incidentally, at a somewhat earlier date the quill feathers of the Trumpeter Swan (*see* page 110) were much in demand for use by artists and calligraphers.

(*see* page 110)

The collecting mania

The urge to collect is perhaps a necessary prelude to the enlightened study of the habits and behaviour of birds. To a primitive mind a bird or an egg normally represents food; later came the desire to possess. Medieval monarchs in Europe liked to have collections of exotic animals and birds to show off to their guests. Sailors of two centuries ago are conventionally depicted as bringing home from their adventurous voyages a brightly-coloured parrot. The author can remember when most English villages had their resident bird-catcher, who operated with nest traps, bird-lime and other devices to meet a demand for singing cage-birds. Many cottagers in the 1920s still kept a bullfinch, goldfinch, linnet, starling, song-thrush or some other locally captured songbird in a small cage in the parlour. It often shared the room with the faded, mounted skin of some other bird—the rarer the better—in a glass case: the inevitable fate of any rarity was to be shot and stuffed. Presumably the motives were pride of possession and love of ornamentation.

In another sense, too, collecting is an essential prelude to field study. Before birds can be intelligently studied at liberty some specimens have to be sacrificed so that detailed examinations can be made of them. How otherwise can we know what we are watching? The science of field-ornithology is necessarily based on the work of museum specialists.

As during the nineteenth century the remote places of the world revealed their secrets to western explorers, foremost among the pioneers who penetrated the new lands were zoologists and botanists sent out to collect specimens of the fauna and flora. Some were employed by museums and similar institutions, some by private collectors, and some worked as free-lances. Towards the end of the century, however, the numbers of private collectors multiplied and their motivation deteriorated. The desire to collect specimens for scientific investigation too often became swamped by the old primeval pride of possession. At its height the fad for collecting eggs and skins became a kind of kleptomania. Collectors, by their very nature, are interested most intensely in rarities, be they stamps, coins, sea-shells or birds' eggs. It follows that when a species becomes rare it attracts the attention of collectors for that very reason. What, for example, would one of the few surviving Great Auk eggs fetch at an auction today? Supposing a tiny surviving colony of Great Auks were to be discovered, even today the collectors would be after them, and conservationists would quickly have to supply an effective system of protection. Collectors certainly harried the Osprey to extinction in Scotland in the early years of the present century, and only constant vigilance protects the nests of those which have returned. Even so, every now and then someone, usually a knowledgeable countryman in the pay of a wealthy collector, slips through the cordon and manages to rob a nest.

When W. H. Hudson, one of the first naturalists to draw attention to the threat to rare birds imposed by collecting, was writing his pamphlet on *Lost British Birds* in the early 1890s, systemic ornithologists decided that the St Kilda Wren (*Trog-*

lodytes hirtensis) should be classified as a separate species. Wrote Hudson:

No sooner had the news gone abroad that lone St Kilda's isle possessed one little song bird of her own—a Wren that differed somewhat from the familiar Wren—than it was invaded by the noble army of collectors, who did not mind its loneliness and distance from the mainland so long as they secured something for their cabinets, and the result of their invasion is that the St Kilda Wren no longer exists.

Hudson was unduly pessimistic. The St Kilda Wren survives, and a recent estimate puts its population at between 400 and 500 birds, which seems a good, healthy total in such a restricted habitat. It has survived, though, in spite of the collectors and chiefly because so many of its nesting-sites are on giddy precipices capable of deterring even the most determined collector.

The Dartford Warbler (*Sylvia undata*) is another species which attracted a great deal of attention from collectors in the late nineteenth century. Hudson, linking it with the Savi's Warbler (*Locustella luscinoides*), which he calls 'the Red Night-reeler' and which is now extinct in Britain, wrote;

The Dartford Warbler has survived not only very severe winters but the destruction of favourite nesting haunts by military camps better than it survived the destruction carried on in Swaysland's time for the supply of private collections. About seventy years ago, when collectors became aware at the same time both of the existence and the rarity of the Red Night-reeler, the usual lively scramble for specimens of the bird and its eggs took place; but it was a bird infinitely more limited in numbers and area than the Dartford Warbler, and not many examples were secured. Its extinction may be said to date back to about the year 1849.

Savi's Warbler was a bird of the Fens and lost its habitat when they were drained. As with so many other species, collectors simply administered the *coup de grace*. The Dartford Warbler lives on gorse-sprinkled heaths in a few localities in southern England but once had a much wider distribution. Collectors undoubtedly played a part in reducing it to its present status, but the remaining pairs tend to be periodically harassed and brought nearer extinction by severe winters and heath-fires, though so far they have always managed to recover, sometimes by the narrowest of margins. After the Arctic-type winter of 1962/3 the breeding population fell to ten pairs.

Many countries which today protect their indigenous birds by law have fewer regulations for exotic species. It is, for example, now illegal to cage any British bird bred in the wild, but there are few restrictions on the keeping of imported birds. Over the past 20 or 30 years, greatly aided by speedy air traffic, a very large trade has developed in small tropical birds, now on sale in practically every pet-shop. Instead of keeping a caged Goldfinch or Linnet the British householder now has his cage of Zebra finches or Budgerigars. The Budgerigar (*Melopsittacus undulatus*) can, of course, now be considered a domestic species, it having bred readily in captivity for a long time. Introduced to Europe from inland Australia in the 1840s, it is now thoroughly acclimatised in many countries and probably has a total captive population of approaching five millions. The need to import new stock captured in the wild has long passed, a statement which also applies to the Zebra Finch (*Taeniopygia guttata*) (another Australian bird), the Canary (*Serinus canarius*), the Barbary Dove (*Streptopelia risoria*) and certain other species.

There is, however, a vast trade in many other tropical birds, often operated by unscrupulous collectors or dealers. Whatever may be the sentiments and regulations at the receiving-end of the traffic, few rules or inhibitions tend to exist at the point of capture. It has been estimated that with some species, and uncommon

115

species at that, the mortality-rate between capture and arrival at the birds' ultimate destination is often as high as 98 per cent—one in 50 survives. Callous methods of capture, ignorance of the birds' diet, despatch in cramped containers for long journeys and general neglect are factors in the horrendous casualty figures. In addition to the capture of live birds for export, there is in many countries a large domestic market for cage-birds. The conventional cages are often far too small and in most instances the trade is entirely uncontrolled. The toll taken by these activities is exceedingly difficult to assess but must be colossal. While few of the species officially considered endangered at the moment seem to be threatened by this traffic, if it continues unabated for much longer there will certainly be additions to the list of birds at risk.

An exception to that statement is the Rothschild's Starling (*Leucopsar rothschildi*), a handsome white-and-black bird which was until recently quite common in certain localities on the Indonesian island of Bali. Bird-dealers have now been so active in its homeland that the population has dwindled alarmingly, and quite possibly its hope for escaping extinction lies in its capacity to breed in captivity. This it has proved able to do.

The decline of the *Amazona* Parrots of the West Indies lies largely in the past, when they were the source of a big proportion of captive parrots brought to Europe by sailors and others returning from 'foreign parts'. In consequence, several species have been rendered extinct (*see* page 70), while others, of which the Bahama Parrot (*Amazona leucocephala bahamensis*), the Puerto Rican Parrot (*Amazona vittata*), the Imperial Parrot (*Amazona imperialis*) and the St Lucia Parrot (*Amazona versicolor*) are examples, have become decidedly rare. The *Amazona* Parrots are still in strong demand in the bird trade, and high prices encourage a good deal of illicit trapping.

The trade in stuffed and mounted birds, happily now moribund in much of Europe and America, still flourishes in some countries, notably in certain tropical lands only recently opened up to tourists. One of the notable victims is the rare and magnificent Monkey-eating Eagle (*Pithecophaga jefferyi*) of the Philippines, mounted specimens of which are offered to tourists as souvenirs. As the total population of the species is now thought to be 100 or less, swift action is needed.

In countries where rare birds are protected by law, collectors of rarities are still active. In most of them the relevant law has from time to time to be invoked to deal with some collector illegally trapping or shooting specimens. The effective conservation of endangered bird-species tends to fall into two phases, first the enactment of appropriate laws, secondly ensuring that the laws are observed. The second aim can be achieved only by constant vigilance and an enlightened public opinion.

Birds as food

Assessed on culinary merit, birds rank high among the animals (in the widest sense of the word) exploited by Man for food. Our modern criteria in this respect evidently differ considerably from those of the past, for our ancestors seem to have enjoyed the flesh of such birds as the Heron, which we would regard as decidedly unpalatable. Perhaps we are not sufficiently hungry—a starving man might well approve of the flesh of a vulture. At an early date men learned to appreciate that a stock of domesticated birds around the tribal settlement was preferable to having to go out and hunt for a meal every day. We know that geese and pigeons were

116

domesticated in Egypt around 300 B.C. and that hens were widely kept in both China and the Mediterranean world before 100 B.C.; ducks and guinea fowl have been kept as domestic stock for the past two or three thousand years. Turkeys and Muscovy ducks are contributions by the New World to our domestic poultry.

The demarcation-line between keeping a population of tame birds or mammals and farming a wild one is ill-defined. Present-day examples are to be found in projects for utilising the big game of Africa and the deer of the northern hemisphere. One alternative is to pen the animals and treat them as domestic stock; the other to leave them at liberty in the wild but to take an annual cull. Primitive men adopted both methods. Where, for instance, they found themselves living in close proximity to an immense population of sea-birds the obvious thing to do was not to try to confine some of the birds in pens but to take an annual toll of both eggs and young birds. A stable human population in such a situation is careful to husband its food resources: one does not cut down the apple-tree to gather the crop of apples. Over many generations the tribe would form a pretty precise idea of how big a toll it could demand. Often the cull would be heavy, but it was never severe enough to endanger the population on which the humans were, in effect, parasitic. In Iceland, the Faeroes and other northern lands the eggs of cliff-nesting birds are still harvested in this way. North American Indians were sometimes prodigal in their slaughter of bison, as for example when they stampeded herds of them over precipices, but they never indulged in an over-kill: always there were plenty left. As we have noted, even the Moas of New Zealand were probably exterminated by Man's domestic animals and by the rats he inadvertently introduced rather than by his direct action.

The extinction of a number of species which has occurred within the past 300 years or so has followed a breakdown in this salutary pattern. Just as Norfolk Island's 'Birds of Providence' and the Cahows of Bermuda were harried to extinction, a similar fate befell the Diablotin or Black-capped Petrel (*Pterodroma hasitata*), which was once recorded as abundant on certain West Indian islands but was almost exterminated by hungry settlers in the seventeenth and eighteenth centuries. The birds are said to have been extracted from their nesting-holes by means of hooks on poles and to have been killed off at a prodigious rate. For many years known only from specimens caught at sea and thought to be on the verge of extinction, the Diablotin was in 1963 found to have a nesting colony of some 4,000 birds on a site in Haiti. There may also be a few much smaller colonies on other islands, though this is not certain.

During the war in the Pacific garrisons, especially of Japanese, were stationed for lengthy periods on small islands and often supplemented inadequate or monotonous diets by taking a toll of local birds. Among the species which certainly suffered from these circumstances were the Megapodes of the Caroline, Mariana and Palau archipelagos. La Perouse's Megapode (*Megapodius laperouse*) has disappeared from a number of the islands which it formerly inhabited and is included in the list of endangered species.

To begin with, the Great Auk and the Dodo were simply exploited for food. Sailors used their carcases for provisioning their ships. It is true that they were often extremely lavish in their assessment of their needs, for as early as 1540 we hear of two ships loading up with Auks at an island off the Newfoundland coast and salting down four or five tons of them in excess of their immediate needs.

Eighty years later Dutch ships were behaving in much the same way to the Dodos of Mauritius. It is possible that, if they had been a resident population, the men who engaged in these massacres would have arrived at a compromise which would have ensured that sufficient birds were left for exploitation the following year. The trouble was that the sailors were transients. Whether they would ever again visit a particular island was doubtful, and even if they had been impelled by motives of prudent housekeeping to leave a breeding-stock the chances were that before long a shipload of sailors of another nationality would call and nullify their fore-thought. So they simply helped themselves and let tomorrow be damned.

Similar considerations seem to have motivated the settlers who exterminated the Passenger Pigeon. As described on pages 37-9, the slaughter was organised on commercial lines by men who were out to make a quick profit from a plentiful natural commodity. In this instance they had as allies the new farming settlers who had no desire for a horde of pigeons as permanent neighbours, pigeons being notoriously partial to farm crops. And no-one who engaged in the holocaust seems ever to have considered, until it was too late, that the extinction of such an abundant species was even a possibility. Not that the foreknowledge would have been likely to make any difference. The massacre in its later stages became geared to a demand for food, not from local consumers but from the inhabitants of distant cities. Restaurateurs in New York and other eastern cities were prepared to pay good prices for supplies of a favourite delicacy with diners who were unlikely to enquire into its source. So, when pigeons suddenly became scarce, the dealers switched their attention to other birds, notably migrating waders.

Thus, the slaughter that had characterised the demise of the Passenger Pigeon was now repeated with curlews, sandpipers, plovers, yellowshanks, godwits and other edible species which passed through the United States on their spring and autumn journeys between their wintering grounds in South America and their nesting-sites in the Canadian Arctic. In the last three decades of the nineteenth century shooting of the migrants persisted on such a scale that the immense flocks were decimated. Two species in particular were brought to the verge of extinction. They were the Eskimo Curlew (*Numenius borealis*) and the Hudsonian Godwit (*Limosa haemastica*). The latter, after teetering on the edge of oblivion, has now happily recovered and is no longer on the danger list. The Eskimo Curlew, once known as the 'Prairie Pigeon' because the enormous flocks in which it appeared reminded observers of those of the Passenger Pigeon, was at the middle of the present century written off as extinct. Since then, however, the appearance on migration in Texas of very small numbers of the bird indicate the existence of an unknown breeding-ground somewhere in the Arctic. The species is now strictly protected.

Although the Heath Hen and Prairie Chicken were ousted from their former habitats largely by the reclamation of vast areas for agriculture, over-kill by shooting undoubtedly also played an important part in the extinction of the Heath Hen, and the decline of the various races of Prairie Chicken to danger-level. It is recorded that in the early days of the settlement of New England it was often stipulated in contracts between employers and servants that Heath Hen should not be served at table more than a few times per week, so abundant were the birds then. Later, on the threshold of the opening of the prairies for settlement, the noise of innumerable Prairie Chicken booming at their mating leks was said to make 'the very earth echo with the continuous roar'. Now the Attwater's Prairie Chicken (*Tympanuchus cupido attwateri*) is dangerously near extinction; the Greater Prairie Chicken (*Tympanuchus cupido pinnatus*) has disappeared from much of its former range though it still occurs in diminished numbers in the north central prairie states; and the Lesser Prairie Chicken (*Tympanuchus cupido pallidicinctus*), found in New Mexico and the neighbouring states, is steadily declining though not yet endangered.

The fact that the Heath Hen and Prairie Chicken were game-birds, obviously related to the European Grouse and Partridges, was obviously a contributory factor in their decline, for they were extensively shot for sport. Domestic animals also took a toll of these ground-nesting species. The catastrophe that nearly overwhelmed the Hawaiian Goose, or Néné, as described on page 54, was similarly due to complex causes, though most prominent among them was the killing for food and sport. As with other geese and ducks, the Néné is unable to fly when it is moulting. At that vulnerable period it therefore used to retreat to volcanic craters on its native Hawaii, where theoretically it should have been reasonably safe. Although the Hawaiian islanders knew of this habit and used to take a regular toll of the moulting birds, the species was in no way endangered until Europeans arrived on the scene. The whaling-ships that called at Hawaii in the late eighteenth and nineteenth centuries then started to kill large numbers of them to be salted down.

In Australia not long ago (in the late 1950s and early 1960s) it was feared that a similar fate might be looming for the Cape Barren Goose (*Cereopsis novae-hollandiae*), a species of the populous south-eastern states. Besides being killed for food and having its eggs regularly collected, this goose was much persecuted by sheep-farmers because of the damage it did, geese being notorious for fouling grassland. The situation has now been stabilised by conservation measures on the offshore islands which are the birds' traditional nesting-sites. Fortunately, too, the Cereopsis is a popular species in wildfowl collections, where it breeds satisfactorily. Another Australian bird declining in numbers though not yet on the danger list is the Mallee-fowl (*Leipoa ocellata*). This bird is a member of the Megapode family, or Mound-builders, which bury their eggs in huge heaps of earth and decaying vegetation that generate sufficient heat to act as incubators. In such mounds the Mallee-fowl lay from 15 to 30 eggs, of good size and decidedly edible. The eggs have always been collected by the Aborigines, but since white Australians have also taken a hand the Mallee-fowl has been losing ground. Introduced foxes have also joined the native Dingoes in digging out the eggs.

Generally, as already emphasised, human communities which regularly exploit bird-colonies by harvesting their eggs are careful to limit their toll to what the colonies can stand. Natural prudence would seem to demonstrate the folly of jeopardising future supplies, but there are some examples of this basic maxim being ignored. The Labrador Duck (*Captorhynchus labradorius*) disappeared from the scene before much was known about it. Until the middle of the nineteenth century it used to spend the autumn and winter on the New England coast, and specimens were occasionally offered for sale in the New York markets, but the numbers recorded were always small. The birds are thought to have nested on islands in the Gulf of St Lawrence and in parts of Labrador, where their eggs are known to have been collected commercially. As the ducks were considered poor

eating, it seems likely that the species, never very common, was forced into extinction by excessive egg-collecting. At present a similar fate may be approaching the Audouin's Gull (*Larus audouini*), a species once widespread throughout the Mediterranean but now confined to a few colonies, of which by far the largest is on the Chaffarines islands, a Spanish possession off the coast of eastern Morocco. This colony is subject to annual harvesting on a severe scale by fishermen, who use the eggs for making a traditional local dish. Now that the species has become scarce, egg-collectors acquiring specimens for collection have also become active.

KILLING FOR SPORT Hunting is exciting. Whether the capture or death of the quarry is to be accomplished by chase, ambush, stealth, ingenuity or direct confrontation, there is for the hunter a quickening of the senses, adrenalin surges through the arteries, and the successful climax is accompanied by exultation or a feeling of profound satisfaction. Small wonder that there is a temptation and a tendency to engage in it more often than is strictly necessary.

Beyond doubt, our primitive ancestors enjoyed hunting for food. The American Indians of the prairies doubtless whooped with delight when they sent a bison herd stampeding over a cliff, killing far more of the animals than they could utilise. The hunting of deer by medieval European monarchs had as its prime purpose the provision of fresh meat for the royal table, but it also gave the king and his courtiers a pleasant day's sport in the open air. African tribesmen need little inducement to trap mammals and birds for zoos. Between killing for necessity and killing for sport there is an infinite number of gradations.

GAME-BIRDS The birds of the Order Galliformes, which includes the Pheasants, Partridges, Quails, Grouse, Guineafowl, Jungle-fowl, Turkeys, Guans and Megapodes, are commonly termed Game-birds. All are good to eat, and most are quite large. Some have long ago been domesticated and now comprise the largest section of our domestic poultry. Others, while remaining ostensibly wild birds, are cropped regularly not only for their food-value but for the sport they afford. The pampered Pheasant is, of course, the outstanding example.

The common Pheasant (*Phasianus colchicus*) is a mongrel in whom the blood of the original type from the Caucasus (*Phasianus c. colchicus*) is mingled with that of the Ring-necked Pheasant (*Phasianus c. torquatus*), the Mongolian Pheasant (*Phasianus c. mongolicus*) and several other less well-known races. Nearly all species of Pheasant are native to Asia, where most of them tend to be birds of mountain-forests. All are spectacularly handsome, with plumage of brilliant colours and bold patterns. They afford a tempting target to any hunter, and not all have been lucky enough to attract the protection that attends *Phasianus colchicus*. Indeed, many are very near extinction. Two of these rare species, the Imperial Pheasant (*Lophura imperialis*) and the Edwards's Pheasant (*Lophura edwardsi*), have as their habitat a limited area of rugged hill-country in central Vietnam. The effect of the long war on them is unknown, but they were uncommon before it started. Equally rare are the Chinese Monal (*Lophophorus lhuysi*) and the Sclater's Monal (*Lophophorus sclateri*), both of which are found on high mountains, to the upper limit of the trees, in south-western China, south-eastern Tibet and perhaps in adjacent parts of Burma and Assam. Both are magnificent birds, much sought after by hunters, as are all the Asiatic pheasants.

The only member of the Pheasant family to be indigenous to Africa is the Congo

Osprey: has become re-established as a British breeding species. *Photo. Eric Hosking*

Peacock (*Afropavo congonensis*), a bird of the deep forests not recognised and identified until 1936. Latest reports indicate that in some places in the rain forests of Zaire it is not uncommon, but insufficient information is available to determine its true status.

The melancholy picture revealed by the catalogue of rare pheasants is relieved by the success attending attempts to breed them in captivity. Handsome and attractive birds, they are popular in any collection, and fortunately most of them breed fairly readily. Of those mentioned, there are captive breeding populations of the Cabot's Tragopan, the Imperial Pheasant, the Edwards's Pheasant, Swinhoe's Pheasant, the White Eared Pheasant, the Brown Eared Pheasant, the Elliot's Pheasant, Hume's Bar-Tailed Pheasant, the Mikado Pheasant and the Palawan Peacock Pheasant. Foremost among the successful breeders of captive birds is Philip Wayre, of the Ornamental Pheasant Trust, in Norfolk, England, who has in recent years returned a nucleus stock of Swinhoe's Pheasant to a specially-prepared reserve in Taiwan.

A related species to the Pheasants, the Horned Guan (*Oreophasis derbianus*) of Central America is said to be under considerable pressure from hunting. It inhabits the mountain forests of Guatemala and the adjacent provinces of Mexico and is thought to be rapidly decreasing in numbers.

THE BUSTARDS Though more nearly related to the Rails than to the Game-birds of the Order Galliformes, the Bustards have long been regarded as game, to be killed for sport as well as for the table. They are confined to the Old World, with species in Europe, Asia, Africa and Australia, the greatest number being in Africa, where several species are still common.

The species nearest extinction is the Indian Bustard (*Chloriotis nigriceps*), a giant of a bird which was once common on India's grassy plains, when India had more grassy, uncultivated plains than it does now. While the British ruled India the princes, maharajahs, rajahs and other potentates made sure, by efficient policing, that no-one other than their own exalted persons hunted the Bustards. After independence, many of the safeguards disappeared, and although in both India and Pakistan the bird is legally protected, the law is too often ignored. Illegal hunting seems to be widespread, and the species is on the decline. In Europe the Great Bustard (*Otis tarda*) has had a history not unlike that of the Indian Bustard. It cannot be classified as a rare or endangered species, for it still survives in good numbers in Russia, Turkey, Hungary, Czecho-Slovakia, Rumania, Central Asia and, less commonly, in Spain, Portugal, East Germany and Poland, but from the rest of western Europe it has been banished. A valued bird of the chase throughout the Middle Ages, its decline began, as in India, with the break-up of the feudal system, and by the end of the eighteenth century it was very rare. A writer in a paper called the *Wiltshire Independent* penned the bird's obituary and, in 1854, throws some light on the reasons for its demise;

There are people now living in Wiltshire who recollect the time when it was the custom of the Mayor of Salisbury to have a bustard as a prominent dish at the annual inauguration feast; and these birds, once numerous on the wild and then uncultivated expanse of Salisbury Plain, could at length only be shot by means of a vehicle so covered by bushes and placed in their haunts as to enable men therein concealed to bring them down at long range. For more than fifty years the Wiltshire Bustard has been extinct, and the Mayor of Salisbury has been obliged to forego his yearly delicacy.

Similar methods are still used in stalking both the Great and Indian Bustards in places where they survive. In spite of the undoubted effects of continual harassment by hunters, however, it is likely that the chief factor in the extinction of the Great Bustard in western Europe was the extension of cultivation. The ploughing up of all available land for food production during the Napoleonic Wars may well have dealt the *coup de grace*. Significantly, a near relation of the Bustards, the Stone-Curlew (*Burhinus oedicnemus*), a shy and secretive bird which favours similar open and desolate wastelands, has been almost exterminated in its former haunts in southern and eastern England as a result of a similar ploughing-up campaign which started with World War Two.

DUCKS AND GEESE In general Ducks and Geese are not today threatened with extinction by shooting. Though much indiscriminate killing does go on, most wildfowlers now belong to organisations which strictly regulate their activities. Realising that the future of their sport depends on the continued existence of adequate numbers of birds, they willingly accept the restrictions of close seasons and limited bags. Their organisations are indeed instrumental in maintaining duck- and geese-populations and are in many instances actively involved in conservation measures. They are, in fact, engaged in taking an annual cull, which is calculated according to what the population can stand.

The situation is less satisfactory in some countries, while in others the present attitude towards shooting for sport has come too late. An outstanding example of a species which succumbed to uncontrolled shooting is the Pink-headed Duck (*Rhodonessa caryophyllacea*), which once lived in the amphibious countryside of what is now Bangladesh, around the mouths of the Ganges and Brahmaputra. Apparently never very common, it was ruthlessly hunted by European sportsmen in the late nineteenth and early twentieth centuries, without regard to close seasons. Its unusual colour pattern—a bright pink head and neck on a brown body— enhanced its attractions for men with guns. The last bird died in captivity in 1944 and as none has been seen in the wild since 1936 the species is presumed extinct.

THE CRANES Though again not strictly game-birds, the Cranes, probably because of their size and therefore the tempting target they presented, have long been treated as such. Even the fish-flavoured Heron was throughout the Middle Ages a favourite bird of the chase, being hunted by hawks. The European Crane (*Grus grus*) has been driven out of western Europe in much the same manner as the Great Bustard, though here one of the chief factors was the drainage of large areas of its former fenland haunts. It is still fairly plentiful, however, in other parts of its range, which extends right across northern Europe and Asia.

The American Cranes have not been so lucky. As related on page 74, their plight has been partly due to the draining of the former wetlands which were their favoured haunts, but of equal importance in their decline has been persistent shooting. The species which has come nearest to extinction is the Whooping Crane (*Grus americana*), which in the mid-1950s had dwindled to a total of only 14 birds. Even in the nineteenth century, however, it was not common, an estimate of its population in the decade 1860–70 being 1,300 to 1,400 in the entire continent. In recent years the numbers have built up a little, and steps have been taken to establish a captive population which should ensure that the species does not become extinct.

The smaller Sandhill Crane (*Grus canadensis*) has a much less precarious status, though its numbers have been seriously diminished by drainage-schemes and shooting. The species is divided into several sub-species, of which the Greater Sandhill Crane (*Grus c. tabida*), the Rowan's Sandhill Crane (*Grus c. rowani*) and the Lesser Sandhill Crane (*Grus c. canadensis*) are in a reasonably healthy condition. The Florida Sandhill Crane (*Grus c. pratensis*) has, however, sunk to a rather low level, a recent estimate putting the population at 2,000 to 3,000 while that of the Cuban Sandhill Crane (*Grus c. nesiotes*) must be considerably lower, though there is little up-to-date information about it.

In Asia the Japanese or Manchurian Crane (*Grus japonensis*) has vanished from most of its ancient haunts but is still found in small numbers on both sides of the river Amur (where it forms the frontier between Manchuria and Siberia), on Lake Khanka and in one reserve on the island of Hokkaido, Japan. Protection and a winter-feeding programme at the Japanese site and in Korea have resulted in a satisfactory increase in numbers, though even now there are only a few hundred birds, but there is also a flourishing population of birds in captivity around the world, for they breed readily in zoos.

A smaller and less spectacular species, the HOODED CRANE (*Grus monacha*) of northern Asia, which nests in the Arctic, is now confined in winter to two valleys in Japan. One on the island of Honshu attracts about 100 birds each winter; the other, in the Iyumi valley on the island of Kyushu, has increased its winter population from 350 in 1958 to about 3,500 today through protection and judicious feeding.

The main wintering grounds of the WHITE-NAPED CRANE (*Grus vipio*) are in South Korea, the winter population being about 2,000. A smaller concentration is found in Japan, where food rations are supplied and where the numbers have increased from 45 birds in 1958 to about 700 at present.

The SIBERIAN CRANE (*Grus leucogeranus*) which nests in Arctic regions of eastern Siberia travels farther south in winter, one group wintering in the Yangtze River area of China, another in a sanctuary in India, in addition to which occasional vagrant individuals turn up with other cranes in Japan. The total population seems to be now more than about 350 birds.

STORKS AND IBISES The killing of Storks and Ibises is usually purely wanton, indulged in simply because they offer large targets. In recent years much indiscriminate shooting of Storks and other large birds on migration has occurred in certain countries of the Middle East, especially Lebanon, where guns are exceedingly numerous and control, in such matters as killing birds, minimal. Protests have been made by West Germany and other countries of north-west Europe, where Storks, which are welcomed and encouraged there, are declining in numbers. Both the White Stork (*Ciconia ciconia*) and the Black Stork (*Ciconia nigra*) are affected, though other factors than shooting are also involved, including, it has been suggested, a trend towards cooler and wetter summers in north-west Europe.

In the Far East the Oriental White Stork (*Ciconia boyciana*) has fared far worse. Once common in Japan, it now has only one known nesting-site there, occupied by only a few pairs. In mainland Asia it breeds in eastern Siberia and perhaps in neighbouring Manchuria but is probably everywhere scarce, though there is little recent news. The Japanese Crested Ibis (*Nipponia nippon*) is in an even worse plight, for it survives only in one small colony on Sado island, which lies off the north coast of Honshu, Japan's main island. Both in Japan and eastern China this handsome bird was once widespread and fairly common but persecution and the destruction of its woodland nesting sites have brought it dangerously near extinction. Its chief hopes of survival would seem to be the discovery of some hitherto unknown nesting-place, perhaps in eastern Siberia.

A species that showed an alarming decline around the middle of the present century is the BALD IBIS or WALDRUPP (*Geronticus eremita*), once widespread throughout much of Alpine Europe, north Africa and western Asia but now apparently confined to a few locations in Turkey and Morocco. Morocco has an estimated population of about 600 birds—less than half of the 1940 population— while the sole site in eastern Turkey harboured in 1977 only 34 birds (13 nesting pairs). Increased human population pressure is undoubtedly a major factor in this decline, but poisoning by pesticide is also contributory. The fall from 120 nesting pairs at Biraçik, the Turkish site, in 1962 to 13 in 1977 coincided with a rapidly increasing use of insecticide. Attempts to revive the veneration with which the Bald Ibis was regarded locally at Biraçik and to increase the area of its nesting-ledges have been only partially successful.

SMALL PASSERINES In general small passerine birds are considered to be beneath the interest of sportsmen in north-western Europe and America. According to the author's recollection, in the early years of the present century they were shot in England only on Boxing Day (26 December) and that probably in conformity with some half-forgotten folklore which decreed that on that day certain small birds, notably the Wren, were ritually hunted. In a number of Mediterranean countries, however, all birds are regarded as legitimate game, and in Italy in particular the shooting-season for small passerines is deliberately set at 18 August, so that the guns can take their toll of migrants from the north. Any birds unwise enough to make their southward journey via the Italian peninsula find themselves running the gauntlet of about 1,700,000 guns, in the hands of excitable humans who do not much care what they shoot. The toll taken of migrants there is estimated at about 200 million birds a year (or 400 million according to another estimate), and in the course of this annual spree the gunners scatter some 52,000 tons of lead shot about the countryside. The massacre attracts increasingly furious protests from naturalists in the northern countries, whose carefully-protected nesting-birds are thus ruthlessly slain, and recently they have been joined by a growing body of public opinion in Italy itself. Similar indiscriminate shooting of migrants and of any small birds occurs also in other Mediterranean countries, including south-western France, parts of Spain and Portugal, Malta and Cyprus, though not on such a colossal scale.

At one period in the recent history of China a campaign was launched to exterminate sparrows throughout the entire vast country. Before the authorities realised their mistake, demonstrated to them by a subsequent alarming increase in insect pests which small birds keep in check, it seems likely that large numbers of small passerines, in addition to sparrows, perished. Little information is, however, yet available.

Towards species of wild life which compete with him for food Man has little mercy. Even suburban householders who erect bird-tables and take a delight in attracting birds to their gardens tend to adopt a different attitude when those same birds begin to devastate their raspberries, currants and plums. It has been known for even dedicated naturalists to engage in unscientific tirades upon discovering that an early-morning heron has completely emptied a garden fishpond of valued fish. The war waged on competitors by primitive peoples whose dinner is being filched is therefore understandable.

Man's competitors —the fish-eaters

Pelicans are among the birds chiefly affected by the war carried on by fishermen against species which compete with them for fish. It is a war that has been going on for centuries, perhaps millennia, and one result has been that two species of Pelican, the White Pelican (*Pelecanus onocrotalus*) and the Dalmatian Pelican (*Pelecanus crispus*), at least one and perhaps both of which nested in the marshes of north-western Europe (including the British Isles) in prehistoric times, are now restricted to the south-eastern extremities of the continent. Their last strongholds are the Danube delta and Lake Mikra Prespa (in northern Greece), both of which are now nature reserves, but their total numbers are now only a few thousands, whereas a century ago the birds were numbered in hundreds of thousands. One factor in their decline was the systematic destruction of some of their nesting-colonies.

In the United States the Brown Pelican (*Pelecanus occidentalis*) experienced a dramatic and sudden decline through the action of pesticides in the late 1960s (*see* page 136). Before that, however, the eastern race of the species (*Pelecanus o. carolinensis*) was so incessantly persecuted by men with guns in the early 1900s that in order to preserve it from extinction one of the first American wildlife reserves was established at Pelican Island, Florida, where happily it remains plentiful.

During the nineteenth century many sea-birds, notably the Gannet, the Cormorant and the Shag, were severely persecuted in Britain because of the damage they were supposed to cause in stocks of sea-fish. In the end, little permanent harm was done to the species, and the Gannet in particular is now a rigidly protected and much appreciated bird, an asset to maritime ecology and an attractive feature of the coastal scenery. Both the Gannet and the Shag have experienced remarkable increases of population in the present century. In New Zealand, however, the New Zealand Rough-faced Shag (*Phalacrocorax carunculatus carunculatus*) has been brought to the edge of extinction, largely through action by fishermen. It had been persecuted both by European settlers and by the Maoris before them and is thought now to have a total population of no more than 500 individuals.

The harassment of the Osprey (*Pandion haliaetus*) has been by anglers, or rather by the keepers who preserve their waters, rather than by commercial fishermen. A cosmopolitan species, the noble Osprey has a distribution that is almost world-wide, and as in many countries it is still quite common it is in no danger of extinction. On the other hand, from certain countries it has been exterminated. Incessant persecution banished it from Britain for more than 50 years. Once a common summer resident in much of Scotland, and in earlier ages in most of England as well, it was last recorded as nesting in 1904 until, unexpectedly, it returned in the mid-1950s. It seems likely that the pair which then decided to nest near Loch Garten, in central Scotland, were migrants on their way to Scandinavia, but the protection now given them in Scotland has been so effective that a pair has continued to occupy the same site annually ever since. Other pairs, probably the progeny of the Loch Garten pair, have now established themselves and there are probably at least 20 pairs nesting in Scotland. The continued protection is now needed against egg-collectors rather than fishing interests, which take a much more enlightened view than in the past of the activities of this undoubted competitor. The birds are still highly vulnerable on migration, on their annual journey to winter quarters south of the Sahara, and a heavy toll is probably taken, especially by Mediterranean gunners.

In America Ospreys are a much more familiar sight, for the birds nest in urban and suburban areas, even atop cartwheels erected on poles for them by hospitable householders. Here, however, and in a number of other countries, they have been falling victim to a more insidious menace, pesticides.

Birds that tend to become the inadvertent victims of the coastal fishing industry in northern waters are the Auks, Puffins and Guillemots. The number of Brunnich's Guillemot (*Uria lomvia*) caught annually in salmon-fishing nets off western Greenland is estimated at more than 500,000.

The eaters of grain and fruit Ever since Man began to cultivate crops he has had to contend with marauding birds, taking their toll of fruit and grain as they ripen. At certain times and in certain places their depredations can be overwhelming, as, for instance in the Sahel countries, south of the Sahara, where, after a favourable season followed by drought, the Red-billed Quelea (*Quelea quelea*) assembles in flocks numbering many millions and migrates to wherever food is to be found. A visitation of Queleas can be as devastating as that of a swarm of locusts. Agriculturists combat the armies with whatever weapons they have, including flame-throwers and poisons, usually without making much obvious impression on their numbers. The news that the Quelea was extinct would no doubt be a matter for great rejoicing by the peasants of the afflicted countries, though they are never likely to hear it. Indeed, of all the bird-species that harass or have harassed men's crops very few have been extinguished by human counter-attacks. The two most notable exceptions are the Carolina Parakeet and the Passenger Pigeon. Both, as has been discussed on pages 38-9, succumbed to a persistent campaign of extermination waged, in the case of the Passenger Pigeon, for several reasons other than the damage done by the birds. Nevertheless, it is doubtful whether the prairies could ever have been cultivated and cropped efficiently while the Passenger Pigeons were present in their original strength. Pigeons of many species and in many lands tend to take a heavy tribute of the farmer's crops, and some kind of adaptation resulting in a diminished and more dispersed population was evidently required of the Passenger Pigeon. It seems to have been incapable of making such an adaptation, or perhaps it was not given enough time.

The demise of the Carolina Parakeet was due more directly to its depredations in the orchards of the south-eastern states of America. One could say that the bird asked for trouble—unwittingly, of course. Not content with taking a toll of ripe fruit, it would invade orchards and fruit plantations in busy flocks, snipping off every fruit before it had even ripened. Naturally, such behaviour was not tolerated, though today the counter-measures would have not been allowed to push to the extreme of extermination.

EAGLES, HAWKS AND FALCONS For several centuries any bird with a hooked beak and sharp talons has been regarded as an enemy by western Man, to be shot at sight or otherwise destroyed. The history of most birds of prey in western Europe and America over the past 200 years is in general a melancholy catalogue of destruction. In Britain nearly every bird of prey has become rare, other than those which have been virtually exterminated, while in North America concern is now being felt even for the Bald Eagle (*Haliaetus leucocephalus*), the national emblem, now reasonably common only in Alaska and western Canada.

The Carnivores

It was not always so. Hawks were once accepted as an appreciated and valued feature of the scene. In the Middle Ages falconry was, of course, a sport of kings and nobles, and the nesting-eyries of all hawks and falcons were thus rigidly protected. The protection was extended to the more plebeian species, notably the Kites (generally supposed in Britain to have been the Red Kite (*Milvus milvus*), but possibly the Black Kite (*Milvus migrans*)), on account of their usefulness as scavengers. A member of the entourage of a Bohemian dignitary who visited London in 1465 recorded that nowhere had he seen as many Kites as on London Bridge and that in London it was a capital offence to kill one. The secretary to the Venetian ambassador to England in 1496 writes of 'the kites, which are so tame, that they often take out of the hands of little children the bread smeared with butter...'

The change in attitude came with the division of the British countryside among great landed estates and with the invention of the breech-loading gun. Throughout the late eighteenth and the entire nineteenth century the birds of prey of Britain, and indeed of most of the world, had a dreadful time. Not only were they shot at sight but all possible devices, including the disgraceful pole-trap, were used to destroy them. Their chief offence was that they preyed on the chicks of the latest objects of sport, the pheasants and partridges. In an age when the natural instinct of a gentleman was to shoot anything that looked interesting or unusual, predatory birds came in for special attention from both gamekeepers and their employers. To them, when guns became freely available, were added farmers, who had similar misgivings about the intentions of hawks towards their domestic poultry. So the birds of prey vanished from the British scene.

A Colonel Birch Reynardson, writing towards the middle of the nineteenth century, states:

About the year 1824, and from before that time to 1828 or 1829, there used to be in that part of the country (around Alconbury Hill, in eastern England) an incredible number of Kites. ... In almost every direction, when travelling by the Stamford Regent Coach, one used actually to see them sitting in the middle of the road, and on one occasion I remember counting as many as twenty-seven in the air at the same time...

By the middle of the century the species was extinct over the greater part of England. It seems to have remained fairly plentiful in the Scottish Highlands until about 1870 but was wiped out within the next 30 years. The Red Kite now survives (in the British Isles) only in central Wales, where not more than about 20 pairs maintain a precarious existence. Though now effectively protected, the chief danger threatening them at present seems to be pesticides, though ceaseless vigilance has to be exercised against egg-collectors.

Similar melancholy histories can be related for nearly all British birds of prey. The Golden Eagle (*Aquila chrysaëtos*) is now a rare nesting species only in the Highlands of Scotland, although it sometimes wanders to other regions out of the

St Kilda Wren
Matthew Hillier

128

nesting season. It is unpopular with sheep-farmers because of the toll it sometimes takes of their lambs. The White-tailed or Sea-Eagle (*Haliaëtus albicilla*) has been completely banished from the British Isles, having been last recorded as a nesting species around the year 1908. Pairs were nesting as far south as the Isle of Wight as late as 1780 and in Cumbria until the 1830s. In that decade a bounty of three shillings was being offered for any Eagle killed, and the reward was often earned by setting out poisoned meat for the birds, this species being fond of carrion. The Marsh Harrier (*Circus aeruginosus*), now confined in Britain to the Broadland district of eastern Norfolk, was once widespread, nesting wherever undrained marshes offered a suitable habitat. Though nesting even in the London area early in the nineteenth century, by the end of the century it was virtually extinct. It was able to stage a return in the 1920s since when, strictly protected, it has managed to hold its own, though latterly suffering from pesticide poisoning.

The New Forest, in southern England, is one of the few remaining refuges of the Montagu's Harrier (*Circus pygargus*), of which perhaps not more than 20 pairs now nest annually in Britain. This is a migratory species, penetrating far south in Africa in winter, so undoubtedly a heavy toll will be taken on its long journeys. It was, however, formerly found over a much wider area and was much persecuted by gamekeepers. To most of Britain the Hen Harrier (*Circus cyaneus*) has been, for the greater part of the present century, only a winter visitor, its last breeding haunts up to the period of the second world war being the Orkneys and the Outer Hebrides. Writers in the 1920s were referring to the species as probably extinct, though until about the middle of the nineteenth century it nested quite commonly in southern England. Since the 1940s, however, the Hen Harrier has staged a comeback, and probably between 100 and 200 pairs now nest in Scotland, northern England, north Wales and central Ireland.

In Britain the Hobby (*Falco subbuteo*), a migratory species, is at the northwestern limits of its range and so may never have been very plentiful. Its present population is believed to be between 75 and 100 pairs, nesting in the southern counties of Hampshire, Dorset, Wiltshire and Sussex. In times past it has suffered from indiscriminate shooting but is now generally protected.

The Honey-Buzzard (*Pernis apivorus*) has geographic limits similar to those of the Hobby and so was never widespread or common in the British Isles. As a nesting species it was confined to the southernmost counties, especially Sussex and Hampshire. Its rarity, and the fact that its food consists of wasps, grasshoppers and other insects and small reptiles, did not save it from the attention of gamekeepers and latterly of egg-collectors. Probably just a few pairs nest in some of their old haunts each year, but the localities are a well-kept secret. As a migratory species, the Honey-Buzzard also suffers considerably from shooting on its bi-annual journeys. The Nature Conservancy Council's booklet, *Bird Conservation in Europe* 1977, states, 'In the Siena region of Italy examination of taxidermists' records suggest that 5,000 diurnal raptors are killed annually'; some Honey-Buzzards will certainly be among them. In one year in the 1960s no fewer than 700 migrating Honey-Buzzards were shot in a single parish in France.

The Peregrine Falcon (*Falco peregrinus*) has suffered from a greater variety of hazards than most raptors. In addition to being shot indiscriminately, like all other birds of prey, and to having its nests robbed by collectors, it was officially hounded almost to extinction during the second world war in order to save military carrier-

129

pigeons from its talons. It was just recovering from that setback when the pesticide problem arose, and this splendid falcon seemed more vulnerable than most. Now it is being further harassed by nest robbers seeking the chicks, which command very high prices from falconers in mid-eastern countries. A census in the mid-1960s indicated that only 68 breeding pairs remained in the British Isles.

A bird of prey entirely lost to Britain, at least for a time, is the Goshawk (*Accipiter gentilis*). A favourite of falconers in medieval times, it was one of the victims of the shooting mania which accompanied the introduction of the breech-loading gun. After having been exterminated in England, it bred quite commonly in Scotland until the decade 1830–40, while odd pairs were reported here and there until the end of the century. Since then there have been an increasing number of nesting records, and the latest information suggests that between 20 and 25 pairs now nest fairly regularly. It is likely that some, perhaps most, of these are birds which have escaped from falconers. The near relation of the Goshawk, the Sparrow-hawk (*Accipiter nisus*) at one time seemed likely to follow it into oblivion. There being no argument about the Sparrowhawk occasionally taking game-bird chicks, the bird was persecuted mercilessly and to deadly effect. Since, however, it was given legal protection in 1966 there has been some recovery.

Montagu's Harrier, now a scarce breeding species in Britain. *Photo. G. H. E. Young*

All hawks in Britain are now on the protected list and in theory should be entirely safe. Persecution still goes on, however, though clandestinely and on a reduced scale. A law is effective only if it can be enforced, and monitoring what happens in private estates is almost impossible. Undoubtedly many hawks, falcons and eagles are still shot by gamekeepers, and it is likely that the outlawed gin-traps are still being used. The danger comes through delegation of responsibility. Often today the landowner does not himself shoot the pheasants reared on his estate but lets the shooting to wealthy clients of many nationalities. The price per day for a gun on some of the best shoots may strike a layman as exorbitant. The client, having paid a large sum for his day's sport, expects to have plenty of birds to shoot at, and the livelihood of the gamekeeper depends on his ensuring that a good stock of pheasants is reared and preserved. Knowing that he will be judged by results, the keeper is under temptation to eradicate anything which may be detrimental to them. Unless he has specific instructions to the contrary, any hooked-beak birds which venture on to his beat are likely to be at risk.

Throughout Europe birds of prey have been and still are victims of similar attitudes. The situation varies from country to country, and protection-laws differ widely. In general they tend to be most effective in northern Europe and least efficient in Mediterranean countries, but there are ample exceptions. In Belgium, for instance, in the 1950s rewards were offered by pigeon-fanciers for killing any birds of prey, which were alleged to be interfering with their sport. The measure was so successful that in 1954 no fewer than 20,000 hawks and other raptors were massacred. Later the annual kill fell off, simply because there were by then so few birds left to slaughter. Even in Norway the bounty offered for killing White-tailed Eagles was withdrawn only a few years ago. In the late 1960s an estimate made by the Société Nationale de Protection de la Nature stated that within the previous 30 years the population of the Golden Eagle in France had fallen by 75 per cent, of the Peregrine Falcon by 80 per cent, and of the Buzzard by 50 per cent. Possibly 15 out of the 36 diurnal species of birds of prey are in danger of extinction in western Europe.

130

Spanish Imperial Eagle—one
of the very rare birds—at its eyrie.
Photo. Eric Hosking

Great Crested Grebe, once rendered rare
through excessive demands for 'grebe
fur'—its downy breeding plumage—but
now happily recovering its former status.
Photo. Eric Hosking

That these birds do not at once appear on the list of endangered species is due to the fact that most of them have a wide distribution in the less populous regions of eastern Europe and Asia. Some of them also occur in America, where too they have experienced some persecution. The Peregrine Falcon, however, was fairly common until the 1950s, even nesting in urban New York. That it is now rare in the eastern states and attracting a complex conservation campaign is due not to shooting but pesticide-poisoning.

Of the birds of prey on the official endangered list the Everglade Kite (*see* page 74) has been brought to the edge of extinction chiefly by the destruction of its habitat. The Galápagos Hawk (*Buteo galapagoensis*), the Hawaiian Hawk (*Buteo solitarius*), the Mauritius Kestrel (*Falco punctatus*), the Seychelles Kestrel (*Falco araea*) and the Spanish Imperial Eagle (*Aquila heliaca adalberti*) have all been brought to a low ebb by direct persecution: sportsmen and poultry-farmers are the main offenders. In Hawaii the persecution has more or less ceased, so the Hawaiian Hawk may now be safe from extermination, though only between 100 and 200 birds are estimated to remain. The Spanish Imperial Eagle is protected in the well-wardened nature reserve, Coto Doñana, though not elsewhere. Its population may be down to 100 birds or less, of which Coto Doñana has seven pairs.

Poultry-farmers have been the chief cause of the downfall of the Galápagos Hawk, which now seems to be confined to a few of the outlying islets—its 1962 population was estimated to be 200 birds or less. The Mauritius Kestrel, an attractive little bird, has undoubtedly suffered because of its local name, *mangeur de poules*, or chicken-eater, a reputation which it does not deserve; only a handful of birds survive. Boys with catapults are said to have played a large part in the decline of the Seychelles Kestrel, a bird too tame for its own good. It has also met with severe competition for nesting- and roosting-sites.

THE VULTURES It would seem logical to expect that Vultures, being large inedible birds which normally do not kill their prey but live on carrion, would be immune from human persecution, but that is not so. Of the four European species of Vulture—the Griffon Vulture (*Gyps fulvus*), the Egyptian Vulture (*Neophron percnopterus*), the Black Vulture (*Aegypius monachus*) and the Lammergeier (*Gypaëtus barbatus*)—are all in somewhat precarious states, largely through shooting. The Egyptian and Griffon Vultures, though more strongly placed than the other two, have suffered also from other causes, notably through eating poisoned baits set out for wolves and other animals regarded as vermin. The Black Vulture has become rare in its last Spanish habitats, though it is still to be found in Greece and Turkey. The Lammergeier, or Bearded Vulture, is a huge bird still common in the Himalayas but now rare in the mountain areas westward, though it occurs as far west as Spain. At one time it was almost extinct in Europe, but in recent years it has re-established itself in the Alps and seems to be on the increase.

It has, however, an African race, *Gypaëtus barbatus meridionalis*, which is considered to be on the danger list. Although its distribution extends over almost the whole continent, its chief stronghold is apparently Ethiopia, from which there are few recent reports. What is known is that in many places the birds are being killed by poisoned carrion put out for jackals. So widespread has that practice become that the Vultures, deprived of their usual food, have taken to killing domestic animals, mainly sheep, which has naturally led to increased persecution by the irate sheep farmers.

In America the magnificent Californian Condor (*Gymnogyps californianus*) has been reduced to a total population of about 50. Its former range extended from the Mexican province of Baja California to northern Oregon and it was apparently quite plentiful in the seventeenth and eighteenth centuries. Now, although legally protected—with a penalty of a fine of $1,000 and/or a year in jail—Condors are still occasionally shot by sportsmen and ranchers, and poison-bait put out for predatory animals is sometimes taken by the great birds; the eggs are also sought after by collectors. At best, the continued existence of the Californian Condor must be reckoned precarious.

The allied but distinct species, the Andean Condor (*Vultur gryphus*), is as yet in no danger, having an enormous range stretching from the Colombian Andes south to the extremity of Tierra del Fuego. It is, however, subject to persecution in many parts of its territory and is, of course, thinly distributed. The *National Geographic Magazine* for May 1971 gives an interesting sidelight on the hazards attending the species. The millions of cormorants which nest on the Guano Islands off the coast of Peru were said to be endangered by Condors raiding the nests for eggs and chicks, so a warden was appointed to drive them away. After a time, the Condors ceased to visit the islands, so the guardian took to visiting the mainland and shooting the birds there, so that he would have something to show his employer in due course and thus be able to keep his job. He claimed to kill at least 50 birds a year, and the reporter saw him fire at and hit nine in one day.

THE OWLS Possessing hooked beaks and sharp talons, the Owls were doomed to the same fate as the Hawks at the hands of gamekeepers and poultry-farmers, though being nocturnal they tended to suffer more from trapping than from shooting. In Britain the two most widespread species, the Barn Owl (*Tyto alba*) and the Tawny Owl (*Strix aluco*), experienced the most persistent persecution. Their carcases were common items on keepers' gibbets, and thousands of Victorian households exhibited a stuffed owl in their parlours. Both species became scarce, and the prejudice against them was a long time dying. Now the Tawny Owl is fairly plentiful again, even nesting in many London suburbs. The Barn Owl, though in no danger of extinction, has been slower to recover, partly because it has lost so many of its former nesting-sites, such as ancient hollow trees and old barns, and partly through pesticide-poisoning. The Little Owl (*Athena noctua*) was introduced into Britain by several landowners in the last quarter of the nineteenth century and, after a few preliminary setbacks, became thoroughly established. Surveying its career over the previous 60 years, Brian Vesey-FitzGerald stated in 1946 that it had steadily increased in numbers and was, if anything, increasing too rapidly. Since then it has experienced a decline and in many districts has even become scarce. The cause is unknown, but pesticides may be partly responsible.

One of the great European birds of prey, the Eagle Owl (*Bubo bubo*), has been exterminated in a number of northern countries and is very rare in many more, though earlier it was quite common. Shooting has been chiefly responsible for the decline. Recently the species has been re-established in southern Sweden, where the last pair had bred in 1937 and the last bird seen in 1950. After an intensive campaign in public relations, several birds were bred and released. They have since been joined by others bred in captivity in England, and all seems to be going well. A similar experiment is now being tried in West Germany.

An owl on the verge of extinction, if it is not already extinct, is the New Zealand Laughing Owl (*Sceloglaux albifacies*), but here the blame lies probably not with direct persecution but with interference to nests and young of this ground-nesting species by introduced predators such as rats, cats and pigs.

Accidental hazards The technical achievements of modern Man have subjected birds to new hazards. Lighthouses were probably the earliest of these new causes of casualties. During big migrations large numbers of disorientated birds dashed against the lights on foggy nights, and indeed much of our early knowledge of bird-migration was based on observations at lighthouses. After a time perches and other safety devices were fitted around the lights, and the toll has now been greatly reduced. A more recent but similar hazard has been created by tall television-masts, which have shown themselves capable of causing heavy mortality among migrants under certain conditions. Power-lines are also a danger, while migrating birds have sometimes been known to collide with high buildings.

Motorways take a heavy toll of birds. A survey made in Britain in 1961 put an estimated annual total of 2,500,000 road-casualties in that country alone, and that was before the construction of the first motorway; the kill is probably much higher now. One reason for the heavy mortality-rate is that on the smooth surface of modern roads—especially those bordered by hedges or trees—their sharp eyes can easily detect there the insects and seeds that have fallen off trees or been blown from the fields. Certain species are more liable than others to road accidents, and the cull is greatest in late spring and early summer, when inexperienced fledglings are learning to fly. Some birds, notably Kestrels, are attracted by the mice and voles which proliferate in the coarse grasses of broad motorway-verges.

From time to time birds collide with aeroplanes or are sucked into jet engines, with results disastrous to both birds and men. No great numbers are involved in the birds, but the hazards to life and machines have impelled men to study the matter intensively. Measures are now taken to ensure that the flight-paths of planes and large flocks of migrating birds do not coincide, and various devices are employed to scare birds off airfields, which they find embarrassingly attractive. One of the most effective measures, used by the air forces and navies of a number of nations, is to patrol the airfields with trained Peregrine Falcons. From being a military hazard in World War Two the Peregrine has thus become a military asset.

In discussing birds of prey mention has already been made of poison-baits. These are usually laid for predatory mammals such as jackals, wolves and foxes, but are often picked up by birds. Where the species concerned is not common, as with most birds of prey, the mortality thus caused can be serious.

Pesticides Attitudes towards birds vary according to one's involvement with them. City-dwellers can afford to be more objective towards, for instance, fruit-eating birds than can farmers whose orchards are being devastated. A missionary in Africa noticed that his class of children would stumble over a prayer in which occurred the line, 'Thank you for the birds that sing'. After some thought he realised that much of their young lives was spent in scaring 'the birds that sing' from the family's ripening crops and that among the few birds whose place in the order of things they could really appreciate were the vultures.

No harvest anywhere is gathered without the expenditure of much thought, preparation and hard work. Upon the reaping of good harvests the wellbeing and very existence of millions of people depend. Anything that can be done, therefore, to diminish the toll taken of the harvest by insect pests (which can in extreme circumstances be as high as 100 per cent) is worth considering. The African peasant sends his children to drive the small birds off his fields, but his more sophisticated counterpart in the western world has a much more powerful armoury of new weapons. They are mainly chemical and they are proliferating at an alarming rate. Since the potentialities of DDT as an insecticide were realised in 1939 more than 1,000 new synthetic chemicals have been evolved for the purpose, and many more are added to the list each year.

With the human species engaging in mass reproduction, nothing but the mass-production of food can keep the burgeoning population from starvation. Hence the trend in agriculture is increasingly towards monoculture, which is now the norm in many countries. Instead of small peasant-plots devoted to a variety of crops, modern food-production deals in vast acreages growing one crop only. Such a colossal concentration of one species of plant naturally leads to the proliferation of the insects and other pests which prey upon it. These infestations build up to such an extent that Man resorts to large-scale spraying of chemicals as apparently the only effective or logical answer. The trouble is that many of the most widely-used pesticides are persistent. They do not exhaust themselves when they have done the work for which they were applied. From the bodies of dead insects they pass into the bodies of any creature which eats them, and there they remain—they are not excreted but are stored in the body-fat. Or, if they do not become lodged in the body of some creature, they seep into the soil and are washed eventually into water-courses and so back to the sea. From there they circulate throughout the oceans of the world until now it seems that no part is free from them. DDT has been found in the bodies of penguins and seals in the Antarctic.

The use of DDT, the related chemical DDD, and the deadly organo-chlorines (the chief of which are dieldrin, aldrin and heptachlor) has now been banned in a number of western countries, but they are still widely employed elsewhere. In high concentrations DDT and its associated chemicals are held to be responsible for mental and nervous disorders, infertility and, to some extent, cancer. Nor are pesticides the only offenders. Other chemicals in common use can have equally deleterious effects. The polychlorinated biphenyls (PCB), which are used in paints and plastics and are evidently a factor in inducing infertility, are similarly persistent and are found now in most organisms, from humans to fish and insects.

Clear Lake, which occupies 650 square miles of California, provides a much-quoted example of the effects of chemical-control of insect pests. It is a recreational lake much frequented by fishermen who were, prior to 1949, irritated by an immense population of biting gnats, of a species known as *Chaoborus astictopus*. After several pilot-schemes the lake was treated with DDD (chosen because it is less toxic to fish than the similar DDT) in 1949, with almost complete success as far as the extermination of the gnat was concerned. By 1954, however, a new gnat-population had built up, and so the treatment was repeated. This time it was

Western Grebe turning its eggs. This species has suffered severely from pollution by pesticides. *Photo. Eric Hosking*

followed by the deaths, on a large scale, of the Western Grebes (*Aechmophorus occidentalis*) which abounded on the lake. A further application of DDD in 1957 was marked by another crop of casualties among the grebes, some of which, when examined, proved to have as many as 1,600 parts per million of DDD in their fat. Later the grebe-population recovered to some extent, though the percentage of young hatched and reared remained low.

In 1968 the Californian Brown Pelican (*Pelecanus occidentalis*) experienced a disastrous breeding-season in its chief colonies along the Californian coast. On Anacapa Island only four young birds survived from 1,000 recorded nests. In 1970 the island produced only one chick. The trouble was that ingestion of DDT had resulted in the egg-shells being so thin that they broke under the weight of the birds. DDT was banned in the United States in 1972, and by the following year the results were already being felt, for 305 chicks were hatched on Anacapa Island. The recovery has since been maintained. A similar disaster struck the Eastern Brown Pelican in Florida and other south-eastern states. A large breeding population in Louisiana was wiped out but has since been re-established by the transference of young birds from Florida.

Pesticide poisoning is most severe in birds of prey, because so many of the small vertebrates which have become contaminated form a large proportion of their diet. The toxins hence have every opportunity to build up in their bodies, resulting in ultra-thin egg shells and also in reduced fertility, fewer eggs being laid. The Peregrine Falcon (*Falco peregrinus*) was affected to such an extent that, although it has an almost worldwide distribution, its imminent extinction was feared. The problem of nesting-failures and the resultant fall in population of the Peregrine were first noted in 1947, when the expected natural recovery from wartime persecution failed to happen. It was not until the early 1960s that the connection between these phenomena and DDT was finally established. Since the use of DDT has been prohibited in the U.S.A., Canada, Britain and a number of other countries, the Peregrine population has stabilised and is showing a slight tendency to increase.

The Osprey is another species which has been seriously and adversely affected by pesticide poisoning, especially in the United States, where experiments have demonstrated conclusively that the fault lies in the eggs, some of which have been found to contain 5.1 parts per million of DDT. In a Connecticut colony of Ospreys, where the mortality rate was especially bad, samples of fish taken from the nests showed that the pesticide-content was five to ten times as high as at a Maryland site, where the nesting success-rate was much better. Even the rare Cahow (*Pterodroma cahow*) has been seriously affected by pesticide-pollution on its oceanic stronghold, Bermuda. Its rate of breeding-success dwindled from 40 per cent to 25 per cent between 1961 and 1966, in spite of imaginative efforts to improve its environment. In 1967 a study of dead chicks and eggs showed an average DDT content of 6.44 parts per million. It could only have been picked up from the sea.

Pollution   Pesticides are, of course, only one of a vast range of man-made substances which pollute the environment. They include oil in various forms, radio-active wastes, chemical effluents, detergents, warfare-gases and heavy metals such as lead which escapes into the oceans in huge quantities in the form of the tetra-ethyl lead used in motor-fuels. Oil-spills from wrecked oil-tankers provide the most spectacular evidence of pollution. The problems created by the wreck of the *Torrey Canyon* off south-west England, including the heavy mortality among sea-birds (estimated at between 50,000 and 250,000), attracted widespread attention and concern, but since then an increasing number of spillages and minor disasters in less publicised quarters of the world have passed with little notice. It is clear that the total number of casualties annually must be very large.

Mercury-poisoning is rife in many lakes in forested regions, mercury compounds being commonly used as fungicides in the processing of wood-pulp. Contamination has reached such a peak that the eating of fish from many lakes in Canada, Sweden, Finland and other northern countries is prohibited, and even the water is unfit to drink. Attention was drawn to the problem in the 1960s by the mortality in such bird-species as the Osprey and the Great Crested Grebe, numbers of which died through eating poisoned fish. Mercurial contamination is, unfortunately, highly persistent; once a lake is polluted it may take many years to purify it.

Little is at present known about the effects on wild life of some of the other metallic residues which contaminate the seas and rivers and the bodies of the creatures which live in them. A mysterious catastrophe which killed possibly 50,000 sea-birds in the Irish Sea in the autumn of 1969 may have been due to poisoning from such a source, for most of the birds were not oiled but had residues of a number of metals—including cadmium, copper, lead, zinc and nickel—in their bodies. One of the problems is that the pollutants which pour into the seas are so varied that we are not dealing with a simple and easily identified substance. Chemicals which may in themselves be harmless can assume a very different character when mixed with other chemicals, producing a deadly brew which is undoubtedly forming in many waters.

Eutrophication, a word meaning enrichment, is a modern phenomenon affecting many shallow lakes and some coastal waters. It arises from an excess of nitrates and phosphates, the residues of chemical fertilisers leached from agricultural land. Effluent from mass-production units of pigs, poultry and cattle and also some detergents contribute to the problem.

Eutrophication

The first result of these substances seeping into shallow waters is greatly to enrich them and to cause aquatic life to proliferate. Wildfowl congregate on such waters to feed on the abundant life. As the nutrient-content of the water rises higher, however, algae and similar organisms increase to such an extent that they use up all the available oxygen. In time the lake, lagoon or bay becomes dead. Masses of decaying algae fall to the bottom and there form deep layers of mud, or else drift about on the surface and pile up on the shores, rotten and stinking: some species produce toxic substances that further pollute the waters. An early and classic example of eutrophication is that of Lake Erie. A survey in 1968 estimated that each year the lake was receiving 37,500 tons of nitrates from farms and 45,000 tons of municipal sewage. The fish-population has declined to the extent that only about 7,000 lb of fish were being caught annually, as against between 20,000,000 and 49,000,000 in the 1920s. On the bottom of the lake is now a mud-layer as much as 125 ft deep in places.

A similar sequence of events is appearing in most European and many American lakes. Some lakes in Sweden and Switzerland, for instance, are so contaminated

Long-tailed Tit, though apparently fragile, manages to maintain its status in Britain. *Photo. G. H. E. Young*

that fish have virtually disappeared and bathing is unsafe. Although in the face of these alarming developments their effect on birds is of minor importance, there can be no doubt that many species of birds *are* affected adversely.

Assets and Liabilities

Superficially the power of flight gives birds such an advantage that it is surprising any species possessing it should ever become extinct. It is significant that a high proportion of those species which have been extinguished were flightless. The Dodo, Solitaire, Moas, Great Auk, Aphanapteryx and a number of the extinct Rails of the Pacific islands are examples of birds which lost the power of flight. Their extinction was directly attributable to that loss. All had evolved in environments which were free from ground predators. Their wings became atrophied and useless because the birds had no need to use them. But when their island homes were invaded by alien predators they soon succumbed: they had no means of escape.

The power of flight

Flight, in one sense, is a synonym for escape. It enables birds to escape not only from predators but from inclement weather. Just how the practice of migration arose is still a matter for speculation, but for millions of birds in the northern hemisphere its practical purpose is to enable them to escape from the northern winters. In summer even the Arctic tundra is alive with insects and provides abundant food for nesting birds, but it is no place for any but the hardiest species in winter. On the other hand, the very ability of so many bird species to undertake long flights imposes its own hazards. The mortality-rate among migrating birds is tremendous. Birds which possess the power of flight are naturally creatures of the air. They live in the air, as a fish lives in water. An extreme example is the Swift (*Apus apus*) which is thought never to alight from the time it leaves the nest till the time, three years later, when it needs to build a nest for its own progeny. For those three years it lives, eats, sleeps and even mates on the wing. Location to such a bird means little; today it may be swooping over London, tomorrow over France.

Swifts and Swallows tend to fly at not higher than 5,000 to 6,000 ft on migration, that being about the altitude-limit at which they can find sufficient insects for food. For many of the smaller migrants, 2,500 ft seems to be about the limit. Larger birds, such as geese and storks, and long-distance migrants such as waders, often fly at altitudes of 10,000 to 15,000 ft or even higher. While some birds apparently prefer to travel over land, taking advantage of land-bridges such as peninsulas and islands, others pay little regard to such amenities. Birds engaged on long journeys over seas inevitably face considerable hazards from storms. The number of American birds which occur in Europe in autumn is an indication of the frequent disruption of flights by adverse weather. Autumnal gales, sweeping eastwards across the northern hemisphere, carry parties of migrants hundreds or thousands of miles off course, and large numbers of these birds must perish at sea.

Those species which use the land-bridges and travel at lower altitudes, of course, face the hazards of predatory humans. As has already been noted, estimates of the numbers of birds shot or netted on migration each year in Europe are around 200 million, mostly in Italy and other Mediterranean countries. The toll may be as much as 25 per cent of all bird migrants in the region. This risk, however, is one which could be and perhaps will be eliminated in due course.

Size

Size tends in general to be a liability in birds. The Dodo, Solitaire, Moas and Great Auk, all large birds, may again be cited as examples of species which have foundered. The extinct Diatryma and Teratornis of America, the Elephant Birds of Madagascar, the Osteodontornis and the Hesperornis were all giant birds. And several of the species now on the danger-list, including the Short-toed Albatross, Trumpeter Swan, Whooping Crane, Giant Ibis, Californian Condor, African Lammergeier, Indian Bustard and Oriental White Stork are decidedly large. Size seems to be a feature developed under stable conditions and relative absence of stress occasioned by enemies. Associated with it are certain characteristics which can prove lethal. For example, the bigger the bird the more food it needs: each large bird or pair of birds therefore requires a large territory for foraging. Where the available territory is limited, the total population is thus necessarily small, as happens on islands.

When the Dodos and Solitaires dispensed with their wings, which they did not need on the predator-free Mascarene Islands, they devoted food and energy from the maintenance of the power of flight to mere size and weight, and this proved their undoing when predators were suddenly introduced. Their large size made them more attractive and more vulnerable to their new enemies and so—their numbers naturally limited by the size of their island habitat—they were soon exterminated.

Reproductive-rates

In order that their population shall not outstrip the available food supply some birds, particularly large carnivorous species, develop low reproductive rates. Some lay only one or two eggs per clutch; some breed only every other year; some take a longish period of years to arrive at maturity and start breeding.

The Californian Condor, for instance, does not start breeding until it is six years old and then lays only one egg every two years. The nesting period—i.e. from the laying of the egg to the time when the fledgling leaves the nest—is no less than five months. The Whooping Crane usually lays two eggs but hardly ever rears more than one chick. The very rare Short-tailed Albatross, like other Albatrosses, does not start breeding until it is eight or nine years old and then lays only a single egg each year. The incubation and fledging period is prolonged. The Monkey-eating Eagle of the Philippines, now on the verge of extinction, arrives late at maturity and lays only one egg a year. The White-tailed Eagle is not ready for breeding until it is five or six years old and then lays only one or two eggs.

A number of birds of prey allow several days between the laying of their eggs, which results in the chicks hatching at intervals. As the young grow, the older ones become aggressive towards the weaker, younger ones, depriving them of food until they die of starvation. The potential reproductive-rate is thus drastically reduced.

Such birds with low reproductive-rates tend to be greatly at risk in periods of rapid environmental changes, as at present. A population can be regarded as safe and stable only when its rate of increase is equal to or greater than its mortality-rate. Thus, birds which delay breeding until they are several years old and then rear only one or two young a year may take too long to compensate for the inevitable casualties.

At the other extreme are birds which arrive quickly at maturity and lay a large number of eggs per clutch or else attempt to raise several families each year. These species are geared to a high mortality-rate, without which, of course, they would soon experience over-population. Many of them are small birds, the natural victims of predators. Thus in Europe the Wren (*Troglodytes troglodytes*) usually lays from five to seven eggs per clutch but sometimes as many as 12 or 14, and it normally rears two broods a year. The House-Martin (*Delichon urbica*), which experiences the hazards of two long migratory journeys a year, lays four or five eggs per clutch but commonly has two broods annually and often three. The Long-tailed Tit (*Aegithalos caudatus*), which seems to be highly vulnerable to severe winter weather, lays clutches of eight to 12 eggs.

One of the most successful species of small birds, the Red-billed Dioch or Quelea (*Quelea quelea*) has a highly adaptable reproductive cycle. In dry years it often does not breed at all but when food is plentiful it nests in huge colonies, covering several square miles with several hundreds of nests in each tree. It has been calculated that from 80 to 90 per cent of the eggs laid produce satisfactorily reared fledglings, and the population builds up rapidly, reaching at its peak an estimated 100,000 million birds in the central African countries which are its home. A species with such reproductive powers would seem to be safe from any disaster and, as noted on p. 127, the Quelea survives the most determined and ruthless attacks by desperate farmers. Nevertheless, it should be remembered that the Passenger Pigeon of America had a similar prodigious population only 150 years ago but is now extinct. The Passenger Pigeon laid only one egg per clutch but compensated for this meagre effort by rearing several broods each season. Pairs kept in captivity produced as many as seven broods per year.

A number of the larger flightless birds, such as the Ostriches, Emus and Rheas, lay large clutches of eggs. Ostriches and Rheas use communal nests which may contain as many as 50 or 60 eggs deposited by a number of females. Usually, however, many of the eggs fail to hatch. Megapodes, Mallee-Fowl or Brush Turkeys likewise lay large clutches, of from 15 to 35 eggs according to species, in artificially heated mounds which act as incubators. They take no care of their young after hatching, however, and the mortality-rate is consequently high. Several Megapodes of the Pacific islands are on the danger-list, though that is chiefly because they were restricted to small island habitats and therefore had small populations to start with.

The familiar Budgerigar (*Melopsittacus undulatus*), still present in enormous flocks in its native Australia in spite of persecution, is an outstanding example of fecundity. It can start breeding within 60 days of fledging and produce several broods at very short intervals. The technique is eminently suitable to conditions in the dry heart of Australia, where the food supply depends on the occurrence of torrential but very erratic rains. The Budgerigar population sinks to a low ebb during periods of drought but can quickly build up to a peak when rain comes.

142

Longevity   Closely associated with reproductive-rates is longevity. To maintain a stable population it needs only for a pair of birds to reproduce themselves before their decease. Most small birds do this in a single year, and therefore their own survival into a second year is not important. Familiar garden or suburban birds kept in captivity may live for five or ten years, but in the wild they seldom do so.

Birds, notably the predators, which rear only one or two young per year and are not mature until they are several years old require a much longer life. It has been calculated that the Californian Condor, starting to breed at the age of about five years, needs to continue breeding, at its normal rate of one egg every two years, for at least 21 years to ensure the survival of a couple of young birds to replace the parents. Its normal life-span of 50 years or so is thus necessary. Most Eagles, Hawks and Falcons similarly have long lives but are subject to a high casualty-rate. Certain other species of birds which combine a fair longevity with some prolificacy have become very common. Examples are the Black-headed Gull (*Larus ridibundus*) with a life-span of up to 25 years; the Blackbird (*Turdus merula*), 10 years; the Starling (*Sturnus vulgaris*), $12\frac{1}{2}$ years; and the Mallard, 10 years (figures quoted for the life-spans are the maxima recorded for ringed birds in the wild).

Diet adaptability   Diet adaptability is an obvious factor in the survival and status of a species. One of the most competitive of all species is the House-Sparrow (*Passer domesticus*) which is almost omnivorous. This bird has spread to nearly every part of the world and has shown itself willing to feed on whatever is available. Several species of Gull, notably the Black-headed Gull and the Herring Gull, have within the present century become scavengers, ranging far inland to fill an ecological niche left by the disappearance of the Kite and the Raven. The Great Tit (*Parus major*) and the Blue Tit (*Parus caeruleus*), both common and highly adaptable species, have over the past few decades developed the habit of pecking holes in the seals of doorstep milk-bottles in order to get at the milk.

With some species, of course, their very adaptability has proved their undoing. The Carolina Parakeets, for instance, could have been forgiven for thinking their millennium had arrived when the settlers of the south-eastern states of America began cultivating fruit, but they took such a heavy toll that the incensed fruit farmers exterminated them. The Kea (*Nestor notabilis*) of New Zealand long existed on a diet of fruit and insects, but with the establishment of sheep-farming developed a habit of pecking at the fat on the backs of sick or injured sheep. The practice naturally earned it the disapproval of the sheep-farmers, with the result that the Kea, a species of Parrot, has now become rare, though not yet officially classified as endangered.

Other species which specialise in their diet are highly vulnerable if their food-source becomes scarce and they are unable to adapt to an alternative. Several of the Honeycreepers of Hawaii retreated to the remaining vestiges of indigenous vegetation as the forests were cleared for cultivation and became either rare or extinct. The Short-tailed Albatross feeds exclusively on squids, in search of which it wanders over vast areas of ocean.

In general it seems that a species' best chance of survival is to adapt itself to a diet of waste products. The products must, however, be indubitably waste, for woe betide any species that finds itself in direct competition with Man.

Adaptation, Conservation & Preservation

As mentioned in the previous chapter, the most successful of bird species in the struggle for survival have been the hangers-on of civilisation. There is nothing like being on the winning side, and beyond argument Man is the most successful vertebrate species in the world today. Those birds which can come to terms with Man's latest experiment in urban living are the best situated of all.

One of the best examples is, of course, the House-Sparrow, which is undoubtedly the most widespread species of land-bird, and one confined almost exclusively to the immediate vicinity of human dwellings. It is now found throughout Europe, North America (except northern Canada), temperate and sub-tropical South America, the Middle East, southern Asia as far east as Malaya, Siberia, Egypt, Morocco, much of southern and eastern Australia, much of New Zealand, and a number of the Pacific islands, including remote Norfolk Island, the Chatham Islands and the Auckland Islands. A writer of 200 years ago would have been able to include only Europe, southern Asia, Egypt and Morocco. Throughout the nineteenth century it spread, of its own volition, across Siberia, reaching the mouth of the river Amur by 1929. The American population derives from a series of small introductions, beginning in New York in 1850, and in Quebec in 1865. By the end of the century it had spread right across the continent. Birds were imported into Cuba in 1850 and to Buenos Aires in 1872. They were introduced to Australia and New Zealand in the 1860s, but they found their own way to some of the outlying islands. House-Sparrows in South Africa are descended from some introduced in Natal in about 1890. Among the world's island groups in which they have become acclimatised are Hawaii, Mauritius, New Caledonia, the Falklands and St Helena. For a notably sedentary species, it is a remarkable catalogue of achievements. Once established in a country they have followed the course of human settlement, often along rivers or railways under construction. Horses, too, have played their part, for the House-Sparrow can derive a lot of its food from horse-droppings. The development of agriculture in Siberia and in North and South America has had much to do with the spread of the Sparrows there. The extreme cold of the Arctic regions evidently sets a limit to their expansion northward, for they have not yet become established in northern Norway, northern Russia, northern Canada, Iceland and Greenland.

Another satellite of human habitations, as abundant in towns as in the countryside (though it has not been deliberately introduced into as many alien lands as the

Red-cockaded Woodpecker
Photo. Kirtley-Perkins
(National Audubon Society Coll./Photo. Researchers Inc.)

California Condor
Photo. Tom McHugh
(National Audubon Society Coll./Photo. Researchers Inc.)

Bittern on nest

Ivory-billed Woodpecker

Japanese Cranes

House-Sparrow) is the European Starling. It feeds on scraps of food thrown out by humans, on food supplied to livestock, on farm crops and fruit, and it is virtually ubiquitous. In America its place is taken by even more plentiful indigenous species, the Grackles and the American Blackbirds, which are closely allied to the European Starling. These birds have multiplied enormously since America became intensively occupied by agriculturists. They breed prolifically around every farmstead and in autumn migrate south to communal roosts in the Gulf states, where they congregate in such numbers that unduly drastic steps, such as spraying with chemicals that saturate their plumage and allow them to die of exposure, have been taken to combat the nuisance.

The menace of the Quelea birds in Africa has already been noted. The Queleas are members of the Weaver-bird Family (the *Ploceidae*), many other species of which are extremely plentiful and tend to be closely associated with settlements and cultivation. Intensive cattle-units, such as beef feedlots, in America, Africa and Australia, attract large assemblies of seed-eating birds, especially various species of Weaver-birds, Starlings (Blackbirds) and Doves.

Another species of Dove which has staged a remarkable extension of range in recent years is the Collared Dove (*Streptopelia decaocto*), which in the 1920s was found no farther north-west in Europe than the Balkans. In the 1930s these Doves began to advance westwards and by 1950 had reached the Netherlands, Denmark and Sweden. They first appeared in Britain in 1952, but now they are found everywhere, even on the offshore islands, and have even pushed on as far as Iceland. They are birds of the farmyard, the suburbs and gardens, feeding largely on waste grains and on food put out for poultry and domestic animals, including that set out to attract birds to bird-tables.

The Feral Pigeon, which is a mongrel based on the wild Rock Dove (*Columba livia*), is common in every city of Britain, but so too is the Wood Pigeon (*Columba palumbus*). In the countryside the Wood Pigeon, target for many guns, is one of the shyest and most wary of birds but in cities, having discovered that it is safe, it undergoes a remarkable change, nesting in parks and feeding on the pavements of squares thronging with pedestrians. In the wild, too, it shows remarkable adaptability. Given the right environment, it often nests communally, large numbers of nests being concentrated into a suitable location, such as a tall-conifer plantation, but if no such site is available it is quite prepared to nest singly. If the Passenger Pigeon could have displayed equal adaptability it might well be alive and flourishing now.

A similar variation in attitude towards humans is noticeable in many species of Duck and Goose. Birds that have been shot at are naturally suspicious of men and on unprotected waters are extremely cautious and suspicious. On lakes and rivers in city parks, however, and wherever experience has taught them they are safe they become as tame as domestic ducks, assembling at the water's edge to solicit scraps from sentimental citizens. Since the number of such refuges has been multiplied, many species of Duck and Goose have been increasing and extending their breeding-range. In Britain examples include the Tufted Duck (*Aythya fuligula*), Pochard (*Aythya ferina*), Pintail (*Anas acuta*), Wigeon (*Anas penelope*) and, naturally, Mallard (*Anas platyrhynchos*). In addition the Coot (*Fulica atra*) has become abundant, while the Moorhen (*Gallinula chloropus*) is almost as familiar as the House-Sparrow. The Moorhen is mentioned here chiefly because of a remarkable difference in attitude towards Man in Britain and America. While in Britain it runs around the feet of pedestrians in city-parks and joins domestic poultry at feeding-time in farmyards, in the United States it retains the skulking, secretive habits of Gallinules in general.

A somewhat similar instance is provided by the Blackbird (*Turdus merula*), one of the commonest and most widespread of birds in Britain, where it is to be seen in almost every suburban garden and even nests on roof-gardens and window-boxes in cities. In continental Europe, however, it has long tended to remain a shy, elusive bird of undergrowth in the wilder parts of the countryside, though this attitude is now changing in some countries. Among other birds which have adapted themselves successfully to city-life are the Kestrel (*Falco tinnunculus*) and the Black Redstart (*Phoenicurus ochrurus*). Both evidently find in the tall buildings of cities a habitat somewhat similar to the cliffs which they frequent in the country-side. The Kestrel nests on ledges among the roof-tops even in central London, while the Black Redstart began to colonise British cities after the bombing raids of the 1940s, nesting in the ruined buildings.

The Fulmar (*Fulmarus glacialis*), a handsome white Petrel, has experienced an explosive expansion of range for different reasons. Just over a hundred years ago it was breeding at only one British station, the lonely island of St Kilda. Towards the end of the nineteenth century it started to colonise other islands off the north and west of Scotland, and its expansion gradually acquired speed and strength until now it nests on suitable cliffs on every coast of the British Isles, except the south-east, and its present British population is probably around 100,000 pairs, perhaps more. An increase in commerical sea-fishing in the North Atlantic and conse-quently in the quantity of offal deposited in the ocean is generally advanced as the chief reason for the increase.

The Gannet (*Sula bassana*) has similarly benefited, though freedom from human persecution, which was once severe, has also helped this species. It too has a probable British population of about 100,000 pairs, and it has in recent years established new colonies in Iceland, Norway and the Channel Islands.

The excavation of gravel from river valleys has in the present century created extensive chains of pits which, as they naturally fill with water, become attractive habitats for certain birds. Some such pools are soon exploited for recreation, but some are retained as nature reserves. One new species which has been attracted to Britain by these new habitats is the Little Rigged Plover (*Charadrius dubius*), which first nested there in 1938 and has now a population estimated at about 200 pairs.

In the western states of America and in British Columbia the Ruby-throated Humming-bird (*Archilochus colubris*) has been greatly assisted by the commercial production of nectar-dispensing devices, which innumerable householders now hang from their verandahs. Humming-birds are naturally increasing.

Opposite reactions by different species to the same set of circumstances are often puzzling. In Britain when the Corncrake disappeared from most of its former haunts, the blame was put on either (a) modern mechanical aids to agriculture, notably the mechanical grasscutter, or (b) modern grassland management, which often involves operations on the land while the birds are still nesting. Either alternative seems logical, but how, then, do the Lapwing, Skylark and Corn-Bunting, which also nest on the ground manage to remain plentiful? What is the

Blackbird—a notable example of adaptability. One of the most plentiful of British birds. *Photo. Dr Alan Beaumont*

146

mysterious factor that spelt doom to the Corncrake but not to these species?

Three obvious ways of promoting bird-welfare and preserving threatened species from extinction are education, legislation and the creation of reserves or sanctuaries. Creating an educated public sympathetic to the needs of birds is largely a development of the twentieth century. Bird-protection societies have been in the forefront of the movement, and a flood of books and television-programmes has helped and continues to do so. Societies devoted to birds operate today in most countries, but in many nations of the Third World they represent a tiny minority. Some of the developing countries have, however, realised that their bird-life is a tourist attraction and protect it accordingly.

Man takes a hand

Legislation to protect birds has a long history, though until recent times it was reserved for species of interest to royalty and the nobility. Hawks and falcons, for instance, were protected from the common folk in medieval times, and the protection given to the Great Bustard and its eggs in the England of Henry VIII is noted on pages 85-6. Today most countries have bird-protection laws, many of them altruistic and enlightened. Some establish close seasons for a number of species which are commonly the target for guns, others give absolute protection to certain species at all times. Passing a law is one thing, however; enforcing it is another. Much depends on the efficiency and interest displayed by the guardians of the law and on the climate of public opinion. Even in the most advanced and humane countries there exist large areas, notably private estates, where police, wardens and the public never penetrate and everything depends on the attitude of the person in charge.

Reserves fall into two categories—general reserves for the preservation of a special type of habitat which attracts a wide range of birds; and reserves established for the specific purpose of protecting one species. An example of the latter type is the island of Torishima (*see* page 109), which the Japanese Government has declared a national monument in an effort to preserve the Short-tailed Albatross from extinction. In England the reappearance of the Avocet (*Recurvirostra avosettö*) at Minsmere on the Suffolk coast in 1946 was sufficient to prompt ornithologists to get the locality declared a nature reserve, where the species has since prospered and increased.

The resurrection of the Takahé (*Nortornis mantelli*) in New Zealand is an example of the success that can attend energetic protective measures. This species was first described from fossil bones in the early part of the nineteenth century. Ornithologists were surprised when a few specimens were obtained in that century, the final one in 1898, but from that time onward for the next 50 years the species was confidently classified as extinct. Then in 1948 a determined search in a remote mountain-district in South Island revealed a surviving population. A nature reserve of 700 square miles was quickly established and various protective measures were initiated, including a campaign against the local stoats which preyed on the eggs and chicks. The Takahé, a large, splendidly coloured gallinule, is now thought to have a reasonably stable population of about 200 pairs.

On Christmas Island, in the Indian Ocean, the Abbott's Booby (*Sula abbotti*) is preserved from extinction by the Australian Government, which officially protects the tall trees in which the last surviving pairs nest. In the Los Padros National Park of California two sanctuaries, one of 1,200 acres and the other of 53,000 acres, have been set aside as Condor reserves, but individual Condors tend to range over such vast areas that it is doubtful whether they will be very effective. The Whooping Crane has been saved from extinction largely by the establishment of a well-wardened reserve at the wintering grounds of the surviving specimens at Aransas, Texas. In West Australia when the Noisy Scrub-bird (*Atrichornis clamosus*), thought for many years to be extinct, was discovered to have a small nesting colony on the slopes of Mount Gardner, near Albany, a reserve of 13,500 acres for the preservation of the bird was set up.

Apart from these specialised sanctuaries, most countries have general reserves or national parks in which most species are entirely protected. Probably the first designated national park in the world was that established at Yellowstone, on the borders of Wyoming and Montana, in 1894—an event which, incidentally, helped to save the Trumpeter Swan from extinction. The effect of national parks in general is to preserve in their present state habitats threatened with change. Many of them preserve large amphibious areas which would otherwise probably be drained and devoted to agriculture. In Europe wetland reserves are to be found in virtually every country, among the best known being the Camargue (southern France), the Coto Doñana (southern Spain), the marshlands of Holland, the Dobrudja (Rumania), Czerwone Bagno (Poland) and Little Balaton (Hungary). In the United States one of the most important wetland reserves is the Loxahatchee National Wildlife Reserve in the Everglades National Park, Florida, one of the last strongholds of the Everglade Kite (*see* page 74). Probably of equal importance is the chain of refuges that act as stepping-stones for migrating birds along the Mississippi-Missouri basin. Much used by geese and ducks, they serve as bases from which wildfowl, pausing on migration, can go foraging in the surrounding stubble-fields after harvest.

More sophisticated techniques are concerned with the manipulation of the nesting-activities of birds in order to save them from extinction. The most straightforward is that of taking eggs or birds from a habitat where they are in danger and endeavouring to establish a captive population elsewhere. When this has been successfully accomplished, the next stage is to return some of the birds to their original home, if the habitat is still available, in the hope that they will recolonise it. One of the outstanding and successful examples is that of the Hawaiian Goose or Néné. In 1947 it was estimated that only 50 Nénés were left alive, a number of them in the private collection owned by Herbert C. Shipman. In 1950 and 1951 two geese and a gander were sent to the Wildfowl Trust which Sir Peter Scott had established at Slimbridge (by the estuary of the River Severn, England), and forthwith started to breed. The gander, a notable sire named Kamehameha after one of the greatest of the Hawaiian kings, is credited with more than 230 descendants before he died in 1963. Meantime the Hawaiian Board of Agriculture had started a new breeding venture for the Néné, and much interchange of stock developed between them and Slimbridge. As the population grew, other birds were dispersed to parks and collections in Europe and America, to avoid dangers from pests and interbreeding, and a wild population is now well established in reserves on the mountain slopes and craters which were the species' former headquarters. The world-population of the Néné has recently been doubling itself every few years.

As noted on pages 93–4, several species of Pheasant are now very rare and may even be extinct in the wild. Some have been saved from probable extinction by aviculturists, among whom one of the most successful is the Ornamental Pheasant Trust, of Great Witchingham, Norfolk, England. Most pheasants, though not all, will breed in captivity and some, notably the Swinhoe's Pheasant, have done well enough to allow a breeding-population to be returned and liberated in their native land.

Not all species of rare birds co-operate with such measures. An attempt to reintroduce the Great Bustard to the chalk downs of Salisbury Plain, England, where once it roamed, ended recently in failure. The Heath Hen gradually drifted into extinction on Martha's Vineyard, off Massachusetts, despite all efforts to save it. Wherever possible, however, what has become known as a zoo-bank is being established for threatened species.

Among old-time keepers of domestic poultry it was common practice to set duck eggs under hens because ducks were notoriously bad mothers. Similarly gamekeepers often used, and still use, bantams to hatch pheasants' eggs. Ornithologists use the same technique to help in the build-up of certain bird-populations which have fallen to a low ebb. It has been tried with notable success with the Whooping Crane, the total population of which in 1938 is thought to have been as low as 14. In 1955 its last breeding-station was discovered in the Wood Buffalo National Park in Arctic Canada, and soon it was realised that a factor in the slow recovery of the species was that although it laid two eggs per year it seldom if ever raised more than one chick. Accordingly one egg was carefully extracted from each of several nests and hatched in an incubator. Later, for this and similar projects, a breeding-centre was set up at Patuxent, Maryland. The experiment has been an encouraging success, and Patuxent has a captive population which has started to breed.

Stemming from it an interesting project has been started to discover whether Whooping Crane eggs and chicks can be successfully fostered by the more plentiful Sandhill Crane. In 1975, 14 of the Whooping Crane eggs taken from Wood Buffalo Lake were given to Sandhill Cranes nesting at Grays Lake National Wildlife Refuge in Idaho. Six young were raised and embarked on the autumn migration to the normal winter quarters of Sandhill Cranes in New Mexico. Two evidently perished en route, but the remaining four wintered satisfactorily and set out on the return journey to Idaho. Unfortunately, the Sandhill Crane has a habit of rejecting its young at about this stage in order to help them to independence before the mating season. The four young Whooping Cranes were at the Monte Vista Refuge in Colorado when this happened, and there they were stuck. What happened to these individuals is not known, but more young Whooping Cranes were hatched by Sandhill foster-parents in subsequent years and the numbers of Whooping Cranes reporting at winter quarters are steadily increasing. In 1977 the total population reached 120. Supposing the young Whooping Cranes hatched at Grays Lake return to breed there, rather than make the journey to northern Canada, they will have a shorter and less perilous migratory journey twice a year.

Similar experiments have been made with the eggs of certain birds of prey, among whom the mortality-rate of young birds in the nest is disheartening. Between siblings in the same nest there is much competition for food and space, so the extraction of surplus juveniles to be reared elsewhere, leaving only those which the parents can easily deal with, is a logical exercise. The technique has been practised with success in Europe with the Lesser Spotted Eagle (*Aquila pomarina*) and the Spanish Imperial Eagle (*Aquila heliaca*). In the United States eggs and chicks have been transferred from Osprey colonies in Connecticut—where there is evidence that the fish collected by the parents contain high degrees of metallic-pollution—to foster-parents in Maryland, where their food is less contaminated.

If all this seems like interfering with nature, conservationists have learned that that is something they cannot avoid. The early idea of a nature reserve was an area in which all wild life could flourish unchecked, but modifications of that principle soon became necessary. Pools and marshy areas became choked with weeds; water-tables sank alarmingly; rank undergrowth suffocated woodlands; predatory gulls played havoc with the nests of terns and waders; grey squirrels, magpies, crows, cats and other efficient creatures took far too heavy a toll of eggs and nestlings. For a nature reserve to function satisfactorily, an ideal ecology has to be planned and maintained as closely as possible. That often involves sacrificing one species to save another. The Brown-headed Cowbird (*Molothrus ater*), for instance, is by no means an objectionable species, but its habit of parasitising other birds by laying eggs in their nests was proving lethal to the rare Kirtland's Warbler (*Dendroica kirtlandii*) when the Cowbirds invaded the limited territory in Michigan where the Warblers nest. So the Cowbirds had to be ruthlessly eliminated there. And on Bermuda it was not until devices were made to exclude the attractive White-tailed Tropic-bird from the burrows of the rare Cahow that the latter started to retreat from the brink of extinction.

The future of many endangered species depends largely on the provision of sufficient and adequately-wardened reserves. More refuges of two types are urgently needed. One is the wetland sanctuary, not only because of the wide variety of birds it attracts but also because the surviving wetlands are being steadily encroached upon. The other is the sanctuary strategically sited to assist migrating birds. North America is much better supplied than Europe with this type of transit-station. The United States and Canada, between which countries there is good liaison, have most of the north–south routes under their control, whereas in Europe the birds have to fly over perhaps a dozen countries with very varying ideas on bird-conservation and protection.

Misgivings have often been expressed by naturalists about the dependence on human beings which results from attempts to build up a zoo-bank or captive population of rare species. Birds bred under sheltered conditions, it is argued, become so accustomed to having food and protection provided for them that they are unable to fend for themselves in the wild. They also lose their fear of Man as a dangerous species. It is basically a fallacious argument. Man has so shaped the environment to his own needs over vast areas of the world that most common species of birds flourish because they have been able to adapt themselves to life as his neighbours. Some, such as House-Sparrows and Starlings, are frankly pensioners or parasites and are none the worse for it. Nor are the many species of ducks which quickly become as tame as domestic ducks in city parks and pools, growing fat on scraps fed to them by the populace.

That kind of relationship between birds and men may be just as natural, if not more so, than the more usual one which sends a bird scurrying for refuge at the sight of a man. Birds nesting in the high Arctic tend to accept the occasional

151

presence of visiting students and explorers with indifference, as do the penguins of the opposite polar regions. It is not necessarily 'natural' for birds to be 'wild'. They are only so when men make them so.

Fear of humans has to be learned. Some species, such as the Dodo and the Great Auk, failed to learn it in time. In the West African state of The Gambia, with which the author was familiar before the tourist influx began, birds of many species were present in astonishing numbers and showed little fear of the African people. The arrival of European tourists in increasing numbers, some of them bearing guns, has made them more wary and timid: a sad reflection on Western civilisation. Already, though, attitudes are changing, and have been doing so throughout the present century. The most encouraging feature of conservation at present is the growing number of people who have become interested in it. A strong body of public opinion in favour of conservation is building up, and the factors which threaten our fauna and flora are coming under closer scrutiny. Though this world is still full of dangers, a species at risk today stands a much better chance of survival than it would have done 20 years ago. But the price of safety is constant vigilance.

Tristram's Grackles. *Photo. Eric Hoski*

Bibliography

ALDOUS, T. *Battle for the Environment* London, 1972
ALI, S, & RIPLEY, S. D. *Handbook of the Birds of India and Pakistan* Oxford, 1968
BIJLEVELD, M. *Birds of Prey in Europe* London, 1974
BOND, J. *Birds of the West Indies* Boston, 1936
  Check List of the Birds of the West Indies Boston, 1950
BRUUN, B. *Hamlyn Guide to Birds of Britain and Europe* London, 1970
CADBURY, C. J. *Silent Death* R.S.P.B., 1980
CARLQUIST, S. *Island Biology* New York, 1974
CARSON, R. *Silent Spring* London, 1963
COLEMAN-COOKE, J. *The Harvest that Kills* London, 1965
CRAMP, S. *Bird Conservation in Europe* London, 1977
CRAMP, S, BOURNE, W. R. P., & SAUNDERS, D. *The Seabirds of Britain and Ireland*
  London, 1974
DARWIN, C. *The Voyage of the Beagle* London, 1845
DELACOUR, J. *The Waterfowl of the World* (4 vols.) London, 1954
DORST, J. *The Life of Birds* London, 1975
DUFFEY, E. *Conservation of Nature* London, 1970
FALLA, R. A., SIBSON, R. B. & TURBOTT, E. G. *A Field Guide to the Birds of New Zealand*
  London, 1970
FITTER, R. S. R. *London's Natural History* London, 1945
FISHER, J., SIMON, N. & VINCENT, J. *The Red Book: Wildlife in Danger* London, 1969
FISHER, J. *The Fulmar* London, 1952
FISHER, J. & LOCKLEY, R. *Sea Birds* London, 1954
GARDINER, L. *Rare, Vanishing and Lost British Birds* London, 1923
GOODERS, J. *Where to Watch Birds in Britain and Europe* London, 1970
GOODWIN, D. *Pigeons and Doves of the World* London, 1967
GREENAWAY, J. C. Jr. *Extinct and Vanishing Birds of the World* New York, 1967
GRIEVE, S. *The Great Auk or Garefowl* London, 1885
HARRISON, C. J. O. (ed.) *Bird Families of the World* Oxford, 1978
HESS, G. *The Bird: its Life and Structure* London, 1951
HOUGH, R. *Galapagos, The Enchanted Islands* London, 1975
HUDSON, R. *Threatened Birds of Europe* London, 1975
HUDSON, W. H. *Lost British Birds* London, 1894
JENKINS, A. C. *Wild Life in Danger* London, 1970
KLOTZ, J. W. *Ecology Crisis* London, 1972
LACK, D. *Darwin's Finches* Cambridge, 1947
  Island Biology Illustrated by The Land Birds of Jamaica Univ. of California, 1976
LITTLEWOOD, C. & OVENDEN, D. W. *The World's Vanishing Birds* London, 1972
MACDONALD, J. D. *Birds of Australia* London, 1973
MANLEY, S. & R. *Islands, Their Lives, Legends and Lore* New York, 1970
MARTIN, R. D. (ed.) *Breeding Endangered Species in Captivity* London, 1975
MATHEWS, G. M. *Birds of Australia* London, 1910–1928
  Birds of Norfolk and Lord Howe Islands London, 1928 (Supplement, 1936)
MUNRO, G. C. *Birds of Hawaii* Rutland (USA), 1944
NELSON, B. *Galapagos, Islands of Birds* London, 1968

NICHOLSON, E. M. *Birds and Men* London, 1951

OLIVER, W. R. B. *New Zealand Birds* Wellington, 1955

PALMER, R. S. (ed.) *Handbook of North American Birds* New Haven, 1975

Readers Digest Assn. *Book of British Birds* London, 1969

ROTHSCHILD, W. *Extinct Birds* London, 1907

ROWLEY, I. *Bird Life* Sydney, 1974

SIMMS, E. *Birds of Town and Suburb* London, 1975

STAMP, SIR D. *Nature Conservation in Britain* London, 1969

STEWART, D. *From the Edge of Extinction* London, 1978

SUMMERS-SMITH, J. D. *The House Sparrow* London, 1963

TAYLOR, G. R. *The Doomsday Book* London, 1972

TEMPLE, S. A. (ed.) *Endangered Birds, Management Techniques for Preserving Threatened Species* Univ. of Wisconsin Press, 1978

TURBOTT, E. G. *Buller's Birds of New Zealand* Wellington, 1967

VESEY-FITZGERALD, B. *British Game* London, 1946

WHITLOCK, R. *Rare and Extinct Birds of Britain* London, 1953

WILLIAMS, J. G. *The Birds of East and Central Africa* London, 1969

WILLIAMSON, K. *The Atlantic Islands* London, 1970

WITHERBY, H. F. *et al.*, *The Handbook of British Birds* 5 vols. London, 1938-41

Index

PLACES